CMC Supporting Papers

The Committee for Economic Development is publishing for the Commission on Money and Credit
THE FEDERAL RESERVE AND THE TREASURY: ANSWERS TO QUESTIONS FROM THE COMMISSION ON MONEY AND CREDIT
and fifty-eight individual essays organized into nine separate volumes, each centered around a particular aspect of monetary and fiscal policy. Their titles and the contributing authors are as follows:

IMPACTS OF MONETARY POLICY

Daniel B. Suits; Robert Eisner and Robert H. Strotz, with a bibliography by G. R. Post; Edwin Kuh and John R. Meyer; Leo Grebler and Sherman J. Maisel; Charlotte DeMonte Phelps; Irwin Friend

STABILIZATION POLICIES

E. Cary Brown, Robert M. Solow, Albert Ando, and John Kareken; Milton Friedman and David Meiselman; Lawrence E. Thompson; Arthur M. Okun; Merton H. Miller; Allan H. Meltzer; Oswald Brownlee and Alfred Conrad

MONETARY MANAGEMENT

Frank M. Tamagna; Warren L. Smith; Clark Warburton; Michael D. Reagan; C. P. Kindleberger; Robert Z. Aliber

FISCAL AND DEBT MANAGEMENT POLICIES

William Fellner; Richard A. Musgrave; James Tobin; James R. Schlesinger; Paul H. Cootner; Irving Auerbach; Ralph K. Huitt; John Lindeman

FEDERAL CREDIT AGENCIES

George F. Break; Jack Guttentag; Ernest Bloch; D. Gale Johnson; Dale E. Hathaway; George S. Tolley; Jack McCroskey

FEDERAL CREDIT PROGRAMS

Stewart Johnson; Warren A. Law; James W. McKie; D. Gale Johnson; James Gillies; Robert C. Turner and Ross Robertson; J. Fred Weston

PRIVATE CAPITAL MARKETS

Irwin Friend; Hyman P. Minsky; Victor L. Andrews

PRIVATE FINANCIAL INSTITUTIONS

Paul M. Horvitz; Deane Carson and Paul Cootner; Thomas G. Gies, Thomas Mayer, and Edward C. Ettin; Lawrence L. Werboff and Marvin E. Rozen; Fred H. Klopstock; E. Gordon Keith

INFLATION, GROWTH, AND EMPLOYMENT

Joseph W. Conard; Jesse W. Markham; Franklyn D. Holzman; John W. Kendrick; Daniel Creamer; Stanley Lebergott; Lawrence R. Klein and Ronald G. Bodkin; Tibor and Anne Scitovsky

TRADE ASSOCIATIONS MONOGRAPHS

THE COMMERCIAL BANKING INDUSTRY
The American Bankers Association

THE CONSUMER FINANCE INDUSTRY
National Consumer Finance Association

LIFE INSURANCE COMPANIES AS FINANCIAL INSTITUTIONS
Life Insurance Association of America

MANAGEMENT INVESTMENT COMPANIES
Investment Company Institute

MORTGAGE COMPANIES: THEIR PLACE IN THE FINANCIAL STRUCTURE
Miles L. Colean, for the
Mortgage Bankers Association of America

MUTUAL SAVINGS BANKING: BASIC CHARACTERISTICS AND ROLE IN THE NATIONAL ECONOMY
National Association of Mutual Savings Banks

PROPERTY AND CASUALTY INSURANCE COMPANIES: THEIR ROLE AS FINANCIAL INTERMEDIARIES
American Mutual Insurance Alliance
Association of Casualty and Surety Companies
National Board of Fire Underwriters

THE SAVINGS AND LOAN BUSINESS: ITS PURPOSES, FUNCTIONS, AND ECONOMIC JUSTIFICATION
Leon T. Kendall, for the
United States Savings and Loan League

_U.S._ *Board of Governors*
of the Federal Reserve System,
and the United States Treasury Department

THE FEDERAL RESERVE
AND THE TREASURY:

ANSWERS TO QUESTIONS
FROM THE
COMMISSION ON MONEY AND CREDIT

PREPARED FOR THE

Commission on Money and Credit

Prentice-Hall, Inc.
Englewood Cliffs, N.J.

PRENTICE-HALL INTERNATIONAL, INC., London
PRENTICE-HALL OF AUSTRALIA, PTY., LTD., Sydney
PRENTICE-HALL OF CANADA, LTD., Toronto
PRENTICE-HALL FRANCE, S.A.R.L., Paris
PRENTICE-HALL OF JAPAN, INC., Tokyo
PRENTICE-HALL DE MEXICO, S.A., Mexico City

© 1963 by Prentice-Hall, Inc., Englewood Cliffs, N. J.

All rights reserved. No part of this book may be reproduced in
any form, by mimeograph or any other means, without permission
in writing from the publishers.

Library of Congress Catalog No.: 63-12487

Printed in the United States of America

C

332.11
U58fe

The Commission on Money and Credit was established in 1957 as an independent organization by the unanimous vote of the Board of Trustees of the Committee for Economic Development. The bylaws governing the Commission on Money and Credit state that "It shall be the responsibility of the Commission to initiate studies into the United States monetary and financial system."

This volume was especially prepared for the Commission on Money and Credit as part of its research program leading to the publication in June 1961 of its final report: Money and Credit: Their Influence on Jobs, Prices, and Growth. It is published by direction of the Commission according to its bylaws, as a contribution to the understanding of the monetary and financial system of the United States. It is one of more than 100 research studies prepared for the Commission by trade organizations, individual scholars, the Federal Reserve System, and the Treasury of the United States.

A selected group of these papers including those of this volume, is being published for the Commission by the Information Division of the Committee for Economic Development in accordance with commitments to The Ford Foundation and the Merrill Foundation, which provided main financial support for the Commission.

Publication of this volume does not necessarily constitute endorsement of such study by the Commission, its Advisory Board, its Research Staff, or any member of any board or committee, or any officer of the Committee for Economic Development, The Ford Foundation, the Merrill Foundation, or any other organization participating in the work of the Commission.

277473

COMMISSION ON MONEY AND CREDIT

Members

Frazar B. Wilde, CHAIRMAN
Chairman, Connecticut General
  Life Insurance Company

H. Christian Sonne,
  VICE CHAIRMAN
New York, New York

Adolf A. Berle, Jr.
New York, New York
(Withdrew to serve as Chairman
  of the U.S. State Department
  Latin American Task Force.)

James B. Black
Chairman of the Board, Pacific
  Gas & Electric Company

Joseph M. Dodge
Chairman of the Board, The
  Detroit Bank and Trust Com-
  pany
(Resigned October 7, 1960.)

Marriner S. Eccles
Chairman of the Board, First
  Security Corporation

Lamar Fleming, Jr.
Chairman of the Board, Anderson, Clayton & Co.

Henry H. Fowler
Fowler, Leva, Hawes & Syming-
  ton
(Resigned February 3, 1961, on
  his appointment as Under
  Secretary of the Treasury.)

Gaylord A. Freeman, Jr.
Vice Chairman, The First Na-
  tional Bank of Chicago
(Appointed April 29, 1960.)

Fred T. Greene
President, Federal Home Loan
  Bank of Indianapolis
(Died March 17, 1961.)

Philip M. Klutznick
Park Forest, Illinois
(Resigned February 8, 1961, on
  his appointment as United
  States Representative to the
  Economic and Social Council
  of the United Nations.)

Fred Lazarus, Jr.
Chairman of the Board, Feder-
  ated Department Stores, Inc.

Isador Lubin
Arthur T. Vanderbilt Professor
  of Public Affairs, Rutgers
  University

J. Irwin Miller
Chairman of the Board, Cum-
  mins Engine Company

Robert R. Nathan
President, Robert R. Nathan
  Associates, Inc.

Emil Rieve
President Emeritus, Textile
  Workers of America, AFL-
  CIO
(Appointed May 19, 1960.)

David Rockefeller
President, The Chase Manhattan
  Bank

Beardsley Ruml
New York, New York
(Died April 18, 1960.)

Stanley H. Ruttenberg
Director, Department of Research, AFL-CIO

Charles Sawyer
Taft, Stettinius & Hollister

William F. Schnitzler
Secretary-Treasurer, AFL-CIO
(Resigned April 28, 1960.)

COMMISSION ON MONEY AND CREDIT

Earl B. Schwulst
President and Chairman of the
  Board, The Bowery Savings
  Bank

Charles B. Shuman
President, American Farm
  Bureau Federation

Jesse W. Tapp
Chairman of the Board,
  Bank of America, N.T. & S.A.

J. Cameron Thomson
Retired Chairman of the Board,
  Northwest Bancorporation

Willard L. Thorp
Director, Merrill Center for
  Economics, Amherst College

Theodore O. Yntema
Chairman, Finance Committee,
  Ford Motor Company

Advisory Board

Lester V. Chandler
Professor of Economics,
  Princeton University

Gerhard Colm
Chief Economist, National Planning Association

Gaylord A. Freeman, Jr.
Vice Chairman, The First National Bank of Chicago
(Resigned April 29, 1960, on his
  appointment to the Commission.)

Leo Grebler
Professor of Business Administration, University of California (Los Angeles)

Raymond W. Goldsmith
Professor of Economics, Yale
  University

Neil H. Jacoby
Dean, School of Business Ad-
  ministration, University of
  California (Los Angeles)

Richard A. Musgrave
Woodrow Wilson School of Pub-
  lic and International Affairs,
  Princeton University

Richard E. Neustadt
Professor of Public Law and
  Government, Columbia Uni-
  versity

Paul A. Samuelson
Professor of Economics, Massa-
  chusetts Institute of
  Technology

Sumner H. Slichter
Lamont University Professor,
  Harvard University
(Died September 27, 1959.)

Edward S. Shaw
Professor of Economics, Stan-
  ford University

Alan H. Temple
New York, New York

Jacob Viner
Professor of Economics,
Emeritus, Princeton University

Staff

Bertrand Fox
Research Director

Eli Shapiro
Deputy Research Director

FOREWORD

Shortly after its organization the Commission on Money and Credit met with the then Secretary of the Treasury, Mr. Robert B. Anderson, and his staff, and soon thereafter with the Board of Governors of the Federal Reserve System and their staff. The meetings enabled the Commission to explore with the aforementioned officials their thoughts as to the nature, range and details of problems and issues which might appropriately be studied by the Commission.

Both the Treasury and the Federal Reserve had set forth their views in detail on many matters of concern to the Commission in testimony before and submissions to, various committees of Congress during the preceding decade. Each was also preparing to testify further before the Joint Economic Committee in the course of its study on Employment, Growth and Price Levels. All these materials were used extensively during the work of the Commission. Nevertheless, there were additional issues and problems on which the Commission wanted to obtain the views of the Treasury and the Federal Reserve or on which it wanted more up-to-date statements.

Consequently, the Commission took advantage of the cooperation promised at the initial meetings and addressed formal inquiries to both the Treasury and the Board of Governors of the Federal Reserve System. These inquiries had been developed in informal discussion sessions between the staff of the Commission and of the Federal Reserve and Treasury respectively. In both instances there was an explicit understanding that the replies were "to become part of the public record of materials submitted to the Commission." Pursuant to this understanding, the replies were released for publication by the Treasury and Federal Reserve.

The replies of the Treasury were prepared and released for publication by the Department of the Eisenhower Administration; they should not be attributed to the Treasury Department of the Kennedy Administration.

Both sets of replies and the questions to which they responded are reproduced in full in this volume in the belief that they will contribute to public understanding of official views on monetary, fiscal and debt management operations and policies. The Commission and its staff are indebted to both the Treasury and the Federal Reserve for their willing and valuable contributions.

December, 1961.   Bertrand Fox
                                   Director of Research

                                   Eli Shapiro
                                   Deputy Director of Research

CONTENTS

Part One   THE FEDERAL RESERVE ANSWERS

Part Two   THE TREASURY ANSWERS

Part One

THE FEDERAL RESERVE ANSWERS

QUESTION I

What are the processes and procedures that are involved in the formulation and the execution of monetary policy? That is, given the customary credit control instruments and the ultimate objectives of price stability, high level employment, and economic growth, how is monetary policy formulated in the short run? For instance, what sort of factors are weighed in determining current policy, what guides are utilized, and what are the immediate objectives of policy?

Among the points of interest within this context are such factors as the meaning and importance attached to the general notion of liquidity in this decision-making process; what specific considerations are looked at in evaluating the current adequacy or inadequacy of the money supply; and whether influence on the level and structure of interest rates is ever an objective of policy?

ANSWER I

Summary

Formulation and execution of monetary policy is a continuous process. The ultimate objectives are, as the question states, price stability, high level employment, and sustained economic growth. The processes and procedures through which policy is executed in the short run are necessarily more specific than these broad goals, but they can never be dissociated from them.

The first section of this answer considers the nature of monetary policy decisions made by the Federal Reserve, with specific reference not only to the liquidity and reserve position of banks and the expansion of bank credit and money, but also to the relationships between the money supply, the use of money, the over-all liquidity of the economy, and interest rates. The second section discusses briefly the principal elements of economic developments in general--demand, employment, prices, and financial flows--that are considered by the Federal Reserve authorities in determining monetary policies. The third section deals primarily with more specific operating guides and procedures that determine day-to-day and other short-run operations by the System in the open market.[1]

Continuous review of economic and financial developments is a prime essential for policy formulation and execution. Implicitly involved in the consideration of policy are three interrelated questions: In what respects is the whole constellation of past and prospective events, as seen at a given moment, contributing to or detracting from price stability, high level employment, and economic growth? In what respects does it lie within the power of the Federal

---

[1]Further more detailed discussions of most of these points are given in answers to other questions.

Many aspects of these various matters are discussed--in some cases more fully--in statements presented by the Chairman of the Board of Governors of the Federal Reserve System to the Joint Economic Committee of Congress in 1959. See particularly Study of Employment, Growth, and Price Levels, Hearings, Part 6A, pp. 1233-35, and Part 6C, pp. 1765-77, 1785-87, and 1800-04. A thoughtful analysis of much the same problems is given in the Memorandum of Evidence presented by Winfield W. Riefler to the Radcliffe Committee; see "Committee on the Working of the Monetary System," Principal Memoranda of Evidence (London: Her Majesty's Stationery Office, 1960).

Reserve to set forces in motion, either to foster the attainment of these goals or to counter any threats to that achievement? What specific action should the Federal Reserve take?

Whatever broad influences may flow from their actions, the Board of Governors and the Federal Open Market Committee are fully aware that the particular economic or financial variable over which they have anything approaching full and direct control is the total of commercial bank reserves. Through this control, they exert a strong influence directly on total loans and investments and total deposits of banks and indirectly some influence on spending, investment, and saving by the public in general. At any given moment, therefore, the choice for Federal Reserve policy lies between various degrees of restraint upon or encouragement to expansion of bank credit through altered reserve availability.

Decisions on the degree of restraint or encouragement to be imposed on bank credit expansion are translated into action principally through Federal Reserve open market and discount operations, with occasional use of changes in reserve requirements and other instruments of policy. Open market operations affect the reserve position of the commercial banks. The bulk of such operations are for the purpose of offsetting the effects of other factors that affect the availability of reserves, most of which are of a temporary or special nature. The net effect of System operations and these other factors determines the availability of reserves for credit expansion.

Federal Reserve open market operations also have other direct and immediate effects upon interest rates in money markets, the money supply, and the general liquidity of money holders. Since these effects are intertwined with other market forces, they are not predictable or measurable. Much greater ultimate effects arise from the action of banks in adjusting their loans and investments to their changed reserve positions and then in turn from the actions of borrowers and depositors in adjusting their uses of funds to the changed availability of bank credit. The over-all magnitude of these adjustments with respect to total volume of loans and investments and of deposits at banks is roughly controllable by Federal Reserve policies. Flows of other funds, however--evolved over time from accumulated savings and outside the control of the banking system-- are of much greater magnitude and generally of greater influence in determining the course of the economy than are those deriving from changes in the volume of bank credit. The ultimate flows of all these funds into particular uses are beyond the direct control of the Federal Reserve. Nevertheless, changes in the availability of bank credit have a marginal influence upon money flows and upon interest rates that, if not properly controlled, can affect economic stability adversely.

Monetary policy exerts its influence largely through the quantitative vehicles of control over the volume of bank credit and
money. Through this channel monetary policy affects the over-all
liquidity of the economy and interest rates, which in turn influence
saving and spending. In determining particular policy actions, consideration must be given not alone to the volume of money but also
to the rate and manner of use of the funds--as reflected in interest
rates, in the over-all liquidity of the economy, and in the total volume of monetary transactions. Efforts must be directed toward
adjusting the volume of bank reserves so as to influence, or to
correct for, these forces in ways most conducive to the maintenance of price stability, high level employment, and economic
growth. It must always be recognized, however, that monetary
policies alone should not be expected to assure the attainment of
these objectives. Monetary policies cannot be relied upon to correct
for imperfections in the economic structure or for imbalances
resulting from actions by others--whether in the public or the private sector.

The Nature of the Monetary Policy Decisions Made by the Federal Reserve

Authority for making monetary policy decisions is shared by
the Board of Governors, the Federal Open Market Committee, and
the directors and officers of the twelve Federal Reserve banks.
Decision as to the current posture of monetary policy is usually
evolved at periodic meetings of the Federal Open Market Committee.
These meetings, which generally are attended by the members of
the Board of Governors and all Federal Reserve bank presidents,
since May 1955 have been ordinarily held at intervals of three weeks.
Although this Committee has specific responsibility for directing
the conduct of open market operations, other related policy actions
are often discussed at meetings of the Committee, and such actions
are determined in the light of the general policy position determined
by the Committee.

At each meeting, the Committee makes a decision as to the degree of restraint or encouragement that should be imposed on bank
credit expansion. Because of the complexity both of the forces at
work in the money market and of the interrelations between developments in the money market and the course of economic and financial events in the economy as a whole, the decisions of the
Federal Open Market Committee with respect to the current emphasis of policy are necessarily expressed in general terms.

The formal record of their decisions is embodied in the policy
directive given to the Federal Reserve Bank of New York, which
executes transactions for the Federal Open Market Account. These
directives, together with a record of the reasons for their adoption

and of somewhat more specific views as to their current application, are published for each year in the Board's Annual Report. The Account Management is guided by this record, as well as by the formal directive, in conducting specific operations to effectuate policies.

Bank credit and the money supply. In operational terms, the principal immediate effect of Federal Reserve actions is to control the supply of reserve funds available to the commercial banking system. On the basis of these reserve funds, the banks make loans and investments, which result in the creation of the bulk of the cash balances that the public holds. Changes in commercial bank credit comprise only a fraction of the total flow of saving and credit in the economy, and changes in the amount of Federal Reserve credit are only a fraction of the changes in commercial bank credit. Federal Reserve and commercial bank credit operations, however, through their indirect effects play a distinctive role in the saving-investment process and in the shaping of the flow of income, expenditure, and output in the economy as a whole.

The banking system as a whole differs from other financial institutions in that commercial banks as a group by expanding or contracting credit largely determine the total supply of money available to be held in cash--currency or bank deposits. This is true because the money made available by the extension of bank credit--however used--must at every moment find lodgement in some bank either as a deposit or in retirement of bank credit (unless held in currency or taken in gold). The amount of money that can be created is a multiple of the reserves made available by the Federal Reserve and is limited by the amount of such reserves that are available.

No single financial institution, however--bank or nonbank--can lend or invest more money than is left with it, and no individual can invest more than he saves or borrows. When expansion of bank credit exceeds the amounts the public wishes to retain in the form of money balances, the excess balances are likely to result in an expansion of spending. Restriction on bank credit expansion to a rate less rapid than that at which the public wishes to increase its money balances will likely lead the public to reduce spending and increase saving in an effort to establish the desired level of money balances.

Since the impact of monetary policy on the economy is transmitted through changes in bank credit and the money supply, it is essential for policy formulation that there be continuous assessment of the adequacy of these magnitudes. This is not an easy task, but it is one that the Federal Reserve, with its power to control the creation of credit and money, must endeavor to perform.

Since the Federal Reserve cannot control the uses that are made of money at the initiative of banks or other holders, monetary policy decisions must be based upon judgment as to the total amount of bank credit and money that is appropriate at any time. Policy cannot be directed toward enabling banks to meet all demands for credit, or any particular demand, that might develop under any conditions. This could result in an undue stimulus to spending and investing, which would derive, first, from increased spending growing out of bank credit expansion and, second, from the creation of a redundant money supply, i.e., excessive liquidity. Special problems arise when some particular type of credit tends to expand at an unsustainable pace or for other reasons threatens the maintenance of economic stability. Such instances raise a question as to whether restraints on total credit expansion should be exercised or whether more selective controls can and should be imposed.

Bank liquidity. The Federal Reserve exerts its influence upon the availability of bank credit, upon the money supply, and upon interest rates, almost wholly by influencing bank liquidity--in contrast to using other types of measures such as direct control of bank lending and investment or direct control of interest rates. In the United States, therefore, bank liquidity--to be distinguished from liquidity of the economy in general--plays a special role in financial and economic processes.

Bank liquidity consists of various elements which may be divided into two broad groups--primary and secondary. Primary bank liquidity relates to the net reserve position of commercial banks. The secondary liquidity of banks resides in their holdings of certain liquid assets, often called secondary reserves, which can be readily liquidated by a bank in order to meet deposit drains or adjust primary reserve positions. These liquid assets include short- and medium-term Government securities, loans to securities dealers, bankers' acceptances, other short-term open market paper, and balances with other banks. Before the 1930's call loans, bankers' acceptances, and interbank balances were the principal secondary reserves; today short-term Government securities are predominant.

The over-all liquidity of a bank is determined by the distribution of its loans and securities between liquid and nonliquid or less liquid components, by the volume of its borrowings, by its capital position, and by the nature of its deposits. Accurate measures of liquidity call for complex and variable formulas. Secondary liquidity of banks is not subject to direct influence by the Federal Reserve, but the Federal Reserve may exert an indirect effect through its control over primary liquidity and over total expansion of bank credit, although the effect would depend on actions by the banks themselves with respect to the illiquid portion of their assets. For example, an increase in member bank reserves would permit banks to improve liquidity by expanding secondary liquid assets, while also increasing their illiquid assets by a smaller proportion. A decrease in reserves, necessitating a reduction in total assets, would mean a decrease in liquidity to the extent that the reduction was effected in liquid assets.

Measurement of the primary liquidity position of banks requires consideration of both positive and negative elements. Positive primary liquid assets consist of balances held by banks with Federal Reserve banks. For liquidity purposes, i.e., for meeting drains on deposits and reserves, reserve balances held in excess of requirements are generally a more significant and useful measure than total reserves. Banks' holdings of coin and currency may also be considered as a part of primary liquidity, but as a rule these holdings are kept at the minimum needed for operating purposes. Beginning in 1960, all of these holdings could be counted as required reserves.

The negative element of primary liquidity for banks arises from member bank borrowings from the Federal Reserve. These provide a vital element of elasticity in the process by which bank credit expansion is restrained or encouraged. Such borrowings, which are obtained at the initiative of the member banks, serve to cushion, where necessary, the impacts on total bank reserves either of Federal Reserve operations or of other factors.

By tradition and by Federal Reserve administration, the cushion provided by member bank borrowing is an elastic one, in the strict sense of the word "elastic," meaning that the greater the use of the cushion, the greater the reverse pressure set up on the borrowing banks to adjust their investment and loan policies and so get out of debt to the Reserve Banks. It is for this reason that member bank borrowing can be regarded as a negative element of bank liquidity that should be deducted from excess reserves to measure the net liquidity position of an individual bank or of the banking system. The degree of restraint exerted by member bank borrowing may be varied by raising or lowering the discount rate charged on such borrowing, relative to rates of interest that banks may receive, particularly on secondary liquid assets.

The Federal Reserve restrains (or encourages) bank credit expansion by reducing (or increasing) the banks' primary liquidity. This is ordinarily accomplished through open market operations. At times changes in reserve requirements may be employed to release or absorb reserves. The effect of these actions, after allowance for the various other factors that influence the availability and use of reserves, may be reflected either in excess reserves or in member bank borrowings at the Reserve Banks. The over-all result for bank liquidity is commonly measured by the figure of "free

reserves" or "net borrowed reserves," which is derived by sub-
tracting borrowings of all member banks at the Reserve Banks from
excess reserves of member banks.

For individual banks, interbank borrowing for reserve adjustments has roughly the same effect on the borrowing bank as borrowing from the Federal Reserve. It differs, however, in its effect on
the credit system as a whole in that no additional new reserves are
made available to the banking system as a whole and no debt is incurred to the Federal Reserve. In our system of thousands of unit
banks, interbank operations--such as interbank balances, borrowing,
and the buying and selling of "Federal funds"--provide mobility to
funds that might otherwise be temporarily immobilized. The lending
bank gives up primary liquidity for the secondary liquidity represented by the asset it acquires, while the borrowing bank obtains
the reserves it needs and incurs a debt, not to the Reserve Bank
but to another member bank.

The effectiveness of the deterrent to bank credit expansion that
is inherent in a reduction in the aggregate net primary liquidity of
the banking system as a result of open market operations is enhanced
by the repercussions through the banking system of actions that individual banks take to adjust their reserve positions, whenever these
actions take a form that involves depositors of other banks. For
example, pressures are transmitted from bank A to bank B, whenever a depositor of bank B purchases securities sold by bank A.
Similarly, in expansionary phases, additions to bank liquidity by
Federal Reserve actions are transmitted through the financial structure and act as an encouragement to monetary expansion.

The existence of an extensive and efficient nonbank market for
Treasury bills and other short-term Government securities contributes greatly to the effectiveness of Federal Reserve restraint
on or encouragement to bank credit expansion. Among bank depositors, there are always ready buyers, at a price, for the securities
sold by the Federal Reserve in its open market operations and for
the securities sold by member banks endeavoring to adjust their
reserve positions. Thus the supply of funds available for other uses
may be reduced. Likewise, when banks have excess reserves but no
present loan demand, they can bid short-term Government securities from nonbank holders and thus add to the supply of money. This
addition to the money supply is likely to seek other uses.

Federal Reserve open market operations that effect cyclical or
longer-term changes in bank reserve positions are ordinarily only
a small fraction of all Federal Reserve transactions in the market
during the course of a year. The bulk of these transactions are directed toward counteracting the effect of various largely temporary
factors that influence the availability of or need for reserves.

These transactions are essential to prevent such temporary factors from causing wide money market shifts that would unduly interfere with the attainment of broad objectives. Ordinarily policy shifts are effected over time through relatively small adjustments in the large operations conducted for short-term purposes.

Generally it can be assumed that additions to the supply of reserves will provide the basis for an expansion of bank credit and bank deposits by a fairly constant multiple. Small variations in the multiple expansion ratio may occur, however, as a result of shifts in the relative proportions of deposits subject to different reserve requirement ratios, the relative preference of the public as between currency and deposits, and fluctuations in the amount of excess reserves that banks choose to hold. On the basis of the present distribution of deposits, the multiple expansion ratio averages nearly seven to one for demand deposits at member banks.

Long experience has shown that any departure from a relatively steady ratio between bank credit expansion and the reserves supplied at Federal Reserve initiative sets forces into operation that tend to encourage bank credit expansion when free reserves exist and to restrain bank credit expansion when net borrowed reserves exist. In a period of vigorous credit demands, for example, the Federal Reserve may increase the restraint on bank credit expansion by not providing through open market operations all of the reserves desired. As a consequence banks would be forced either to increase their borrowings at the discount window or to limit their credit expansion. Conversely, in a period of contraction, the accompanying decrease in required reserves brings about an increase in excess reserves or permits banks to reduce borrowing, thereby encouraging credit expansion or relaxing restraint without Federal Reserve action.

The significance at any given time of net borrowed reserves (or free reserves) as a factor tending to restrain (or encourage) bank credit expansion depends on at least five things: (1) the magnitude of the free reserves (or net borrowed reserves); (2) the level of short-term money rates relative to Federal Reserve discount rates; (3) the vigor of actual current demands for bank credit; (4) the existing level of total bank liquidity; and (5) the variations among different classes and groups of banks with respect to the conditions just named.

Federal Reserve decisions to impose a certain degree of restraint or encouragement on expansion of bank credit and money are something very different from a precise determination of the actual expansion of bank credit or of the money supply. Rather, these decisions relate to the setting into operation of forces to resist or accentuate other forces that affect the course of bank credit. The state of bank liquidity at any given moment and the changes in liquidity that are constantly occurring influence the level and structure of interest rates. This effect is reflected primarily on short-term money market rates and secondarily, sometimes with a considerable lag, on bank lending rates. Ultimately, because of the fluidity of financial markets, the whole structure of interest rates is affected, although, as elsewhere explained, the particular pattern of rates is largely determined by other forces in the credit markets.

The use or velocity of money. Changes in the volume of bank credit and the money supply are not determined by the banking system alone but also depend upon decisions of borrowers as to credit demands. Changes in the use of money grow principally from the decisions of borrowers, of holders of money, of spenders, and of nonbank lenders. From the standpoint of performance of the economy, it is not the holding of money but the use of money that counts. Amounts held, to be sure, may influence decisions as to the use of money. If new money created keeps moving to holders who do not want to hold more cash, the flow and the turnover of money can expand rapidly. Experience shows that the rate of use or velocity of money varies significantly over short periods of time, as well as over long periods.

Even though Federal Reserve operations exercise their influence primarily through the quantity of bank credit and the money supply, policy decisions cannot be made exclusively in terms of the level or rate of change of the money supply. Monetary policy must take into consideration variations in money turnover, which have an important influence on the course of economic events. Variations in money turnover need not be considered as a bar to the effectiveness of monetary policy if policy formulation takes them into consideration, although they may at times complicate its task.

General liquidity. A related reason why Federal Reserve policy decisions cannot be made solely in terms of money supply goals is that economic decisions are influenced by all elements of liquidity, including holdings of other assets as well as of money balances. The concept of general liquidity used here refers to liquid asset holdings of the nonbanking sectors of the community. Decisions of spenders and lenders are likely to be affected by the degree of their liquidity existing at any point in time and by variations in their liquidity over time.

Many types of assets possess qualities of liquidity, namely the ability to use as or to convert into means of payment at will, with little or no risk of loss in face value. Some types of assets, such as time deposits at banks and savings and loan association shares, are redeemable at fixed values. The obligors are expected to be in a position to assure liquidity for such claims. For certain other types of assets, liquidity depends upon shiftability among holders, or marketability, whereby holders of such assets wanting spendable funds may exchange these assets for the idle cash balances of others without the creation of new money. Short-term paper of high credit-worthiness offers such liquidity. In addition, assets, such as long-term bonds, which otherwise would not be classified as liquid, might be given liquidity by Federal Reserve action. If the Federal Reserve should follow a policy of purchasing any particular assets at prices that would not penalize offerings, then such assets in effect become as liquid as money.

Particular actions available to the Federal Reserve to restrict general liquidity outside the banking system are limited. Regulation of margin requirements, which reduced trading on brokers' credit to minimal amounts, has effectively limited the volume of stock market call loans, which before the 1930's provided an important type of liquid asset. Liquidity of time deposits at commercial banks can be restricted to some extent by rules as to conditions of withdrawal, which are incorporated in regulations relating to reserve requirements and to payment of interest on such deposits. The Federal Reserve, however, has no similar power with respect to deposits at mutual savings banks or to shares of savings and loan associations.

Because of the predominant position of short-term Government securities in the holdings of noncash liquid assets--and also because of their importance in money market adjustments--debt management policies of the federal government may exert highly important influences on the use of money and on general liquidity. This influence may be exerted through shifts in the maturity structure of the public debt available to others than the Federal Reserve and federal government funds. The practice of some governmentally chartered agencies of selling short-term obligations in order to make long-term loans may also have an influence.

The Federal Reserve can, to some degree, affect the maturity distribution of the public debt held by the public--bank and nonbank--by changes in System holdings of particular securities. Operations for such purposes, however, are restricted, in part because of the need to maintain a high degree of liquidity in the System portfolio to make possible its large short-term variations, and in part because of the uncertain effects on the functioning of the Government securities market. For these reasons Federal Reserve operations in Government securities are conducted principally with a view to affecting the volume of bank reserves and are usually confined to the short-term sector of the market, which is broader and more flexible than other sectors.

For the month-to-month decision-making of the Federal Open Market Committee, the changes in noncash components of general liquidity that are most directly relevant are those that are most closely related to current changes in the money supply. If an increase in the money supply occurs through bank acquisitions of Treasury bills from nonbank holders, the degree of general (nonbank) liquidity rises, although aggregate nonbank holdings of all types of liquid assets do not. Conversely, if the banks to expand loans sell short-term Government securities to nonbank holders, general liquidity may rise even without an increase in the money supply. Shifts between demand and time deposits have a similar significance, although the impact on securities markets and interest rates may be somewhat different.

Transfers of security holdings between banks and nonbank holders, or among nonbank holders in exchange for deposits, it may be noted, provide some of the characteristic processes by which monetary velocity may increase during a period of economic expansion and rising interest rates or decrease when interest rates decline. An increase in noncash liquidity outside the banking system is not necessarily a hindrance to or a limitation on the effectiveness of monetary policies. It may imply merely that the public wishes to hold such assets rather than idle cash balances. Or it may, under some conditions, imply that more restraint is required than would otherwise be necessary upon the creation of additional money through bank credit expansion. To the extent that credit demands are being met through the borrowing of savings other than through the banking system there is less need for bank credit expansion. Such expansion might add excessively to the volume of cash balances.

If nonbank holders desire to shift from other liquid assets to money, monetary policy should be designed to discourage or facilitate such shifts, according to the prevailing state of economic activity. If there are pressures on resources, the creation of additional money is restrained and holders of assets desiring to obtain cash have to find buyers other than banks. In periods of slack in economic activity, on the other hand, monetary policy attempts to increase general liquidity by making reserves more readily available to banks, and through this to encourage expansion in bank credit and the money supply. In essence, it may be said that Federal Reserve policies influence general liquidity by influencing the availability of money, rather than by attempting any direct regulation of nonbank holdings of other types of liquid assets.

Financial developments in the United States in 1959 and 1960 provide an example of a situation in which monetary policies were adapted first to large increases in credit demands, in nonbank lending, in general liquidity, and in monetary velocity, and then to a shift in these tendencies. In 1959, exceptionally large amounts of credit demands--both government and private--were met with little or no expansion in the money supply. Banks provided substantial amounts of short-term loans to businesses and individuals, but obtained the funds to meet these demands by selling Government securities to nonbank buyers. Nonbank lenders absorbed not only these sales of securities by banks but also large net additions to the outstanding public debt, and they increased their holdings of other assets as well. The funds for these purposes came in part from current savings and in part from activation of already existing cash balances, which had been built up during 1958, when monetary policy was directed toward encouraging monetary expansion. In 1959 funds were attracted into uses other than cash holdings by the higher interest rates that resulted from the pressures of the large credit demands along with restraint on bank credit expansion.

Under these circumstances, adequate credit was available to maintain a high degree of economic activity without creation of additional money that could have exerted undue pressures on available resources. This experience is an example of how monetary policy can be effectively applied in limiting unnecessary expansion of bank credit and creation of money when credit and liquidity needs are being otherwise met.

During 1960, in contrast, credit demands declined considerably from the record level of 1959, reflecting not only a shift from a large federal government deficit to a moderate surplus, but also a decrease in private credit demands. Monetary policy shifted gradually from restraint to encouragement of bank credit expansion. Interest rates declined. Banks met a moderate, though reduced, loan demand and added to their holdings of Government securities, while reducing their borrowings from the Reserve Banks. The money supply declined somewhat in the first half of the year but increased in the last half; the public's holdings of time deposits and savings association shares increased considerably; but nonbank holdings of U.S. Government securities declined. Monetary velocity, however, was maintained at a higher level during 1960 than in previous years. General liquidity of the nonbank public, as measured by holdings of liquid assets, which had been built up greatly in 1958 and 1959, showed a much smaller growth in 1960, but indebtedness also increased less.

Interest rates. Interest rates serve as an essential allocator of resources in the whole process of saving and investment, and in the day-to-day functioning of the money and credit system. Changes in interest rates and concomitant changes in bond prices have pervasive influences on incentives to invest and save. Individuals, businesses, and financial institutions, as borrowers or investors, are all likely to be affected in some degree by changes in the cost of borrowing money or in the capital value of their financial assets. Since the impact of changes in interest rates on borrowing costs and capital

values ultimately influences spending and saving decisions, monetary policy by influencing interest rates can have an effect on these
decisions.

The level and structure of interest rates prevailing in credit and
capital markets at any given time reflect a complex interplay of
demand and supply forces. Credit and monetary policy, which affects
primarily the quantity of bank reserves and in turn the volume of
bank credit and the money supply, functions as only one supply factor in interest rate determination. The great bulk of the supply of
funds available for lending arises from the savings of the public--
past and current; bank credit usually comprises only a small portion
of the total. It is often a marginal factor, the importance of which
may vary according to the state and composition of economic activity and expectations.

Monetary policy, it seems clear, can never be the sole determinant of the credit supply and therefore of the supply forces that
influence interest rate levels. In other words, it cannot at will
determine the level and pattern of interest rates through its influence on supply. Monetary operations necessarily have to permit the
interplay of total demand and total supply forces to be reflected in
interest rate changes. As is described below in the discussion of
Federal Reserve operating guides and procedures, rate changes
often provide monetary authorities sensitive clues to the direction
and intensity of pressures in the credit markets.

Federal Reserve actions to implement monetary policy are
generally focused on the volume and availability of bank reserves
rather than on any particular level or pattern of interest rates.
Federal Reserve actions designed to impose or maintain a desired
degree of restraint or encouragement on bank credit expansion consist principally of market operations in short-term Government
securities. Operations in short-term securities have minimal direct effects upon the structure of securities prices and interest
rates, although the indirect impact on the level of interest rates
arising from the effects of System operations on bank credit expansion may be substantial. The nature of these indirect effects is
determined by the market itself.

Under some circumstances, however, monetary policies may for
a short period be purposefully directed toward cushioning supply or
demand changes tending to have temporarily disturbing effects on
market patterns of interest rates. This may occur, for example,
during a period of Treasury financing or when some seasonal or
similar temporary influence is affecting rates to an excessive degree. International movements of funds that can be attributed to
interest rates differentials may call for policies aimed particularly
at influencing interest rates. There may also be cyclical develop-

ments in which operations directed toward affecting the structure of interest rates may appear to be appropriate.

As a matter of general practice, however, Federal Reserve policies are administered so that basic changes in the saving/investment relationship and variations in demand and supply among different segments of the market can be reflected in changing levels and structures of interest rates.

Principal Factors Influencing Policy Decisions

Decisions made by the Federal Open Market Committee as to the degree of restraint or encouragement that should be imposed on bank credit expansion cannot be interpreted or illustrated by any precise mathematical formula. The process of decision-making proceeds by successive approximations. That is to say, the Committee reviews at each meeting information covering a wide range of economic and financial developments, and forms a judgment as to whether its previous decision regarding the degree of restraint or encouragement of bank credit expansion was in fact appropriate or not, and whether it is still appropriate. If it is not, the Committee then considers what changes should now be made in direction or in degree of encouragement or restraint on bank credit expansion.

Information required for the broad and continuing analysis of economic forces pertinent to policy decisions is almost unlimited in scope. Information available at any time is limited and judgments must often be based on incomplete facts. Even more important than the information itself are the judgments that must be made in interpreting the data: for example, judgments as to the stage of the business cycle the economy has reached, involving views as to whether consumption, saving, and investment are in balance or are showing signs of disequilibrium; judgments as to the climate of expectations about price movements, equity values, and interest rates; and judgments as to the trend of the international balance of payments. It is in the light of judgments such as these that decisions must be reached as to the appropriate degree of restraint or encouragement to be imposed on expansion of bank credit.

Price stability and economic growth. Basic to the formulation of monetary policy are the national objectives of price stability, high level employment, and economic growth. Satisfactory achievement of these objectives depends on actions of the Congress and the Executive and on actions of people in all walks of life. Disturbances to economic stability and growth may arise in many ways. Generally, the roots of the trouble develop long before overt signs are clearly seen. In an industrial economy, growth tends to proceed irregularly through cycles of advance and recession or pause. Some cyclical variation may be the unavoidable result of the self-correcting forces of the market system. A flexible price system is essential for maintaining balance between production and consumption of particular goods and services. At times structural imbalances develop that cannot be corrected by general public policies.

The task of public policies is to endeavor to detect forces of disturbance and to temper excessive movements in one direction or another so far as possible. Federal Reserve powers contribute most to the achievement of the national objectives of price stability, high level employment and economic growth when they are so exerted as to minimize price inflation or deflation, to damp down expectations of sudden and violent changes in commodity prices or in equity values, and to prevent unsustainable expansion or discourage harmful contraction in bank credit. The immediate task of Federal Reserve policy is to decide upon the degree of restraint or encouragement to be imposed on bank credit expansion consistent with achievement of national objectives. This may mean helping to check unstabilizing developments in the economy influenced by credit factors when they become apparent. It also means helping to prevent such disturbances from occurring.

Federal Reserve policies, it needs to be kept in mind, are exerted through influencing the total volume of bank credit and money. It lies beyond the powers of the Federal Reserve to promote growth of particular segments of the economy without affecting other segments in ways that may or may not be desirable. It is likewise difficult or impossible to restrain particular activities without exerting general restraint.

Clearly actions by the Federal Reserve alone cannot assure the attainment of the broad national objectives. Attempts to assure continuous stimulation of over-all growth through bank credit expansion, regardless of other developments, might incur the risk of inflationary or speculative developments that would be unsustainable and thus create instability and unemployment or they may merely result in the accumulation of idle cash balances with little perceptible effect in the economy. Monetary policies cannot be expected to prevent or correct imbalances that might develop as a result of particular governmental actions, of structural imperfections in the economy, or of mistakes of judgment made by private businesses or individuals with respect to the amounts and prices of goods and services they offer. It may at times be unwise to endeavor through monetary policies to prevent the adjustments in the economy that such imbalances may inevitably entail, although Federal Reserve actions might help to ease the adjustment process. Any such imbalances and their causes must at all times be taken into consideration in determining policies. Their existence may call for more restrictive, or justify less restrictive, policies.

It follows that in formulating policies the Federal Reserve authorities must be cognizant of developments with respect to production, employment, and prices, as well as the financial variables more directly affected by monetary policies. They must appraise the course of developments and make judgments as to any emerging imbalances and their causes. These analyses require the assembly and interpretation of a large amount of information in many aspects of the economic situation--foreign as well as domestic.

The flow of funds. Broad influences of monetary policy, reaching beyond the money market to affect economic and financial developments in the economy at large, can be traced through two sets of channels of cause and effect: on the one hand, those connected with bank lending and investment, and on the other hand, those connected with changes in the liquidity of the economy. It is never possible to trace these two sets of influences in complete detail. They are, moreover, an integral part of the broader complex of the flow of funds that reflects changes in income and consumption, saving and investment, and portfolio management.

Monetary policy is more or less limited in the scope of its direct influence. It operates through the channel of bank credit, which constitutes a relatively small portion of total credit and the total flow of funds. Over the past ten years since the Treasury-Federal Reserve Accord, the net increase in the total of credit and equity market instruments has generally been between $30 billion and $60 billion a year, while the amount supplied by the commercial banking system has averaged about $6 billion. Of total bank credit only about half is reflected in a growth of the money supply, as narrowly defined to include demand deposits and currency; the remainder represents savings held in the form of time deposits and bank capital. The bulk of funds for investment or other borrowing comes from savings other than those created by or channeled through the banking system.

In exerting a direct influence over the total of commercial bank loans and investments, however, monetary policy may play a marginal role in the flow of funds and in the saving/investment relationship. Maintenance of equality between total investment outlays and the amount of voluntary saving that corresponds with a high employment level of income at stable prices is an essential for sustainable economic growth. Monetary policy, by restricting the creation of additional bank credit and permitting interest rates to rise at times of relatively full utilization of resources when investment outlays are tending to press unduly against the flow of voluntary saving, aims both to restrain investment outlays and to encourage saving. In periods of recession or slack, monetary policy helps to encourage investment and other spending by making bank credit more readily available to supplement the flow of loanable funds emanating from savers. Any other policies under the circumstances would contribute to instability.

An important analytical device for summarizing the flow of saving into investment and for placing the various elements of this flow in perspective, both in relation one to another and in relation to flows of current income and expenditure, is the Board's compilation of flow-of-funds accounts for the economy as a whole.[2] The flow-of-funds accounts are a convenient vehicle for analyzing the mutual impact of the various financial and nonfinancial groups in the economy and of the adjustment process among the various financial markets.

Operating Guides and Procedures

Open market operations necessary to effectuate the policies adopted by the Federal Open Market Committee are carried out by the Manager of the Federal Open Market Account at the Federal Reserve Bank of New York. The Management is guided by the broad directive that has been formally adopted by the Committee, by the discussion of the current economic situation, and by such specific instructions as may be expressed at the Committee's meetings. The instructions given and the essential points of the discussion, including a summary of the factors and reasons upon which the decisions were based, are incorporated in the Record of Policy Actions published each year in the Board's Annual Report. The Manager of the Account is expected to use his special and expert knowledge of market conditions, along with a great amount of statistical material on market trends in judging the specific actions needed to maintain or bring about the conditions indicated by the Committee's directive. Operations are conducted within the limits imposed by various operating procedures that have been adopted by the Committee.

The principal specific factors considered by the Management in determining short-term operations may be summarized as follows:

---

[2]This compilation is available in its present form by years since 1946 and by quarters since 1952. Figures are published quarterly in the Federal Reserve Bulletin. An example of its use for current analysis is found in the text of the Board's Annual Report for 1959. Availability of the flow-of-funds accounts has improved the ability to analyze each type of credit flow to each major sector simultaneously in terms of (1) the total credit flow of that type, (2) the whole pattern of capital market flows, (3) the other sources of financing utilized by the sector, and (4) the sector's need for funds in relation both to its income and its expenditures.

(a) <u>Bank reserves.</u> The particular immediate purpose of open market operations is to keep banks supplied with a volume of reserves adequate to support the volume of bank credit and money considered appropriate. As previously pointed out, the bulk of Federal Reserve operations are directed toward counteracting the effect of various largely temporary factors that influence the availability of or need for reserves. In the course of a year the gross volume of System open market operations may exceed $10 billion; net changes in total holdings in any one week may equal several hundred million dollars; and the net change from the seasonal low point of the year in the spring to the high point in December customarily averages about $1.5 billion.

These repetitive variations in the Federal Reserve portfolio are almost wholly for the purpose of covering normal seasonal movements in required reserves (resulting from similar movement in deposits) and in currency. Large, sometimes erratic, fluctuations in Federal Reserve float also call for some offsetting action, although precise offsets are generally not possible or necessary. Fairly large day-to-day or week-to-week operations are needed to cover these and various other temporary or occasional factors that influence the availability of reserves. Other large changes in System holdings over extended periods have been made to counteract the effect of gold movements. The task of meeting these temporary and special needs is in essence not a policy matter, but a technical operating problem of measuring or otherwise detecting such variations and making prompt adjustments to them. As explained later, the net amount of Federal Reserve operations designed to cover cyclical variations and growth in credit and monetary needs seldom exceeds $1 billion in the course of a year.

For short-term operating purposes, the essential immediate guide is the volume of total bank reserves that is adequate to meet the current needs of member banks for required reserves against their deposits plus some volume of excess reserves. The volume of reserves supplied relative to minimum needs or desires of banks represents the degree of restraint on or encouragement to credit expansion. The figure of "free reserves" or its negative counterpart "net borrowed reserves" provides a convenient and significant working measure of the posture of policy at the time. This figure, which is the difference between member bank excess reserves and member bank borrowings at the Reserve banks at any one time, is readily and promptly obtainable on a daily basis with a reasonable degree of accuracy. It is also a device that is better adapted than its components taken separately for estimating and projecting the net impact of regular variations in factors affecting reserves.

The general level of free reserves prevailing over a period of time may be viewed as an indicator of the degree of restraint or

ease that exists in the money market. Although figures for free or
net borrowed reserves are useful for current operational purposes,
and serve as a general indicator of policy, they must be considered
in the context of changes in the total reserve position of member
banks. The particular level of free reserves that may be needed to
achieve the objective of policy may vary from time to time depending on changing economic conditions. To maintain free reserves at
some particular level might under circumstances of vigorous credit
demands mean providing reserves to meet all demands. Under conditions of slackening credit demands, maintenance of the same
level might mean an actual reduction in the supply of reserves or
an increase in borrowings, with pressure for credit liquidation
rather than encouragement to expansion.

(b) Bank credit and money supply. Broader guides to policy
operations are provided by the consequences of changes in reserve
availability on the amount of total loans and investments of banks
and on the money supply. Assumptions or estimates as to these
elements underlie the current and projected figures for total reserves and free reserves. The Open Market Committee in its de-
liberations has in mind what conditions with respect to the availability of bank credit and growth in the money supply would be an
appropriate end of policy at the time.

In conducting its operations to carry out the Committee's decisions as to reserve availability, the Account Management must
adjust its operations to cover seasonal and other temporary variations in monetary and credit needs, as well as in other factors
that affect reserves. Average seasonal swings in currency in circulation cover a range of more than $1 billion in the course of a
year, and there are fairly wide temporary movements around holi-
days; seasonal swings in required reserves ordinarily amount to
somewhat less than $1 billion (reflecting seasonal variations in the
volume of bank deposits of about $5 billion). There are also sig-
nificant temporary variations in required reserves incident to
Treasury financing operations and to periodic large tax and dividend payments.

Growth in reserve needs resulting from monetary expansion
might average $1 billion a year, or only $20 million a week. Cyclical
movements generally amount to less than $1 billion in the course
of any 12-month period. Because of wide, purely temporary, and
partly unpredictable variations in the money supply, as well as in
other factors affecting reserve needs, it is difficult to relate day-
to-day Federal Reserve operations precisely to a particular level
of the money supply. Cyclical and growth changes in reserve availability are usually the net result of relatively large, partly offsetting short-term operations.

(c) <u>Money rates</u>. The role of interest rates both as an objective of and as a guide to Federal Reserve policy has already been noted. As pointed out, the Federal Reserve policies generally are directed toward providing an appropriate volume of reserves and not toward establishing or maintaining any particular level or pattern of interest rates. Such rates are determined by the forces of the market, one of which is the supply of bank credit. At times, however, when special circumstances are affecting the market, the Federal Reserve may act directly to influence prices and yields of securities. The level of market rates is also to some extent influenced by the Reserve Bank discount rates.

In operations to effectuate policies adopted by the Committee, interest rate movements perform a distinctive and important function as an index of the course of market forces. Alterations in sensitive money market rates, such as those on Treasury bills, may furnish the Account Management a delicately attuned signal of market forces and guide for the timing of operations.

Federal Reserve operations are generally so conducted as to minimize their influence on the structure or pattern of rates. In order to avoid unnecessary System interference with the functioning of the market and to inform market participants of the usual nature and scope of Federal Reserve intervention in the market, the Open Market Committee has adopted a number of operating procedures to be observed by the Account Management in conducting open market operations. In brief, these working rules, which may be changed at any time by action of the Committee to meet special situations, relate to the maturities of Government securities in which transactions can be conducted, to operations in securities involved in a concurrent Treasury financing, and to operations directed toward changing the structure of the System portfolio.

<u>Conclusion</u>

Federal Reserve policies, directed toward the broad ultimate objectives of fostering price stability, high level employment, and sustained economic growth, are determined by the policy-making authorities of the System on the basis of a great many considerations. They are put into effect operationally through control over bank reserves. It is principally through the channel of bank reserves that Federal Reserve policies influence the volume of bank credit, the money supply, and interest rates.

In determining the volume of operations needed at any time in order to provide reserves adequate for changes in bank credit and the money supply that would best contribute to the broad objectives of policy, allowance must be made for seasonal and other temporary variations in factors that affect the supply of or demand for reserves. In dollar amounts these temporary variations are much greater than cyclical or growth needs.

Decision as to the appropriate amount of bank credit and money at any time is made in the light of a great number of variables: supply and demand conditions in markets for goods and services, the volume of employment and production relative to available resources, movement of the general level of prices, the general liquidity of the economy, the availability of credit from nonbank sources, the strength of prevailing credit demands, and the rate at which the existing money supply is being used. It must be recognized that bank credit supplies only a relatively small portion of the total credit needs of the economy, but the maintenance of this portion at an appropriate amount is of considerable marginal importance in helping to make possible sustainable economic growth.

Movements of interest rates are determined by the interaction of borrowing demands of all kinds upon the available supply of lendable funds. Bank credit is only a portion of this supply. Federal Reserve policies and operations do not aim at long-term control of the level or structure of interest rates. Normally the free interplay of supply and demand forces on the course of interest rates enables such rates to perform essential allocative functions. Interest rate changes are an essential part of the mechanism through which monetary policies ultimately influence the decisions of borrowers and lenders. They serve as a significant indicator of market developments that are relevant to the determination of such policies.

QUESTION II

Is monetary policy less appropriate or less effective under conditions of "cost-push" or "demand-shift" inflationary pressures than under conditions of "demand-pull" inflation? Is it possible to differentiate in practice as to when one or the other of these situations is dominant?

ANSWER II

Summary

Business fluctuations in the United States since World War II, while differing from one another in many ways, have had features in common with respect to the interactions of demands, output, costs, prices, and profits. The description of these relationships provided below indicates that the problems of inflationary pressures arise during the expansion phase of the business fluctuations characteristic of industrial economies, when demands are expanding. In the early stages of a business expansion, production and employment are likely to increase without generating widespread upward pressures on prices and costs. Continued expansion in demands eventually generates upward pressures on prices and costs as output in some industries reaches high levels in relation to capacity and unemployment is reduced. If the pace of expansion is moderate and competitive conditions are maintained, increases in prices and costs are likely to be confined to a relatively few markets. On the other hand, if demands expand rapidly and expectations are ebullient, increases in prices and costs are likely to become widespread.

With respect to the second of the two questions raised, once the process of inflation is under way, it is usually not possible to determine whether the dominant influence on prices stems from "cost push" or "demand shift." Since prices of goods and services represent costs to someone, increases in costs are one of the ways by which inflationary pressures are transmitted through the economy. At the same time, increases in some costs are promptly reflected in income payments and thus exert an influence on demands. Through this interaction of demands, prices, and costs, the inflationary process is initiated, and once in operation, the demand and cost elements interact in such a manner that they cannot be disentangled as separate and distinct forces.

In the chain-reaction process of demands, prices, and costs, the most direct influence that monetary policy can exert is on demands for goods and services. Through its influence on credit availability and on liquidity, monetary policy endeavors to maintain a climate of demands and expectations during business upswings that is conducive to a high rate of utilization of available resources without widespread upward pressures on prices and costs. Should upward pressures nevertheless develop, monetary policy can help to restrain them. Appropriate monetary policy can limit the funds that may be made available through bank credit to finance the expansion in demands stimulated by the income effects of price and cost increases, by expectations, and by other forces.

When business activity is high, prices generally are advancing, and the community expects continuing advances in prices, a monetary policy that restrains the use of bank credit is an appropriate and necessary tool. Whatever the causes or the means of propagating inflation, expansion of bank credit would influence both spending and expectations and so would provide additional impetus to the price-cost spiral. Under these conditions, individual and group efforts to hedge against inflation or to protect against it by tying contractual arrangements to price indexes would tend to aggravate inflationary forces.

In appraising the effectiveness of monetary policy, a number of factors must be considered. The formation of policy, first of all, depends on current assessments of developing business and financial conditions and, despite improvements in economic intelligence over the years, it is not possible always to judge accurately the strength of the forces developing. Other activities of the federal government, furthermore, have an impact on levels of production, employment, and income, and thus they influence needs for greater or lesser degrees of monetary ease or restraint. These policies, consequently, may complicate or simplify the task and they may inhibit or enhance the performance of monetary policy. Government policies that affect the functioning of markets and those that directly affect prices--such as import duties and quotas and antitrust policies--also bear on the effectiveness and results of monetary policy. The degree of market power exercised by private groups also may affect the sensitivity of markets to current and prospective demands. If monopoly power were widespread, it could have an influence on the effectiveness of both monetary and fiscal policies in pursuing their goals.

Nature of Cost-Push and Demand-Shift Explanations

Controversy over causes of postwar inflation has focused mainly on developments since 1954. On the causes and nature of the episodes of inflation in the earlier postwar years, there appears to be widespread agreement. World War II left a legacy of accumulated demands for goods of all kinds, and methods employed in financing the war resulted in highly liquid financial positions. When wartime price controls were removed, effective demands at current prices were considerably in excess of supplies in virtually every market.

When the Korean War began in mid-1950, memories of war-induced shortages and price increases provoked protective buying by consumers and businesses, here and abroad. In both periods of inflation, costs as well as prices rose and there were large shifts in the composition of demands, but the influence of strong demands in originating and sustaining price advances was by far the predominant one.

In the 1954-57 inflation, demands were not strong in all markets simultaneously, and the advance in prices was moderate in comparison with the war-related experiences. In view of these circumstances, several interpretations of the period since 1954 have emphasized the independent nature of costs. Another interpretation has stressed rapid changes in the composition of demands. What is common to these interpretations is that they have attributed primary importance to rigidities or to autonomous elements in markets for goods and services and have given little or no weight to the role of aggregate demands. From these theses, further interpretation is drawn that use of general instruments of restraint on aggregate demands in order to check such price increases would be ineffective or would incur unacceptable social costs in terms of unemployment of human and material resources.

The "cost-push" approach to the explanation of price inflation seems fundamentally to assume that costs are more or less independently determined by market power and, therefore, little can be done about them. Prices are set by administrative decisions to cover all costs, including a satisfactory margin of profit, without regard to current or prospective demand conditions. Production is scheduled to conform to sales at these prices.

In such circumstances, it is said, government policies--monetary and/or fiscal--must operate to provide demand sufficient to assure maximum output and full employment at the wages that are the result of labor-management agreements and at the prices businessmen--and, sometimes, public agencies--deem necessary. Otherwise, output and employment will be held or reduced below attainable levels, but there will be no appreciable restraint on advances in price levels and labor or other costs.

In practice, however, the extent to which the price of a product can be raised is limited by actual or potential competition from other products or from imports; these checks are strengthened by government policies that operate to restrain demands and prevent ebullient expectations from developing. Competitive constraints on prices strengthen resistance to increases in costs and at times may exert downward pressures as businessmen attempt to maintain or increase profit margins. The influence on costs may take such forms as programs to raise productivity, various efforts to economize on the use of materials, control of administrative and other types of salaried employment, or resistance to increases in wage rates and fringe benefits.

The "demand-shift" explanation of the type of inflation experienced in the 1954-57 business expansion rests on a combination of factors. Inflation, it is said, originates in the general excess demands which temporarily emerge as the economy passes from recession to full employment, and from the excess demands in specific sectors that often remain after the aggregate excess has been eliminated. Inflation is perpetuated and spread throughout the economy, the argument proceeds, by the influence of costs in wage and price determination and by the relative insensitivity of prices and costs to decreases in demands.

In this view, particularly as it relates to the 1954-57 business expansion, demands increase and full employment is reached without generating upward price and cost pressures. Then, a rapid shift in the composition of demands is reflected in excess demands in some sectors and insufficient demands in others. Because prices are more sensitive to increases than to contractions in demands, a general rise results as prices advance in those sectors where demands are increasing rapidly and decline by smaller amounts or not at all in those sectors where demands are decreasing. General monetary and fiscal policies appropriate to combat an inflation arising out of excess aggregate demand are not suitable, it is contended, to combat an inflation arising out of excess demands in particular sectors of the economy.

The composition of demands relative to the composition of available resources has an important bearing on developments in business expansions. The problems of inflationary pressures, however, are likely to arise well before demands and output reach the limits of capacity, partly because the use of marginal production facilities raises costs. Problems of inflation certainly arise before output reaches capacity in all major sectors because resources are not highly mobile. In 1955 and 1956, for example, output was well below capacity in the basic textile industries but very close to capacity in the basic metals industries. As E.A. Goldenweiser wrote in 1941:

> It should be mentioned ... that there is no clear-cut line at which an increasing number of bottleneck advances in prices passes over into a general inflation. The development of a number of bottlenecks in many leading commodities may be the introductory phase of a general inflation. It can occur long before the entire country is operating at full capacity, because neither plant capacity nor labor supply is completely mobile. The existence of unused capacity in some industries may not prevent great shortages of capacity in others, and the presence of large numbers of unskilled workers without jobs may not prevent grave shortages in many skilled lines. So long as these instances of shortages are scattered and relatively few the situation is not properly described as inflation and can be handled by nonmonetary remedies. But it may become general long before full capacity is achieved. It should be kept in mind that it is the available supply of goods and not the theoretically possible supply that must meet a growing demand in order to prevent inflation.[1]

---

[1] E.A. Goldenweiser, "Inflation," Federal Reserve Bulletin, (April 1941), p. 292.

The demand-shift approach treats the milder, peacetime inflations of the sort experienced in 1954-57 as something different
in kind from the type often associated with wars, whereas the difference appears rather to be one of degree. The immobility of
resources is more obvious in the former cases, but it is not confined to them. In the more severe inflations, immobility of resources
also limits shifts to areas of strongest demands, but its existence
and influence are concealed by the general excess of demands.

In an economy with high and rising standards of living and many
other features fostering change, demands are not likely to expand
in such a way that their composition is always in balance with the
location and types of existing plant and other resources. In business
expansions, imbalances are likely to exist, and they are not likely
to be precisely the same from one expansion to the next. Such imbalances operate to attract the newly available resources (and
savings) into the sectors of strongest demand pressures.

Patterns of Price and Cost Changes in Business Fluctuations

Prices are determined by the interaction of a number of factors
functioning continuously in many different types of markets, and
there is an unending process of market adaptation to changes in
the various factors. While business fluctuations differ from one
another in important respects, they all have features in common
with regard to the interactions of demands, output, costs, prices,
and profits. Reviewing the process of change during postwar business expansions and contractions in this country, certain relationships and patterns of behavior are discernible.

Periods of expansion. Early in expansions of business activity,
prices usually are rising in markets for "sensitive" industrial
materials--that is, the materials whose prices are most responsive
to short-run changes in demand. For rubber, hides, and some other
sensitive materials, world production cannot be increased much
(if at all) in the short run in response to rising demands. As a result, increases in demands are rather promptly reflected in price
advances and may alter the international flows of commodities.

Production or supply can be increased in the short run for other
sensitive materials, such as scrap metals, wastepaper, copper,
lead, zinc, and lumber. Because increases in output are accompanied by rising costs per unit of output or because of other conditions of supply, expansion in demands is reflected in price rises
which provoke increases in supply. Price trends for a group of
these sensitive materials often suggest the direction and strength
of demands before other types of data for the same time period
become available.

Many foods and foodstuffs--including livestock, poultry, and some crops--also conform to the type of market behavior described for sensitive industrial materials. For these, however, the response of domestic demands to cyclical and secular income changes is slight (the income elasticity of demand is low). Substantial changes in output may occur, however, mainly because of variations in weather, swings in the hog and cattle cycles, or rising productivity. Consequently, price fluctuations for these commodities usually reflect changes in supplies to a greater extent than they reflect shifts in demands.

Agricultural commodities subject to federal support programs are largely protected from the price-depressing influence of large increases in production. At the same time, the existence of stocks previously accumulated in the process of supporting prices has limited in recent years the response of prices to a crop failure or other events that reduce production and supply.

For most industrial materials other than those described as sensitive, supply is expansible in the short run until some relatively high rate of capacity utilization is reached. This is true for steel mill products, paper products, many chemicals, cement, brick, and other materials. In the early stages of expansion, variable costs per unit of output are not likely to rise as increases in output are accompanied by gains in productivity and wage rates do not rise much. Fixed costs per unit and average costs per unit decline, and profit margins as well as total profits rise. Expansion in demands for these materials is accompanied for a time by rising output and supply without widespread advances in list prices. Absorption of freight and other concessions from list prices which had developed during the previous recession tend to be reduced during the early stages of expansion. These changes in actual prices are not reflected in the established price indexes, which are based mainly on manufacturers' published price lists.

The behavior of wholesale or manufacturers' prices of most finished industrial products in the early stages of expansion is much like that described for the second group of industrial materials--for similar reasons. Therefore, increases in their prices early in expansions are likely to be restricted in scope.

Continued expansion of demands eventually generates upward pressures of costs on prices of industrial materials in the second or nonsensitive group and on prices of finished products. The upturn in costs is primarily a consequence of higher levels of output in relation to available manpower and material resources.

Contrary to the suggestion sometimes made that pressures of demand against resources available to produce specific products cannot possibly contribute to increases in their prices and costs until operations are at 100 percent of capacity, costs of production often begin to rise before output approaches such high levels. The plant and equipment existing in an industry at any time is of varying age and efficiency. As demands expand, less efficient facilities must be used if output is to be increased to fill the rising volume of orders. Partly because these marginal facilities have to be activated, over-all productivity advance slows and may actually cease or be reversed. This contributes, along with increasing wage rates, premium payments for overtime, and advances in prices of some materials consumed in the industry, to rising costs per unit of output.

Price- and cost-raising pressures of demands in specific industries, furthermore, may become widespread enough to constitute a general problem before output reaches high rates in relation to capacity in all major industries. Usually, some industries are growing while others are not, and some regions are gaining while others are losing business. A number of important bottlenecks may develop even while unused capacity exists elsewhere. These developments also contribute to a higher level of frictional unemployment of labor than might exist otherwise. A judgment that output in the whole economy is at a high rate relative to plant capacity does not require that there be no margins of unused capacity, any more than "full employment" means that there are no persons looking for jobs.

Given variations in the timing and intensity of demand and cost pressures among industries, governmental policies to further expand aggregate demands in order to raise demands and output in those industries where capacity is not being intensively utilized would intensify demand pressures on those industries where output is already close enough to capacity to result in rising costs and higher prices. Consequently, while a higher level of aggregate demand might increase total output somewhat, it would also accentuate upward pressures of demand on prices.

An additional and important aspect of these developments and relationships is that an expansion of capital outlays is likely to be stimulated well in advance of full utilization of plant capacity. Business enterprises always have some capital replacement needs, and additional capital expenditures in most cases reduce costs or increase sales potentials. Incentives to undertake new commitments for expansion as well as for replacement are intensified if business managers expect higher levels of demand for their products from both secular growth and cyclical expansion. Since it ordinarily takes many months before new facilities can be acquired and efficiently integrated into the production process, business managers must plan expenditures to increase capacity well before output reaches the limits of their ability to produce.

Among the elements of cost, attention in recent years has been focused on changes in labor costs, partly because wage rates have risen persistently and labor costs are an important part of total variable costs. In major industries, where changes in wage rates tend to be industry-wide, such changes occur at a particular moment in time and they usually are widely publicized. On the other hand, changes in productivity, which operate in the direction of offsetting the effect of wage rate increases on labor costs per unit of output, occur over a period of time. Also, the advances are likely to vary considerably from plant to plant and from one producer to another.

For many industries, average measures of productivity show more cyclical variability than wage rates, rising in the early stages of expansion, leveling off as output approaches capacity, and declining in the early stages of recession. This pattern of change is probably accentuated by the short duration of the business fluctuations of postwar experience. Many new facilities are put in place late in expansion—or in the early months of recession—and there is some time lag between installation and their efficient operation. When there is such a lag, the resulting productivity gains may appear late in recession and early in expansion.

Partly for this reason, unit labor costs tend to decline in the early stages of expansion when productivity gains generally exceed increases in wages. As expansion develops, unit costs turn up because productivity advance slows and the rise in wages continues and possibly accelerates. In recession also, unit labor costs typically rise in certain industries as output per manhour declines.

Meanwhile, capital consumption and other relatively fixed costs—by definition—do not vary with the level of output. On a per unit of output basis, therefore, they show an inverse correlation with output, decreasing when output is rising and increasing when output is falling.

Cyclical variations in costs per unit of output, which result in considerable part from swings in production, are not accompanied by similar variations in prices. Consequently, profit margins fluctuate more widely than labor and other costs per unit of output, generally moving in the opposite direction. In the early stages of expansion, profit margins rise sharply; in later stages, they level off or decline; in recession, they decline decidedly.

The preceding review of price and cost influences indicates that in early stages of economic expansion, production and employment are likely to advance without generating widespread price and cost pressures. While wage rates and prices of certain materials increase, margins of profits over costs widen and are likely to approach their cyclical peaks. After expansion has progressed for a time, however, upward price and cost pressures build up, primarily because output in some industries has reached high levels in relation to capacity and unemployment has been reduced. As described earlier, less efficient plant facilities must be used and productivity advance slows or is reversed. At the same time, reduced unemployment and enlarged profit margins intensify pressures for increases in employee compensation.

With demands strong and output in some industries already at high levels in relation to capacity, the subsequent behavior of prices and costs is strongly influenced by the rate at which over-all activity has been expanding and by expectations. If the pace of expansion has been moderate, competitive conditions are maintained within most industries, between industries serving common markets, and between domestic goods and goods produced abroad. In these circumstances, increases in prices and costs are likely to be confined to a relatively few markets and are unlikely to be very large.

On the other hand, if demands have been expanding rapidly and assessments of prospects are highly optimistic, increases in wage rates and fringe benefits are likely to be large and price advances extensive. Increases in wages will be propagated throughout industry and may directly cause further expansion in demands for goods and services. Price advances may indirectly contribute to expanding demands by generating expectations of additional advances.

Increases in the price indexes will further contribute to cost increases through escalator provisions of labor, rent, and other contracts. Some state and local taxes and fees may be raised to cover the rising costs of current services and higher costs of school, highway and other construction. These taxes are also reflected in the consumer price index used for escalation purposes. And thus an interacting inflationary process of demands, prices, and costs can get in full operation.

Implicit in this description of price behavior for industrial commodities is the fact that relatively few markets conform to an ideal competitive model. In the competitive model, prices are determined by the interaction of buyers' bids and sellers' asking prices in the market; the individual seller has no significant influence on total supply and therefore has no discretion except with regard to his acceptance or rejection of the going price or how much he will supply at that price. This type of market behavior is approached most closely in markets for livestock, some other agricultural commodities, and the industrial materials earlier described as sensitive.

Markets for industrial commodities, on the contrary, are generally characterized by "imperfect" or "monopolistic" competition.

Prices in these markets often are described as "administered." In such industries, a producer must make decisions regarding the pricing of the product--including all the price-related decisions associated with quality, design, and selling techniques. These pricing decisions are based on judgments of what sales would be at different levels of prices, on calculations of what costs per unit would be at various levels of production, and on the behavior of competing producers and products. Thus pricing decisions take into account, in addition to demand, the range of forces affecting production and costs, just as sales, production, and costs are influenced by pricing decisions. Producers must attempt to find a price that is in harmony with all the relevant short- and long-term demand and cost considerations, but without knowing precisely what will most effectively accomplish this aim.

The fact that prices are set by the decisions of producers implies a degree of market power--stemming from the nature of the product and the nature of the production process--but it does not connote full monopoly power. On the contrary, market forces--including competition within the industry and from other domestic or foreign products or alternative sources of satisfaction--are constantly working to alter past price decisions.

Rates for utilities, freight, public transportation, insurance, and postage are also administered prices, as are rates for many other business and consumer services. Both the cost and demand conditions encountered in the service industries vary widely. Some services are produced under conditions affording opportunities for basic technological improvement and productivity advance while for others such opportunities are limited. Some are primarily labor while others have a higher commodity content. Prices of some services are very responsive to local labor market and related economic conditions while others are subject more to nationwide forces. Some are regulated by public commissions and still others are stipulated fees for public services. In particular instances, service prices follow trends in wage rates fairly closely.

The result of most of these influences is that inflationary pressures in the economy are transmitted to services via increases in costs. For the regulated prices, advances may lag considerably behind the initiating causes and may occur in many instances even after business expansion has given way to recession.

Periods of recession. During contractions in demands and activity, changes in prices and costs and in the relationship between them are determined mainly by the duration of the contraction and by developments in the preceding expansion. In a prolonged and severe depression, accompanied by distress sales and substantial decreases in prices of existing assets, strong downward pressures develop on prices of currently produced goods and on wage rates and other elements of production costs. Since a contraction of this severity has not occurred since World War II, attention may be confined to the milder recessions experienced since then.

In recession, prices of sensitive industrial materials generally decline. Contraction in domestic demands and decreases in prices may reduce domestic supply by altering international commodity flows and/or by making marginal operations unprofitable. For the nonsensitive materials, analysis is complicated by the tendency of producers to change prices by varying concessions and discounts from unchanged list prices. While it is known that net or actual prices fluctuate more widely than list prices, little information is available to show the degree of change in actual prices.

List prices tend to be maintained in the early stages of contraction and if the recession proves to be brief, recovery in activity begins before many list-price cuts have been made. When it becomes clear that demands are reviving, the list price for a product on occasion is lowered to conform to actual transactions prices--because the operation of new facilities or some other development causes demand-cost relationships to be fundamentally different from those on which producers had been basing their decisions.

In describing the behavior of nonsensitive materials during business expansion, it was emphasized that producers' price decisions are based largely on calculations of costs at various possible levels of output as well as on judgments about demand. When demands contract and production is reduced, many elements of costs do not decline. Wage rates, for example, are maintained--or may actually increase in some lines owing to the terms of long-run labor agreements. The tendency of wage rates to be maintained was characteristic also of the mild recessions of prewar years.

Even in an administered price market, individual producers, faced with declining demands, have an incentive to reduce prices in order to increase sales, if they think competing producers will not also reduce prices. This goes far to explain the preference of producers for unpublicized price cuts--for price cuts brought about through concessions rather than through reductions in list prices. In certain situations, however, there may be incentives to publicize price reductions by cutting list prices: a cyclical contraction in demand for a particular material may be accompanied by competition from a new and lower cost source of supply or a new substitute material, or it may be accompanied by a change in the methods of production that appreciably reduces costs.

The recession behavior of manufactures' prices of most finished industrial products is similar to that of the nonsensitive materials.

To the extent that prices of materials decline, however, downward pressures on prices of finished goods are intensified. Prices of services tend to resist forces of decline in recession. In many cases, they rise further because of the increases authorized by regulatory agencies on the basis of earlier increases in costs, but the rate of rise in average prices of services slows down.

To summarize, prices of many sensitive materials typically decline in recession. These commodities have little weight in broad price indexes, however, and their influence currently is much less than in the indexes available for prewar years. Declines in prices of some other commodities are likely to be concealed in concessions from stable list prices. Still other prices, however, may resist any downward adjustment to declines in aggregate demand in moderate recessions.

If the previous expansion was accompanied by inflationary developments and appreciable increases in levels of prices, the increases are not likely to be fully erased during mild business recessions, giving rise to what has been called the "ratchet effect." If, however, price increases in the previous expansion were small, they may be subsequently offset as the competitive pressures that develop during recession, domestic and foreign, strengthen incentives to cut costs and to reflect these reductions in the form of lower prices. This emphasizes the importance of containing growth in credit and in demands for goods and services during periods of economic expansion and of preventing a climate of expectations conducive to large and widespread advances in prices and costs.

Developments Since 1954

The interpretations of the functioning of the market system which have led to skepticism about the efficacy of general measures of public policy have been supported almost exclusively by analyses of the 1954-57 business expansion. A comparison of developments in the period with the process described above will tend to show that the originating causes of inflation in the 1954-57 expansion--as in other periods of expansion characterized by inflation--were strong demands and overly optimistic appraisals of prospects. Once begun, the inflation was sustained by persistence of strong demands, by demand-price-cost-demand interaction, and by generation of widespread expectations of continuing inflation.

The business expansion that began in the spring of 1958 had not, through the spring of 1960, led to large and widespread increases in prices, as producers endeavored to hold down and reduce costs. Comparison of this period with both the process described previously and with the 1954-57 experience shows that the growth in final demands, while substantial, was reasonably well balanced and moderate in relation to available resources.

The 1954-57 expansion. Recovery from recession began in the second quarter of 1954. Expansion of consumer buying and residential construction activity was followed shortly by a shift from liquidation to accumulation of inventory. This was a period of rapid industrial expansion abroad, and foreign demands were contributing strength to domestic markets.

Prices of sensitive industrial materials began to rise in the spring of 1954, as shown in Chart II-1, and were back to the pre-recession level by the spring of 1955. By that time, prices of some other materials and producers' equipment also had been raised. Changes in wholesale prices of industrial commodities from June 1954 to June 1955, and over succeeding 12-month periods, are shown in Table II-1.

TABLE II-1

Wholesale Prices

(Percent Increase)

	June 1954 to June 1955	June 1955 to June 1956[1]	June 1956 to June 1957	June 1954 to June 1957
Industrial commodities	1.8	4.9	3.2	10.2
Materials	2.4	5.4	2.9	11.0
Sensitive	5.4[2]	5.4	-2.6	8.1
Other	1.3	5.4	4.9	11.9
Finished goods	.9	4.2	3.7	9.0
Consumer	.3	2.6	2.5	5.5
Durable	.5	3.5	3.0	7.2
Nondurable	.2	2.1	2.1	4.5
Producers' equipment	2.1	7.9	6.1	16.9

[1]Well over half of the increases in this period occurred during the second half of 1955. The rate of increase in prices in that period was faster than after the end of 1955 when the rapid shift in the composition of demands is said to have become a major influence.
[2]The rise in this group began in March 1954, and from that time to June 1955 amounted to 7 percent.

Source--Based on Bureau of Labor Statistics data.

Industrial production reached a new high in the spring of 1955 and continued to expand, while the labor market tightened. Sales and output of autos far exceeded previous records, under the influence of price concessions, radical changes in design, and a shift in credit terms to considerably longer maturities and lower downpayments. The volume of residential building was exceptionally

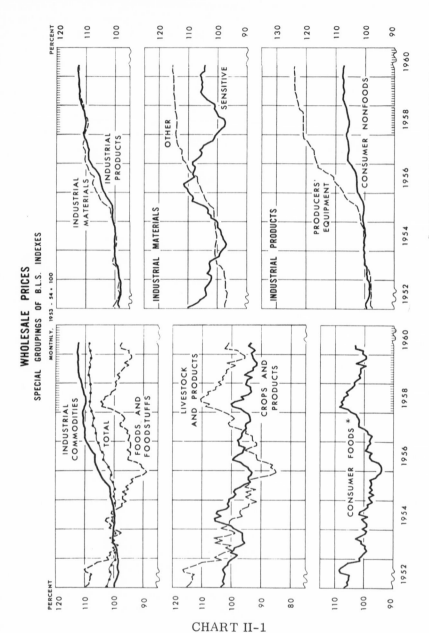

WHOLESALE PRICES
SPECIAL GROUPINGS OF B.L.S. INDEXES
MONTHLY, 1953 - 54 = 100

CHART II-1

large, and production of other consumer durable goods and business plant and equipment all advanced. Even though steel production reached capacity levels and output of other primary metals was at peak rates, metals were in short supply, and capacity was under mounting strain in many other important industries. Business profits after taxes increased considerably. This intensified incentives to expand capital investment and also provided some of the needed funds, with the result that business investment plans rose sharply.

These were the conditions and expectations in mid-1955, when some important labor contracts were negotiated. Demands for large increases in wage rates and fringe benefits were strong, and re-sistance to them was weak. In the auto, steel, and certain other major industries, large increases were agreed upon, and these lib-eral contract terms were negotiated for the most part without work stoppages.

Given the demand conditions and prospects of the time, prices could be and were raised to cover not only the increases in wage rates but also advances in other costs such as those resulting from the sharp increase in hiring of nonproduction or salaried workers. Costs of materials and supplies were also advancing. Partly be-cause of the lagged effects of the World War II and Korean War inflations on the book values of the stock of real capital, depreci-ation charges were higher in relation to sales than in earlier postwar periods of rising economic activity. A widespread rise in prices of industrial commodities erupted in mid-1955 and a price-cost spiral was set in motion.

By the spring of 1956, the rise in business capital expenditures-- which had been stimulated partly by the surge of consumer buying in 1954-55--reached boom proportions. Total spending by govern-ment was also rising. Economic activity abroad continued to increase and foreign demands for United States products gained further in strength. Meanwhile, some categories of demand were increasing less rapidly than earlier and still others, such as demands for autos and new houses, declined.

Curtailments in output in some of these lines in 1956 released resources and thus permitted expansion elsewhere. Unemployment remained low. For the most part, pressure of demands against capacity in basic industries was maintained. The capital goods in-dustries depend on many of the same materials and types of labor as are required in the auto industry. Similarly, industrial and com-mercial construction use essentially the same labor and some of the same materials consumed in residential construction.

In the industries producing basic metals, for example, the op-erating rate was about 93 percent of capacity in mid-1955, when

the advance in prices became widespread among industrial commodities. By the end of 1955, the rate was up to 97 percent. New
capacity was being installed in these industries during 1956, and at
least some of it became fully available for production during that
year. While rated capacity increased 4 percent from the end of
1955 to the end of 1956, output rose 3 percent, so that the year-end
operating rate was 96 percent. Some other industries producing
basic materials also maintained very high operating rates.

Expectations of continuing prosperity remained strong in 1956,
despite decreases in sales of autos and housing. The decrease in
automobile sales came to be regarded as a normal falling-off from
the extraordinarily high levels of 1955, and expectations in the
industry and elsewhere were for a renewed rise after introduction
of new models toward the year-end. The capital goods boom that
began in 1955 continued through 1956 and into 1957.

Price and wage developments in 1956, then, were dominated
by strong demands, by shifts in the composition of demands for
finished durable goods, and by ebullient expectations. Prices of a
few sensitive materials declined: prices of lumber declined after
February 1956 in response mainly to the decrease in residential
construction; and in the spring of that year, copper prices began
to decline--from very high levels associated with strikes--as supplies caught up with demand. Prices of most industrial commodities,
however, continued to increase.

In lagged response to the inflationary developments begun in
1955, moreover, the Consumer Price Index began to rise in early
1956. This rise resulted in wage increases based on escalation
clauses in existing contracts and intensified demands for other
large wage increases. In the summer, long-term contracts negotiated in the steel, aluminum, and some other industries, provided
for liberal annual increases in wages and fringe benefits and automatic cost-of-living adjustments.

In early 1957, prices of industrial commodities rose further--
reflecting partly a working through of earlier increases in prices
of materials and other costs and partly the fact that the expectations
of inflation continued to be widespread. Concurrently, rising prices
were limiting sales, and inventories were increasing. After nearly
three years of expansion, the seeds of recession--invariably sown
in a boom--were beginning to germinate.

By the autumn of 1957, wholesale prices of industrial commodities had risen about 10 percent from the early 1954 level, the total
wholesale index 7 percent, and the Consumer Price Index 6 percent.
Given the strength of demands and the optimistic nature of expectations, increases of these magnitudes over a three- to four-year

period are perhaps not extraordinarily large. Nevertheless, the rise in prices would have been larger had monetary policies not been restrictive. Developments through the period emphasize the need for vigorous efforts to contain the growth in demands for credit and for goods and services during periods of economic expansion and to prevent the generation of a climate of expectations conducive to widespread advances in prices and costs.

The 1957-58 recession. In the early autumn of 1957, more than three years after the upturn in business, expansion gave way to recession. A capital equipment boom by its very nature cannot be indefinitely prolonged. Exceptionally high rates of capacity expansion, rapid rise in equipment prices, and reduction in business liquidity eventually weaken incentives to make additional outlays. A decline in business capital spending will usually entail a period of inventory liquidation for capital goods industries, with reduced employment in these industries. Secondary effects of these developments are reductions in business inventory holdings, employment, incomes, and demands generally. The recession that began in the autumn of 1957 was of this type--although other elements were present, including cutbacks in defense ordering and contraction in foreign demands for U.S. exports.

Recession was not accompanied by widespread liquidation of credit and distress sales, however, and the basis was soon formed for recovery and renewed expansion, in part because of the increased availability and reduced cost of credit. Policy actions had operated to restrain the use of bank credit for speculative purposes during the expansion, and then operated in recession to encourage expansion in bank credit and increase the liquidity of the economy.

During the recession, prices of sensitive industrial materials declined, as the chart shows, with the average returning to the early 1954 low. While it is likely that various forms of concessions from list prices developed for other industrial commodities, list prices generally were maintained and, in fact, were raised further for some commodities. The failure of list prices to decline may be attributed in part to continuance of expectations of rising prices, to additional increases in costs arising out of commitments made during the preceding boom, and to the brevity of the recession.

Expansion since early 1958. When recovery in business activity began in the spring of 1958, average levels of prices were appreciably higher than in early 1954--when the previous recovery began. Expectations of continuing upward creep in prices remained widespread. The reality of expectations of inflation became obvious not so much in the behavior of commodity markets but in a further advance in common stock prices to new highs and a continued increase in land values. Moreover, interest rates turned up promptly and long-term rates which had declined only moderately in the recession, quickly approached or reattained prerecession highs.

The pattern of demands, production, productivity, prices, and profits through the first year of expansion was similar in many important respects to the comparable period of recovery from the 1954 low. Consumer buying expanded rapidly, housing starts closely paralleled the rise of 1954-55, and liquidation of inventories slowed down and then gave way to accumulation toward the end of 1958. Constant dollar Gross National Product reached a new high in the fourth quarter of 1958 and industrial production exceeded the 1957 prerecession peak by March 1959. Prices of sensitive industrial materials responded to expanding demands, rising about as much in the first year of economic expansion as in the comparable period of 1954-55.

However, growth in final demands was less rapid than in the comparable period of 1954-56. Consumer buying of autos rose less sharply--for a variety of reasons, including higher prices and no important further easing in credit terms in contrast to the marked liberalizing of terms in 1955. Moreover, merchandise imports rose substantially while exports changed little. In recent years, there has been a considerable improvement in the ability of other industrial nations to satisfy their own requirements and also, partly because of price advances in this country, to compete with American manufacturers of many materials and finished products in domestic markets as well as in markets abroad.

Consequently, while consumption of materials in manufacturing reached a new high in the spring of 1959 and inventories were being accumulated at a rapid rate (stimulated in part by the expectation of interruptions of supply by strikes), the margins of capacity over output for most major materials were somewhat greater than in mid-1955, and greater than during any other period of high-level activity since World War II. The margins were not large, but their importance was magnified by the fact that they existed simultaneously in several industries whose markets overlap. Government policy actions and policy pronouncements, furthermore, lessened the expectation of rising prices. Altogether, there was more uncertainty in the outlook, and prospects were for more intensive competition.

From the spring of 1959 to the spring of 1960, therefore, developments were quite different from those in the comparable period after the spring of 1955. One of the most obvious differences was the development of strong resistance to cost increases as manufacturers were less confident of their ability to pass them on in the form of higher prices. Specifically, strong resistance to demands for increases in wages and fringe benefits in the steel and other industries, as reflected in prolonged work stoppages, resulted in generally smaller increases. Gains in productivity, meanwhile, were as large as or larger than in the earlier period. Salaried employment, which had declined more in the 1957-58 recession than in previous recessions, increased less rapidly than in the 1954-57 expansion. Advances in prices were limited, and wholesale prices of the various groups of industrial commodities were nearly stable.

QUESTION III

Granted that stability of employment and prices are conducive to economic growth, are there any ways in which the monetary authorities can contribute directly to growth in addition to aiming at stabilizing employment and price levels?

ANSWER III

Summary

The monetary authorities can and do contribute directly to growth in ways over and beyond the pursuit of stabilization policies. An expanding population requires expanding employment opportunities, and stability can be maintained in a growing economy only when demand grows sufficiently, year by year, to provide the increase in job openings needed to keep pace with labor force growth. The monetary authority recognizes and accommodates this need for employment growth in the course of its stabilization activities, in which the objective is long-run expansion of money supply and bank credit consonant with maximum sustainable growth in output and employment.

High levels of total demand expanding at sustainable rates provide an optimum climate for investment leading to further growth in the economy, and the monetary authority contributes to growth in so far as it contributes to such a climate. Within the capacity limits set by labor force growth, however, expansion of total output can be accelerated only by speeding the rate of productivity advance, mainly through research, development of new products, and modernization of capital. Hence a direct contribution to growth by the monetary authority "in addition to aiming at stabilizing employment and prices" would take the form of an influence toward higher rates of productivity increase. To achieve faster productivity increase without inflation, such an influence must act to shift the composition of total demand and production, within the output capacity limits of the economy, toward activities that are most effective in stimulating productivity.

The forms of monetary policy instruments now in use are ill-suited to an objective of altering the structure of demand. These instruments are intended to provide for appropriate growth in total money supply and bank credit with minimum direct influence on individual credit markets or areas of production. Composition of output is determined by structure of private and government demands in competitive markets in relation to output capacities. If monetary policy actions were to be used as a direct instrument in aid of faster productivity growth, therefore, they would have to be modified to include some form of control or pressure on credit markets tending to shift demands into the types desired. While measures to exert such pressure might be devised, they would probably be seriously destabilizing to total demand if effective, and if held to limits that would not be destabilizing might be ineffective in shifting demand.

Monetary policy has an important contribution to make toward faster growth, but only as one part of a broader public program for growth that would include tax measures, expenditures, and debt management as well as monetary measures. Adjustments of prices and costs in the private economy so as to obtain optimum demand conditions are also essential for maximum growth. In almost any form of public program, the monetary contribution would be to exert a stabilizing influence on demand and prices; the initiating force in shifting output structure is most appropriately sought in other public agencies and in the private economy.

Introduction

In considering the contribution that monetary policy can make to economic growth, it is useful to distinguish sheer expansion of activity--growth in labor force, employment, and productive facilities--from rising productivity--growth in output per person or per worker or per hour worked. Growth in the sense of rising activity is closely related to population growth: When population is increasing the economy must expand merely to provide the new job opportunities needed for a growing labor force, to generate the output needed to maintain existing standards of consumption, and to provide the schools, housing, roads, and other facilities that should increase together with population. Growth in productivity, on the other hand, makes possible that combination of rising living standards, increased leisure, and more effective national strength that we have come to expect from growth.

Growth in total activity and growth in productivity proceed together, of course, and are interrelated with one another, since investment to accommodate population growth usually raises productivity at the same time. The distinction between activity and productivity is nevertheless significant in this discussion, since monetary policy stands in markedly different relationship to these two elements of growth.

Growth in total activity. Growth in aggregate employment and production is a direct concern of the Federal Reserve under existing legislation, in particular the Employment Act of 1946. One of the aims of monetary policy is, in the language of the Employment Act, to provide "useful employment opportunities...for those able, willing, and seeking to work..." With labor supply continually expanding, employment opportunities must also increase continually at any fixed level of employment but along a growth trend that parallels the growth in labor supply and that keeps unemployment as low as possible.

An important area of Federal Reserve efforts toward adequate employment growth lies in the work of the twelve Federal Reserve banks in analyzing business opportunities and in encouraging improvement in financial facilities in their districts. To the extent that industry can be attracted to areas where available workers live, frictional and structural unemployment in the economy can be substantially restrained.

If employment, for any reason, does not grow rapidly enough to absorb net additions to the labor force, the resulting rise in unemployment may be merely cyclical or it may also reflect a longer-run tendency toward stagnation. Short-run and longer-run developments are always difficult to distinguish in current affairs, but for economic policy the distinction is important and should be attempted to the extent possible. Policy measures to stimulate demand, such as tax changes and credit programs, can take many forms, some flexibly adapted to short fluctuations in business, and others necessarily more permanent in form. The measures used should suit the developments taking place, and some appraisal of those developments is essential in choosing forms of policy measures.

The scope of choice in monetary policy, however, is limited within the present framework of powers of the monetary authorities. Broadly speaking, the actions available to the Federal Reserve to foster long-run expansion of employment take the same form as actions to offset cyclical tendencies toward recession. For both purposes measures are taken to stimulate demand generally and investment demand in particular through expansion of bank credit availability and the money supply. Expansion to offset recession tendencies is needed only sporadically, of course. Expansion to provide for growth proceeds continuously, on the other hand; it constitutes a basic policy objective underlying all others, and stabilization actions are in effect temporary departures from this objective to counter short-run imbalances between demand and capacity.

While the growth objective can be viewed as separate from and underlying stabilization goals, however, there are no specific or separate monetary actions to provide for growth. In current operations, credit policy becomes restrictive when total demand expands too fast in relation to growth in labor force and plant capacity or is of such a nature as to threaten stability, and policy leans toward ease when demand is not expanding fast enough to keep pace with labor force growth. In the process money supply, liquidity, and credit availability expand over the long run at rates consonant with maximum sustainable economic growth. But the actions leading to this expansion are fully integrated with stabilization actions and are indistinguishable from them.

In following the directive of the Employment Act, then, monetary policy accommodates employment growth directly in the course of stabilization activities. There is not a contribution to growth here "in addition to," in the words of Question III, "aiming at stabilizing employment and price levels." Provision for adequate sustainable growth in money supply, credit availability, and financial facilities are essential if employment and activity are to be maintained at high and expanding levels. Question III, however, focuses on other forms of contribution to growth that the monetary authority might make. In terms of the distinction mentioned earlier between growth in total activity and productivity growth, such other contributions would take the form of aids to faster productivity growth. The following discussion follows this focus and is concerned primarily with contributions that monetary policy might make toward higher productivity.

Growth in productivity. Monetary policy has a far more diffuse relation to productivity growth than to employment growth. Higher production per capita can originate in many ways. It can come from increases in the proportion of the population in the labor force, from lengthening of the work week, from shifts of demand away from low-productivity industries toward high-productivity industries, and from deepening of the uses of capital relative to labor in production.

The fundamental source of rising productivity, however, lies in innovation and development of new products, new services, and new methods of production. An economy can deliberately undertake, in a war or other emergency, to expand output by working longer hours, bringing marginal workers into the labor force, and operating more equipment on a multiple-shift basis, but there are

inevitable limits to growth by such routes. Growth in living standards and economic strength can be continuous only if it is based
on creative ability to see and exploit new opportunities for doing
things better. Both elements are essential--the new ideas themselves and the application of those ideas to economic activity.
Without new ideas an economy must continually borrow from abroad
in order to maintain its international competitive position. And new
ideas fall on sterile ground unless there are both willingness and
resources to put the ideas to work.

Historically, the direct sources of productivity growth have
interacted continuously with one another. Competitive pressures
to reduce costs in individual industries result in rising productivity
that releases resources for other uses. New products and product
improvements are introduced that create new demand to absorb
these resources as well as capture demand from existing products.
In the process the new industries demonstrate to existing ones new
materials and new ways to produce that raise productivity further
in older industries. Growth in demand for individual products may
increase productivity through new possibilities for large-scale
production. Materials shortages stimulate research that results in
new materials more useful than the vanishing ones. Wars and threats
of wars, although absorbing resources wastefully, also result in
development of new processes and products. And the innovations
that make up this process occur in all areas of economic activity--
production, marketing, consumption, government--with continuous
cross-fertilization.

The following discussion considers ways in which this complex
process--the creating, developing, and exploiting of new ideas
wherever they occur in the economy--might be stimulated or speeded
by monetary policy. More specifically, the questions considered are
(1) the relation of existing forms of monetary influence to productivity growth, (2) the possibilities for larger investment spending as
a route to faster productivity growth, and (3) the contribution that
additional powers, such as selective credit controls, might make to
productivity.

As a goal of monetary policy, high rates of productivity growth
must be coordinated with other monetary objectives--high employment and price stability. There is no inevitable conflict between
these two sets of goals, but from time to time a need arises to
emphasize one aim more than another. The discussion below suggests that with appropriate use of public powers outside the realm
of monetary policy, such temporary conflicts can be largely avoided.

Existing Forms of Monetary Influence

Federal Reserve policy actions ordinarily take forms intended
to have the least possible specific effect on particular markets.

The aim of monetary policy is to provide for a volume of bank credit and money supply consistent with general price stability and with high and expanding total demand. The composition of that demand--in terms of consumption goods and services, capital formation, and government operations--is allowed to reflect the interaction of millions of individual decisions in the market as to what to buy and what not to buy.

These demands are continually changing with shifts in the capacities and desires of the nation, and it is the function of competitive markets to respond sensitively to these shifts in order to meet demands as they arise. With the structure of demand largely determined by market forces, the function of monetary policy is to promote, in so far as bank credit and money supply are factors, an aggregate of such demands that grows continuously and consistently with expansion of the labor force and productive capacity in the economy.

In this role, monetary policy exerts a permissive rather than initiating influence on productivity growth. Prosperity with price stability provides an optimum climate for growth through ventures into new ways of doing things that involve risk and uncertainty. Such conditions help to minimize both the fear of unemployment, which inhibits willingness to compete and to make mistakes, and the fear of inflation, which generates drives to buy too much of existing forms of capital rather than to explore new forms. Both of these fears inhibit economic development, and when they are minimized by high levels of activity and stable growth rates, the economy is given the greatest freedom to expand productivity through discovery and experiment.

In its general form, however, monetary policy is not in a position to aim at stability in the economy as a whole and at the same time to discriminate in favor of specific forms of demand that speed growth. A policy of credit ease adopted in order to aid specific investment in growth would stimulate other forms of spending as well, and if total demand were high could lead to an inflationary condition in the economy. And an opposite policy of credit tightness to raise saving and to suppress nongrowth demands for credit would restrain growth investment as well and tend toward underemployment and inadequate total demand.

The relative competitive positions of growth and nongrowth demands for credit are virtually impossible to assess, since credit demands arising from growth are as various in form as the sources of growth that create them. This can be seen by considering the different sources of credit used to finance innovation in such forms as railroad dieselization, modernization on farms, research and development for defense goods, construction of toll highways, and development and marketing of new industrial equipment. While many others might be mentioned, these are enough to indicate that credit to finance productivity growth has come from established security market channels, from banks, from government aid, from equity investments by individuals in small firms, and from internal saving by business. Where capital cost has been a dominant consideration, as in toll highways, the demand for funds has been sensitive to market conditions. In many forms of new product development, on the other hand, market prospects tend to override other considerations.

With this diversity in growth financing, it is apparent that monetary stabilization policy has no distinctive effect on growth demands for credit. These demands compete directly with other borrowing in all parts of the credit market. By operating in the credit market at as general a level as possible, the Federal Reserve minimizes its specific influence on individual segments of the market. The effects of stabilization activities on growth demands for credit are thus as diffused and various as effects on other forms of credit demand, and growth investment is neither hindered nor helped differentially by credit conditions of restriction or ease that may occur with varying levels of business activity. A climate of economic stability is, nevertheless, important to technical progress and development over a broad range of activities. It constitutes a major contribution of monetary policy to growth under existing conditions.

Policies for Higher Investment and Saving

The question remains whether alternative forms of monetary policy might be adopted that could contribute to productivity growth as well as to employment growth by favoring credit demands leading to growth as against other forms of demand.

Most proposals for stimulating growth in the U.S. economy include measures to increase the rate of business investment spending. These measures are advocated on the basis of both long-run and short-run considerations. In the long run, higher capital outlays would contribute to growth primarily by modernizing plant and equipment more rapidly and raising the trend of growth in labor productivity as a result. For the immediate period increased investment would also serve to expand total demand and to halt the gradual rise in unemployment rates that has been occurring in recent years.

In so far as total demand is slack in the economy, monetary measures to stimulate capital spending through credit ease are generally consistent with, and indeed part of, stabilization policy. The rising unemployment rate reflects an excessive tendency toward saving in the economy relative to investment demand, and expansion of capital spending will help to correct the imbalance.

As a route to more adequate employment growth, therefore, raising investment outlays does not present new problems to monetary authorities specific to the policy goal of a higher rate of growth in the economy.

When total demand and employment are already at high levels, however, the problem of expanding investment spending is broader and more complex. An increase in capital outlays in these circumstances requires a parallel increase in saving if inflation is to be avoided. There are thus two sides to the problem, and the policy steps needed to raise investment may be separate from those needed to raise rates of saving. Whether separate or combined, however, influences on saving and on investment must be coordinated reasonably well if stability is to be maintained.

General monetary measures to tighten or to ease financial markets, however, tend to have opposite influences on saving and investment. This is an essential characteristic of monetary policy as a stabilizing force in the economy. To raise saving and investment together requires a different and broader form of policy action in which the existing instruments of monetary policy can play only one part.

The requirement for expanding investment and saving together is, in general, some form of structural change in economic relationships among groups or types of income. Tax benefits in favor of investment are of this type, since they would shift tax burden away from investors in new capital goods and toward noninvestors. Other tax measures, such as small business investment company provisions, and various forms of government lending programs or credit guarantees alter structure to increase credit availability to certain types of capital outlays independently of monetary actions.

The extent of structural shifts needed to increase productivity appreciably is difficult to predict. It depends on the responsiveness of business in expanding outlays as a result of the shift, on the effectiveness of higher investment in raising output per manhour, and on the measures needed to expand saving. Applied as a broad-scale incentive, the required shift may not be feasible and a more narrowly focused device may be necessary, combining direct subsidies and increased government saving. Whatever the form, however, the effect is to shift income and demand in ways that give investment goods a more favorable position than they presently have.

Structural shifts such as these are based either directly or implicitly on governmental tax and borrowing powers and on use of these powers to divert income and resources from one area to another in the economy. The monetary authority has no comparable command over flows of funds and hence no comparable ability to shift the basic structure of income and spending relationships. Monetary policy must act within the existing structure when it operates through general controls on bank reserves and money supply.

Monetary policy unquestionably has a role in a broader public program of higher private capital formation, however. While tax and other legislation can be devised that would tend to raise both saving and investment rates, the effect in practice would be, in general, a greater upward influence on one than on the other. Such programs, that is, might be destabilizing in some degree--inflationary if investment demand responds more and depressive if saving shows the greater response. Imbalance should of course be avoided within the program to the extent possible, but monetary policy will inevitably play a part in countering both the short-run and long-run residual pressures that emanate from the program.

Stability is important to growth under existing conditions, with investment determined mainly by market factors. A stabilizing influence is even more essential when public policy measures are expressly shifting economic structure in order to accelerate growth. While the economy has shown great resilience in the postwar period, a program to alter structure might produce shocks potentially dangerous to over-all balance. Measures to preserve balance--monetary, fiscal, and other--would then have to assume a correspondingly enlarged role in public policy in order to avert those dangers.

Selective Credit Controls

The preceding discussion has indicated that general and non-discriminatory forms of policy actions now available to the monetary authority contribute to growth as a stabilizing force in an expanding economy. While stability is essential to sustaining growth, general forms of policy action can only accommodate growth rates determined elsewhere in the economy, whether in competitive markets alone or with specific assistance from government. General forms of policy instruments, that is, have not the scope in themselves to accelerate growth directly by altering the structure of demand and income.

There remains the possibility that selective credit controls in some form can make a direct contribution separate from stabilization. Direct controls on specific types of credit can in fact have some of the ability to affect economic structure that is found in taxing powers. Regulations that prohibit lending on terms mutually acceptable to sellers and buyers have a number of influences on income, spending, and credit market flows that shift demand structure away from that of a free market. If suitably constructed, therefore, a system of direct controls might contribute to a shift of credit from nongrowth to growth demands and to a higher economy-wide rate of saving.

Many forms of regulation can be designed to divert credit flows to or from specific uses. In the U.S., direct controls have been limited largely to terms of lending for consumer credit, home mortgages, and stock market credit. Bank examination procedures have an element of direct control, but the focus in examinations has been on soundness of individual banks' positions rather than economic policy. Securities regulation, control of nonbank financial institutions, and limits on savings deposit interest rates have similarly had objectives other than influence on the level and structure of demand. If it appeared appropriate, however, controls of these types could be reoriented toward influencing demand structure and could be integrated into larger programs of economic policy to expedite growth.

The first function of such controls as aids to growth would probably be to restrain consumer demands for credit. With consumers forced to accumulate savings to a greater degree before buying houses and durables, production resources would be freed to expand output of business capital goods, while credit markets could be eased without threat of inflation. Such controls could of course be extended with parallel effects so as to discriminate among industries, among regions, or among types of firms if the need for such extreme measures appeared to exist.

Direct controls could very probably be used only in conjunction with specific government inducements to higher business spending, since by themselves the credit controls would undoubtedly be deflationary. Their effect in depressing consumer demand, that is, would be stronger than the influence of credit ease toward expanding business investment, particularly since the restraint on consumers would in itself depress investment demand. Such controls would thus be used not as a direct aid to growth but rather as a catalyst to government-induced business investment.

Before undertaking a system of direct controls as part of a growth program, however, the very substantial problems associated with them should be understood and balanced against potential benefits. Selective credit controls are a common instrument of policy in a number of countries, but the U.S. economy has characteristics that make this form of control distinctively difficult to administer. With a large and diversified geographic area, with thousands of individual commercial banks, finance companies and mortgage lenders, and with a generally impersonal relationship between government and the financial community, selective controls are awkward, costly, and onerous to enforce effectively. When continued over extended periods, moreover, such controls tend to be subverted by changes in credit market relationships, and the form of control must be continually adapted to follow these market shifts. Selective controls should thus be undertaken only if they can produce the desired result--greater growth--reliably and efficiently on a permanent basis and if no more palatable alternative device exists.

Historically, consumer credit and mortgage controls have been used only on temporary bases, for the specific purpose of holding down inflationary pressures during a massive shift of resources into and out of national defense activities. In each situation the need was specific, urgent, and short run, and the types of influence exerted by the controls discernible.

In applying direct controls on financial markets in aid of a national growth program, the first question is whether there is a need that is as specific. It is important that the need be specific as to types of output desired and that it be recognized by all major sectors of the economy. Regardless of the importance or urgency of the need, no policing of direct controls can be effective unless it relies primarily on the cooperation and good faith of the public.

The concept of growth is poorly suited to a national program requiring this degree of public cooperation. Productivity growth is a complex and broadly based process in the U.S. economy, and successful innovation springs from interaction of many different forms of demand and competitive responses to demand shifts. Financing of new techniques makes use, as mentioned earlier, of all forms of credit channels, both in development and in application to production. In a subject as far ranging and diffuse as growth, therefore, it is not surprising to find broad differences of opinion among groups as to the purposes, nature, and sources of growth. And without a reasonable concurrence on the value of a credit control program will become increasingly diluted with time, particularly if used aggressively.

Selective controls also have a more specifically economic difficulty. While the aims visualized for a program to speed growth are many, there is clearly a need to preserve balance in the economy as it expands. Balance is difficult to define in this context, but broadly it refers to capacity to produce at all times the kinds of goods and services that the public wants and in the proportions desired. A program for growth should ideally shift resources into investment, education, research, and so forth for the purpose of expanding--sooner or later--a structure of output that meets the public's demands as they would appear in free markets.

If this is the goal of growth, selective controls are an inappropriate and even dangerous tool of policy. The purpose of direct controls is always to shift demand structure away from free-market form. As part of a program to increase total research, development, and modernization outlays, controls would inevitably restrain investment and research in the industries where final demand was restricted and thus warp the capacity of the economy to meet the structure of demand that will be most satisfactory to the public. Thus a monetary instrument that is effective in wartime, when private consumption preferences must be subordinated, can be quite out of place in a different setting of economic policy.

Distortion of demand structure is part of the underlying and fundamental objection to selective controls in the United States, that is, that such controls contravene the decision of competitive markets in determining output structure. Maximum freedom of private choice in use of resources remains a major tenet of economic policy and should be qualified only when critical national needs can be met in no other way. To suppress this freedom in order to improve the general public welfare would very probably be self-defeating. With the broad objective of encouraging innovation and modernization wherever they are most fruitful in the economy, selective controls would be in contradiction to the goal and a hindrance to achieving it.

Government Programs for Growth

The potential for promoting balanced growth at higher rates through monetary policy appears small when compared with possibilities for specific government programs in growth expenditures financed through taxation. On the investment side the government is in a position to present explicit capital demands to the economy, whether in the form of research or in physical facilities that the government deems strategic to growth. In so far as policy looks to growth for defense purposes, these demands would presumably be most immediately for military equipment and technical education, but they need not be restricted to such areas. Government research in agriculture has, for example, had striking consequences for farm productivity. On the saving side, the taxing power can be used just as explicitly to generate saving by the government that is needed to finance the extra investment spending.

As in the case of a government effort to stimulate private investment, a direct public investment program can create instabilities in the economy in so far as private responses result in differences between demands for investment and saving. Counteracting these disturbances would be part of general stabilization policy, both fiscal and monetary, and is not a direct part of a growth program.

Conclusion

The concept of economic growth is one of the least specific in public affairs. The meaning of growth, the objective of a public policy on growth, and the urgency of the need are all subjects on which there are wide differences of opinion. The processes of economic growth are complex interactions among many types of forces in the community and in spite of intensive study remain little understood. It is still not possible to state in operating terms the extent to which individual activities are sources of growth and the extent to which they are only uses of growth.

To be effective, therefore, public policy to stimulate growth should have specific objectives as to types of growth and should work toward those objectives by direct means. Attempts to stimulate growth at a very general level, with diffuse goals and indirect channels of influence, may be misdirected if the forces at work are not well understood. The result can be no more than unwanted distortion of economic structure. The role that monetary policy can have in promoting growth is affected by these considerations.

It is in the problem of adjusting continuously to many forms of growth pressures that monetary policy has its most immediate relation to growth policy. The first function of any monetary authority is to provide the means of payment and associated bank credit needed by an operating economy. As the economy grows these needs also grow, and the monetary authority must stand prepared to meet them.

Monetary policy should in particular be closely coordinated as a stabilizing element in any government program for direct participation in growth investment and saving, serving here to offset inadvertent or even intentional imbalances of receipts and outlays related to such a program. Irrespective of growth considerations, monetary policy must always take government expenditures and receipts into consideration, since these are major factors affecting current economic conditions. The stabilizing functions of monetary policy in relation to a growth program, therefore, are not likely to be markedly different from the normal functions served by monetary policy.

QUESTION IV

It is frequently claimed that both (a) the existing high corporate income tax rate, and (b) the volume of internal financing now undertaken by business firms, reduce the responsiveness of business firms to monetary policies. What is your view regarding the validity of these claims? What is their significance with respect

to the effectiveness of monetary policy and the relative impact of monetary policy upon various sectors
of the economy?

ANSWER IV

Summary

The answer to the first part of this question is limited to the
specific point raised with respect to corporate responsiveness to
monetary policy under conditions of high income tax rates. It does
not attempt to assess other economic effects of such tax rates,
which may indirectly affect adversely the economic climate in which
monetary policy operates.

The first allegation, that high corporate income tax rates reduce the responsiveness of business corporations to monetary
policy, may be questioned on two grounds:

1. The relative reduction in rate of return with a given increase
in interest cost is the same when taxes are high as when they are
low. This is so because income taxes reduce all items of deductible
expense and most taxable income by the same proportion.

2. High income tax rates may influence corporate investment
policies and corporate external financing practices in certain ways
that might increase rather than reduce corporate responsiveness
to monetary policy.

With respect to the second claim that heavy reliance on internal
funds by businesses as a group blunts their responsiveness to monetary policy, three considerations may be noted:

1. Many businesses rely much more heavily on borrowed funds
than is suggested by aggregate statistics for the business sector.

2. Cost of credit is only one factor influencing business borrowing decisions. Responsiveness to changes in the cost of credit will
depend in large part on the relative importance of noncredit factors,
e.g., the urgency of the project to be financed.

3. The customary proportions of internal vs. borrowed funds
in a company's total financing may have little effect on its decision
as to whether to undertake a particular investment that requires
outside financing.

It seems doubtful that the impact of monetary policy on other
sectors of the economy is directly and significantly affected by

either the existing high corporate income tax rate or by the heavy reliance on internal funds by the corporate sector as a whole.

The claims referred to relate to the responsiveness of business firms to monetary policy, by which is apparently meant responsiveness to changes in the cost and availability of loanable funds. The reasoning proceeds that, because of high tax rates and heavy internal financing, firms are more or less insensitive to the rising cost and reduced availability of funds during periods of excessive credit demand and accompanying policies of monetary restraint. In examining these claims, one should keep in mind that monetary policy influences but does not determine interest rates and credit availability.

Effect of Existing High Corporate Income Tax Rate

It is important to note at the outset that this part of the question relates to the differential effect of historically high vs. historically low income tax rates on corporate responsiveness to changes in monetary policy. It does not relate to what effect the mere existence of a corporate income tax may have on the attitudes of corporate managements. Nor does it relate to the general question of corporate responsiveness to changes in the cost of money, independent of the tax factor.

High corporate income tax rates, such as those presently in effect, undoubtedly influence the form that corporate financing takes. They may have some effect on the general level of interest rates and of corporate investment, though the effect would tend to diminish the longer tax rates remained at the same high level. Many observers feel that high tax rates also reduce corporate responsiveness to cost increases, and therefore to monetary policy as it affects the cost of money. While there are no recent empirical studies on this point, the logic of the situation suggests that the level of income tax rates as such should not significantly affect corporate responsiveness to monetary policy.

The claim that monetary policy is less effective under conditions of high tax rates usually focuses on the effect of credit restraint on the cost of credit rather than on credit availability, i.e., on corporate responsiveness to interest rate increases. The argument as frequently advanced is that much greater increases in interest rates are acceptable when tax rates are as high as they are at present, than would be the case if they were lower. This is because, with interest payments deductible for tax purposes and with the federal income tax rate on most corporate income at 52 percent, the Treasury in effect pays more than half of a corporation's interest costs.

Thus, it is said, the restraining influence on corporate borrowing of a given increase in interest rates is greatly reduced. Or, put another way, much larger increases in interest rates are required to produce the same response that a much smaller increase would produce if tax rates were lower.

In focusing on interest rates, however, it should be noted that interest cost is only one element in the profit and loss statement. The claim that corporations are less responsive to interest rate increases when tax rates are high could be, and frequently is, made about other deductible costs. Moreover, if an income tax rate of 52 percent is viewed as offsetting more than half of a corporation's interest cost, it must also be viewed as offsetting the same proportion of every other deductible cost, and as absorbing more than half of a corporation's receipts.[1] This is, of course, not the way income taxes are computed, but applying a rate of 52 percent to the net of receipts and deductible expenses is equivalent to applying that rate to each of the separate items. In effect, income taxes reduce all items of income and expense by the same proportion, and this means that the relative importance of interest as a cost is the same whatever tax rate is currently in effect.

At any level of tax rates, the worth of an expenditure of funds will be gauged in light of the net return it will provide. Because income taxes reduce both receipts and deductible expenses by the same proportion, a rise in interest cost produces the same relative reduction in after-tax return (assuming gross return is unchanged) regardless of the level of the tax rate, so long as the tax rate is the same at both levels of interest cost. This relationship can be illustrated most conveniently by use of a simple arithmetic example.

Chart IV-1 shows, for a $10,000,000 plant earning $1,500,000 per annum before interest and taxes, the return after interest and taxes that would be earned under different combinations of tax rate, interest rate, and financing method. If the investment is financed entirely by borrowing, as in the left-hand section of the chart, an increase in the interest rate from 3 percent to 5 percent reduces the net return by one-sixth, whatever the tax rate may be. That is, at a 25 percent tax rate, the return is reduced from 9 percent to 7 1/2 percent, at a 50 percent tax rate, from 6 to 5 percent and, at a 75 percent tax rate, from 3 to 2 1/2 percent.

Thus, the absolute reduction in return with a given increase in interest rate is smaller the higher the level of tax rates, but the relative reduction is the same at all tax rate levels. Since this

---

[1]Dividend income and capital gains are exceptions, of course, since they are taxed at less than 52 percent.

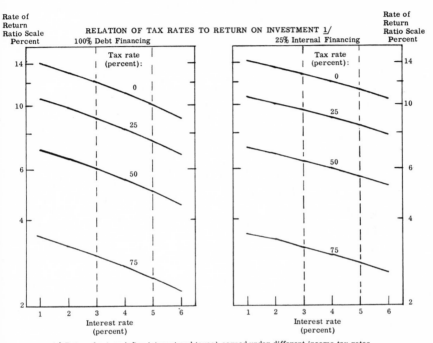

Rate of Return Ratio Scale Percent

RELATION OF TAX RATES TO RETURN ON INVESTMENT 1/

Rate of Return Ratio Scale Percent

100% Debt Financing   25% Internal Financing

Tax rate (percent):

Interest rate (percent)

1/ Rates of return (after interest and taxes) earned under different income tax rates, interest rates and financing arrangements, if return before interest and taxes equals 15 percent of cost of investment.

CHART IV-1

relative effect is independent of the level of income tax rates, the fact that the federal tax rate on most corporate income is currently 52 percent, rather than, say, 25 percent, seems unlikely to have much direct influence on corporate responsiveness to interest rate increases.

While the claim that income taxes reduce corporate responsiveness to cost increases is usually made with respect to high tax rates, it seems less likely to obtain under conditions of high but fairly constant rates than under conditions of rising tax rates, and/or of strong anticipation of a change in tax rates. When tax rates are rising rapidly, with the new high level expected to be temporary, a small net addition to current costs may promise substantial future income benefits.

A certain laxness with respect to cost control reportedly was fairly common in the early years of World War II. In this period, effective tax rates, which had ranged between 10 and 14 percent throughout the 1920's and 1930's, rose to 40 percent by 1941 and to 56 percent by 1943.[2] But effective income tax rates, though now below their wartime peak, which included the excess profits tax with its high marginal rates, have remained at historically high levels for nearly twenty years.

After so extended a period of high federal income tax rates, it does not seem logical to assume that there are many corporate managements today who consider the effect of income taxes on costs alone. They must be mainly concerned with the combined effect of rising costs and high taxes on net earnings. It seems reasonable to assume that, in a competitive industry where rates of return are not regulated or protected, most companies faced with an increase in any cost will consider alternative actions. These alternatives may include economizing on other costs, avoiding the cost increase in whole or in part, accepting lower profits, or accepting a lower profit margin.

Interest is like any other deductible cost in this respect. Even though, for most companies, it is a small cost relative to total sales, it may be relatively large for an individual project. In general, the longer run the project (i.e., the slower the pay-out period and/or the longer the maturity of the debt incurred to finance the project), the greater the relative importance of interest cost.

The analysis thus far has taken no account of what may be an important indirect effect of high taxes on corporate investment

---

[2] Effective rates are measured here by the ratio of federal income and excess profits taxes to the earnings of corporations reporting a net income.

policy. The figures plotted on Chart IV-1 assume the same gross rate of return, and the same range of interest rates, under each assumed tax rate. It may be that both borrowers and lenders have such fixed goals with respect to after-tax returns that funds will not be supplied by lenders, nor demanded by borrowers, unless the pre-tax return is greater when tax rates are high.

The expected profitability of a proposed investment is, of course, greatly affected by the current and expected levels of tax rates. Under the assumptions with respect to gross return and financing method used in the left-hand section of Chart IV-1, the after-tax return with interest cost at 3 percent would amount to 9 percent if taxes were levied at a 25 percent tax rate, but amounts to only 6 percent at a 50 percent tax rate. In order to obtain a 9 percent return at the present higher tax level, the gross return, as may be seen from Chart IV-2, must be 21 percent rather than 15 percent. That is, the investment must "pay out" in five years rather than in seven years.

If a corporation has sought to maintain its after-tax return at approximately the same level regardless of the level of tax rates, projects that would have been undertaken when taxes were low may not be undertaken when taxes are high. This would, however, have more effect on the general level of corporate investment under different tax rates than on the responsiveness of corporate borrowers to changes in interest costs under conditions of constant tax rates.

If, on the other hand, in a period of high tax rates, a company has reluctantly lowered its profitability requirements with respect to new investments, any further reduction resulting from a rise in interest cost may induce the corporation to postpone or cancel a proposed investment. In other words, a reduction in after-tax return from 6 to 5 percent may be less acceptable than the same absolute reduction from 9 to 8 percent, or even than the same relative reduction from 9 to 7 1/2 percent.

There are no reliable studies of the minimum net return that corporations consider acceptable under particular circumstances. It probably varies with the nature of the project, with the pressure of competitive factors, with long-run expectations as to markets, costs and prices, and perhaps, as suggested above, with the level of tax rates.

There probably is such a minimum, however, and it greatly affects a corporation's response to rising interest rates. Referring again to Chart IV-1, suppose a company will go ahead with a certain proposed expansion that is expected to yield a gross return of 15 percent, if it is reasonably sure of a net return of at least 6 percent. At present tax rates, it can obtain this return and finance the

TAX RATES AND REQUIRED RETURN ON INVESTMENT 1/

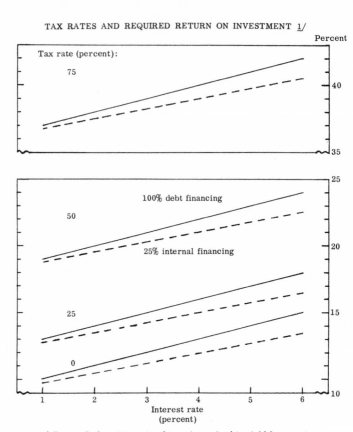

1/ Return (before interest and taxes) required to yield 9 percent
   return (after interest and taxes) under different income tax
   rates, interest rates and financing arrangements.

CHART IV-2

project entirely with borrowed funds, only so long as it can borrow at 3 percent or less. At half present tax rates, it could pay as much as 7 percent interest.

If an increase in borrowing costs occurs, the company can still obtain the minimum yield it has set by reducing the proportion of borrowed funds used and financing a part of the project with internal funds. Such a response is the desired objective, of course, of a policy of restraint that is expected to encourage corporations to rely more heavily on internal funds and to economize on borrowed cash. Suppose the company is able to finance one-fourth of the cost of the project with internal funds. Then the expected net return from the investment will remain at 6 percent or above until the interest rate reaches 4 percent, as the right-hand section of the chart shows.[3]

With different assumptions as to expected gross return on the proposed investment and/or as to minimum net return required, the point at which the company's investment and borrowing decisions are significantly affected by rising interest costs will be different. Under any reasonable set of assumptions, however, there comes a point at which the rise in interest rates reduces the after-tax return to a level that is not acceptable. There seems no logical reason for assuming that this point comes more slowly when tax rates are high. It may, in fact, come faster for the company that has not been able to offset historically high tax rates with historically high pre-tax rates of return.

Moreover, high taxes have one very important influence on corporate financing that may indirectly increase corporate responsiveness to monetary policy. This is their influence on the form which corporate external financing takes. With interest payments, but not dividend payments, deductible in computing taxable income there is a strong incentive, for those corporations that are in a position to make a free choice, to favor debt rather than stock financing. The higher the income tax rate the stronger the incentive, other things being equal, and the higher must be the level of interest rates relative to stock yields before equity financing has a net cost advantage.[4]

---

[3]For simplification, the calculations underlying the chart make no allowance for the cost to the company of foregoing alternative investment income from internal funds used to finance the company's own expansion.

[4]We ignore here the inherent cost advantage of equity financing that derives from the fact that dividend costs may be lowered or eliminated at the discretion of the company, while interest costs are fixed. Many large companies, however, feel committed to maintain their dividend rates and are extremely reluctant to reduce or omit payments.

At a 50 percent tax rate, the interest cost of debt must be double
the dividend cost of stock in order to eliminate the cost advantage
of debt and make equity financing an economical alternative to
borrowing. At a 25 percent tax rate, the debt cost need be only one-
third greater. This means that avoidance of rising interest rates
by shifting to stock financing is likely to be less feasible when tax
rates are high than when they are low--a factor tending to make
corporate outlays more sensitive to credit restraint under conditions of high income tax rates.

Effect of Heavy Reliance on Internal Funds

The bulk of business investment during the postwar period has
been accomplished without recourse to outside financing. Over five-
eighths of the funds used by nonfinancial corporations, as a group,
to expand their fixed and working assets in recent years has come
from internal sources. As may be seen from Table IV-1, the composition of these internal funds has changed markedly since the early
postwar years. The relative importance of other major sources of
corporate funds has not changed significantly during the postwar
period, though their dollar magnitude has increased substantially.

TABLE IV-1

Gross Sources of Corporate Funds
(Percentage Distribution)

Source	1947-50	1951-55	1956-59
Internal sources	62	61	64
Retained earnings	39	25	19
Depreciation allowances	23	36	45
New security issues	17	21	21
Increase in bank loans	6	8	6
Other sources	15	11	10
Total	100	100	100

Note: Percentages shown are derived from Department of Commerce
estimates of sources and uses of funds by corporations (other than
banks and insurance companies), as published in the Economic Report of the President. Gross sources were computed separately for
each year, and in general are equal to the sum of all positive changes
in net worth and liability accounts and all negative changes in asset
accounts; thus, "other sources" comprises increases in accrued
federal income taxes, other current liabilities or miscellaneous
noncurrent liabilities, and any decreases in cash balances, U.S.
Government security holdings, accounts receivable or any other
asset. Percentages for each period shown above represent the
average of percentages for each year of the period.

Reflecting primarily the record plant and equipment programs undertaken by business since the end of World War II, the bulk of all corporate internal funds now represent allowances for depreciation of existing facilities, and the more volatile component--retained earnings--accounts on the average for a greatly reduced proportion of corporate internal funds. In dollar terms, depreciation allowances have risen steadily from $5 billion in 1947 to about $21.5 billion in 1959, while retained earnings, which averaged about $11.5 billion in the 1947-50 period, have been lower ever since and averaged less than $9 billion in the 1956-59 period.

Even though, as a group, corporations finance most of their asset expansion out of their own savings, it does not appear entirely valid to characterize business firms as being relatively unaffected by monetary policy. In the first place, dependence on internal funds varies considerably from company to company, and even from industry to industry, as the following table indicates.

Some companies finance exclusively with internal funds, just as some consumers purchase their automobiles for cash. Among large corporations, extremely high dependence on internal funds appears to be characteristic only of railroads and most manufacturing industries. In the case of electric and gas utilities, large retail trade companies, and the largest communications company, internal funds supply only three-eighths to one-half of total funds used, and among sales and consumer finance companies practically all asset expansion is financed with credit. Thus, if the impact of monetary policy on businesses is a function of the degree of dependence on external funds, then a significant share of the business sector is considerably affected by the availability of credit.

Second, cost of credit is only one of several factors affecting business decisions to borrow. Other factors, related to the urgency of a proposed outlay that would require outside financing, include expectations as to sales and earnings, estimates of present vs. future costs, prices, and availability of materials, and the need to improve margins by modernizing or diversifying. Standards of what constitutes "urgency" may be influenced by the relative availability of credit and its cost, but it is probably safe to say that the less urgent the outlay the more crucial becomes the credit factor. In fact, public statements of corporate officials confirm that it is the less urgent, or less immediately profitable, projects that are most likely to be postponed when credit is restricted.

Third, the weighing of credit cost and availability against non-credit factors affects the decision as to whether to borrow on a particular occasion, and the customary importance of internal funds in a company's total financing may be largely irrelevant. Thus, if a railroad feels under much less pressure to expand than does an

TABLE IV-2

Importance of Internal Funds to Corporations in Selected Industries
(Percent of gross sources)

	Total internal funds		Retained earnings		Depreciation	
	1955	1956	1955	1956	1955	1956
All corporations	59	57	24	22	35	36
Large corporations:						
Manufacturing	69	58	35	27	33	31
Food	68	61	35	31	33	30
Tobacco	53	57	43	46	9	11
Rubber	49	63	27	32	22	31
Petroleum	80	66	46	36	34	30
Chemicals	65	63	29	25	36	38
Iron and steel	63	66	30	30	32	36
Nonferrous metals	70	70	48	47	22	23
Machinery	57	37	25	16	32	22
Automobiles	53	47	23	11	30	36
Other transportation equipment	31	31	18	19	13	11
Railroads	70	70	37	34	33	35
Electric power	44	42	17	17	27	25
Communications	36	38	14	17	22	21
Retail trade	43	49	25	31	18	19
Consumer finance	11	10	11	10	1/	1/
Sales finance	2	7	2	7	1/	1/

1. Negligible.

Note: Source of data for all corporations, as well as definition of gross sources, is as noted in Table IV-1. Figures for large corporations in selected industries are based on Federal Reserve compilations for about 300 nonfinancial corporations and about 110 finance companies; data are available for the 300-company sample only through 1956.

electric utility, a restrictive monetary policy may have much more impact on the former's credit demand than on the latter's, despite the fact that railroads typically rely much more heavily on internal funds than do electric utilities (70 percent vs. 40 percent, as may be seen in Table IV-2).

A final consideration is that monetary policy has indirect effects that may impinge strongly on companies that make only moderate use of credit. For example, an individual manufacturing firm that relies very largely on internal funds for financing its own outlays may nevertheless find its current and prospective sales, and therefore its incentives to expand, greatly influenced by credit conditions if its ultimate customers tend to finance their purchases of the company's products largely with credit.

Effects on Other Sectors

It seems doubtful that the present high corporate tax rate significantly affects the impact of monetary policy on noncorporate borrowers. While it might influence the attitudes and goals of lenders who are subject to the corporate income tax, the over-all effect of this influence would appear to be quite small.

Less than one-fourth of all public and long-term private debt is held by lenders who are subject to the corporate income tax. More than one-half is held by institutional investors that are largely or entirely exempt from the tax. The remainder is held by individuals and miscellaneous investors. This composition of debt ownership, together with other nontax factors that influence the cost and availability of funds to different classes of borrowers, would seem to minimize the influence of corporate tax rates on the responsiveness of lenders to monetary policy.

It also seems unlikely that the heavy reliance on internal funds by businesses as a group has much direct influence on the impact of monetary policy on other sectors of the economy, except in certain stages of a cyclical upturn or downturn. Particularly in the early stages of an economic expansion, the volume of funds generated by rising sales may increase faster than outlays, and businesses may be able to provide funds to other sectors, thus moderating the impact of a restrictive monetary policy. Similarly, in early stages of economic contraction, businesses may find their earnings declining while their outlays are still rising, and may need to restrict the credit they make available to their consumer and business customers. It should be noted, however, that the major component of internal funds--depreciation allowances--shows little cyclical variation.

QUESTION V

One frequently stated objection to an anti-inflationary monetary policy is that it is not very effective unless the brakes are applied so vigorously as to make it "too effective" and precipitate a sharp decline in the securities markets and thereby in business activity. Are small changes in interest rates likely to be effective in stemming inflationary pressures? If not, what is your evaluation of the alleged danger that, to be effective, interest rates might have to rise so far (or bond prices fall so far) as to disrupt the securities market?

ANSWER V

Summary

Relationships between interest rates, monetary policy, and the functioning of securities markets are highly complicated. Accordingly, this question cannot be answered satisfactorily without taking into account many economic forces, including changes in bank credit and the money supply, which affect changes in interest rates and security market movements and which, in turn, are influenced by them.[1] Moreover, it should be emphasized that monetary policy works not only through the effects of interest rates on spending but also through the effects on spending of changes in cash balances and of nonprice rationing of credit. In this frame of reference, the question may be answered in summary as follows:

(a) In a developing inflationary situation, increases in interest rates will largely depend on the extent to which private and public demands for funds are outrunning the supply of funds at pre-existing rates. The pressure on interest rates will tend to be greater when inflationary psychology is pervasive and rising interest rates as well as rising prices are expected. Nonprice rationing of funds in the market, which usually occurs to some extent, may be expected to substitute in part for increases in rates.

(b) In the short run, monetary policy affects both the course of interest rates and general credit availability. In arriving at judgments as to action, monetary policy focuses primarily on the volume and availability of bank reserves rather than on any particular level

---

[1]The answer to the first part of this question can be considered as an elaboration and translation to a specific context of some of the general points made in the answer to Question I.

or pattern of interest rates. Thus, anti-inflationary monetary policy functions by restraining the supply of bank reserves. In this way, it limits the demands that can be satisfied through bank credit. Under conditions of strong credit demand, interest rates will then tend to rise, though unevenly in different sectors of the market, and the tendency toward rising interest rates will be accentuated as monetary policy endeavors to compress the total supply of credit towards the amount generated by the current savings decisions of the public. The rise in rates may come sooner and perhaps be sharper, of course, if market participants generally expect rising interest rates.

When credit demands are slack relative to the supply of savings, interest rates will tend to decline. In these circumstances, monetary actions to increase the availability of bank credit will accentuate the downward trend of interest rates.

On a recent occasion, an international balance-of-payments deficit was made larger by a credit outflow in response to higher short-term interest rates in major foreign markets than prevailed in this country. These conditions made it necessary to pay greater-than-usual attention to the level and structure of interest rates in the shaping of monetary policy. They also resulted in an experimental extension of open market operations from short-term Government securities to those of longer maturity, thus modifying the direct market impact of System transactions.

(c) When rising interest rates appear to be the result of inflation-generated expansion in credit demands, with tendencies toward an unsustainable volume of business transactions, monetary restraint will be called for. Rising rates will themselves help to discourage some credit demand and enhance the volume of credit available to other users. In exerting this influence, the extent to which rates will rise depends on the effects of higher interest rates in restraining marginal investment outlays, in stimulating the flow of marginal saving into lendable forms, and in inducing conservative portfolio policies on the part of financial institutions.

(d) Over the past decade of flexible monetary operations, marked advances occurred in interest rates from cyclical lows to cyclical highs in expansion periods. Variations in short-term rates were especially wide--reflecting the typically high sensitiveness of such rates to changes in money market conditions--but were not greater than in many earlier cycles. While continuing to vary within a narrower range than short rates, long-term rates adjusted more promptly to turns in the economic cycle, and showed a greater amplitude of fluctuation, than did long rates in earlier periods. Variations in both short and long rates in the past decade helped to

limit and correct developing imbalances in saving and investment.
In restraining inflationary credit developments, the rate increases
that have occurred were supplemented by nonprice rationing of
available credit among different borrowers, including increased
use by lenders of required compensatory balances and loan repayment provisions less attractive to borrowers.

It is difficult to determine what the consequences would have
been of attempts by monetary action to keep rate changes smaller
than they were, but in view of the strength of inflationary pressures
during the expansive periods of economic cycles over the past
decade, it seems likely that, assuming the same fiscal policy,
smaller rises in interest rates would have been at the cost of a
less effective monetary policy. In other words, the over-all result
of efforts to dampen cyclical rate advances might well have been a
greater increase in price levels, some progressive impairment of
the saving-investment process, and still wider cyclical fluctuations
in economic activity.

(e) The alleged danger that a rise in interest rates to be effective will disrupt the securities markets assumes that the distance
which interest rates will ultimately have to move in a period of
inflationary economic expansion uniquely determines that danger.
A detailed examination of the relationship between interest rate
changes and functioning of securities markets makes it evident that
comparatively large cyclical changes in interest rates per se need
not disrupt the functioning of the securities markets, at least as
long as these changes do not occur too abruptly. On the other hand,
failure of the fiscal and monetary authorities to pursue adequate
anti-inflation policies when these are needed would pose a real danger of disrupting the economy, including its financial mechanism.
Actually, sharp changes in market rates are neither a necessary
aim of monetary actions nor a requisite for their effectiveness.
Indeed, most Federal Reserve operations are undertaken to prevent
disruptive effects of strong seasonal and other transient influences
on either supply or demand, and thereby on interest rates, in credit
markets.

(f) There is, of course, no present basis for judging whether
inflationary pressures in years to come are likely to be "small" or
"large," in whatever way these terms may be defined. Nor is there
any present basis for predicting how "small" or how "large" will be
the interest rate changes accompanying a monetary policy restrictive
enough to prevent inflation. So long, however, as monetary and fiscal policies of the federal government provide a framework conducive to economic stability and sustainable growth, movements of
securities markets and interest rates should tend to be self-limiting
and unlikely to interact in any disruptive way.

Formation and Functioning of Interest Rates

Interest rates are formed in credit markets as the supply and demand for funds seek a balance, and the resulting interest rate levels and movements serve to allocate funds among alternative and competing uses. Changes in the willingness to lend and in borrowing demands are the result of a number of forces at work in the economy, but three important and interrelated influences are the nation's saving and investment tendencies at given levels of income and interest rates, changing expectations related to future economic activity and financial market conditions, and the actions of monetary authorities in regulating bank credit and money.

Imbalances between the nation's willingness to save and its investment demand--that is, between its willingness to refrain from current consumption and its desire to use domestic resources for the production of capital goods or to invest abroad--are reflected in interest rate movements to a greater or lesser extent depending on a number of circumstances. At times when the use of productive capacity is declining, for example, investment demands are likely to fall relative to savings, tending to reduce interest rates. Rising real investment in such conditions will lead to greater output and to additional saving out of the resulting higher real incomes.

When the economy moves toward full resource utilization, and particularly if inflationary tendencies are present, interest rates are likely to rise to a greater extent. Inflationary pressures are often generated as the economy moves toward near-capacity utilization of its plant and equipment. At those times, investment demand is likely to exceed what the public wishes to save, with resulting pressure on interest rates (and prices), since the extent to which saving might be increased out of a rise in real income is limited. These pressures become intensified during periods when expectations of continued inflationary conditions are widely prevalent. In such periods, savers attempt to hedge against the expected inflation by, among other things, purchasing equities rather than debt obligations; as a result, stock prices typically rise rapidly, stock yields decline, and interest rates rise further. Borrowers, on the other hand, make further demands on credit markets since they expect cost and price conditions to be less favorable at a later point or because the cost of borrowing may seem small relative to possible speculative profits.

While the main outlines of interest rate movements are determined by continuing changes in the balance between investment demands and the public's willingness to save, the Federal Reserve, through the effect of its actions on bank reserve positions, has an important marginal influence on the timing and size of changes in the supply of loanable funds. Furthermore, expectations as to System policy may have a strong short-run and temporary impact on the money and capital markets.

When there are inflationary pressures, the Federal Reserve limits the availability of bank credit in an effort to keep growth in spending in line with the resources available to satisfy demands without inflation. Limitations on the extent of bank credit expansion combined with strong credit demands will tend to cause market interest rates to rise.

A general rise of interest rates under these conditions might be dampened for a time if the Federal Reserve supplied more bank reserves. Expansion of bank credit in order to permit satisfaction of credit demands at pre-existing interest rates would, under conditions of near-full employment of resources, result mainly in rising prices and would force the monetary value of both saving and investment to rise without relieving a shortage of real resources. In this process incomes would be redistributed and resources reallocated, reflecting differences in the ability of economic groups and sectors to participate in the general advance in prices of commodities, services, wealth, and equities.

Pronounced tendencies for interest rates to rise, furthermore, would be checked only temporarily if inflationary expectations were pervasive. Indeed, if such expectations were not already pervasive, they would clearly become so if the Federal Reserve followed policies of tolerating, rather than resisting, inflationary trends. Thus, in the absence of a comprehensive system of official resource rationing and price controls, the Federal Reserve cannot establish rates contrary to market forces; any attempt to do so would be self-defeating.

The changing degrees of restraint on or stimulus to monetary expansion over time are attempts at successive approximations to the needs of a constantly evolving economic situation. The chain of events set in course by monetary policy in turn influences the character of future policy. For example, a situation of strong credit demands and restraint on monetary expansion is typically accompanied by rising interest rates, and in turn the rate increases help to modify economic activity and the continued need for restraint. Thus, the degree of monetary restraint that needs to be applied is affected by the extent to which interest rate rises limit spending, especially that financed by borrowing, and encourage saving. It is also affected by the extent to which rising interest rates and the accompanying decline in portfolio values may discourage lending by reducing the liquidity of lending institutions.

The interest rate sensitivity of the demand for and supply of funds has been the subject of extensive consideration in the liter-

ature of economics. While there is disagreement as to the precise
degree of sensitivity, it is agreed that changes in interest rates
and in associated changes in terms of borrowing affect marginal
borrowers who undertake investments in which borrowing costs
are fairly significant--including certain inventories as well as
housing, public service facilities, and many types of commercial
and industrial construction. Changes in the level and structure of
interest rates also seem to have an influence on the supply of funds
through their effect on marginal saving-spending decisions and on
the portfolio preferences of savers. These and other effects were
all reflected, in varying degree, in changes in the flow of credit and
in economic activity during the past decade, when interest rates
moved flexibly in response to varying conditions in credit markets
and thus served as an essential aid in the effort to maintain economic stability.

Credit Availability and Interest Rates

The interest rates prevailing in credit markets are not uniformly responsive to changes in credit availability relative to demand. Some rates respond with a lag and at any particular time may
not reflect accurately the existing supply and demand situation. In
some cases, the stated interest rate may not change, but the rate
may be effectively varied through changes in other factors such as
the amount a bank requires a borrower to leave on deposit or the
extent to which lenders acquire assets at a discount or a premium.

In market sectors where interest rates tend to be less flexible,
lenders give more emphasis to nonprice factors in allocating funds
among borrowers whenever credit demands press actively against
the supply of funds. While lenders always tend to be selective to
some degree in satisfying borrowers, they adhere to stricter lending standards and screen credit-worthiness of borrowers more
carefully when credit demands are strong and market conditions
are tight. Borrowers then become obliged to shop more intensively
in order to find lenders whose loan standards and terms they can
meet, and some borrowers will fail to find such lenders. Thus, an
increase in demand for funds relative to supply not only causes
interest rates to rise but also has a direct effect on the readiness
and extent to which borrowers can obtain funds.

Federal Reserve anti-inflationary actions, therefore, tend to be
accompanied by both rising interest rates and more emphasis by
lenders on credit standards and other nonprice factors in allocating
funds. Counterrecession actions taken by the System, on the other
hand, tend to be associated with declining interest rates and reduced
emphasis by lenders on nonprice influences.

Range of Interest Rate Variation

Since the restoration of flexible monetary policy in 1951, the range of fluctuation in long-term interest rates has widened from that of the preceding 15 years. The range, however, has not been greater than during many cycles preceding the Great Depression of the thirties. Short-term rate adjustments to shifts in monetary policy have characteristically been rapid. Yield movements on longer term obligations, although of smaller amplitude than on shorter term securities, appear to have quickened in recent cycles, compared with earlier ones.

There are no simple explanations for the extent and pattern of interest rate movements since 1951. Certainly, our experience is too brief and the analytic tools of economics still too incomplete to permit any freehand generalizations. Nevertheless, some significant factors can be pointed to.

In the past decade or more, there occurred a rather marked upward shift of the interest rate structure as a whole in many countries, including the United States. In the United States, this followed a period of exceptionally low rates, brought about during the depression of the 1930's and arbitrarily maintained during war time and for a period thereafter. With the structure of interest rates at a higher level, there should be no surprise that fluctuations in market rates during the past decade exceeded those of the two preceding decades.

Apart from this, there are other important considerations. Experience shows that, in a period of active economic development and growth, one important factor is the limited (or even conflicting) effectiveness of measures other than monetary policy in curbing the recurrent inflationary pressures generated by an unduly rapid expansion of credit demands. Monetary policy can limit the availability of bank credit and, to a degree, of credit in general, but by itself it is not equipped to prevent or correct serious imbalances that might have their origin in the unwise spending or investing of available funds, whether their source is in bank credit or other savings forms.

Over the past decade, furthermore, the trend in public debt has been upward, with some increases in periods of strong economic expansion and rising private demands for credit. The net effect of the government's fiscal policy in these periods and for the decade as a whole has been to absorb savings. Consequently, the supply of funds has been less than would otherwise have been available while the demand for funds has been augmented, thereby enlarging the gap obtaining in credit markets between the demand for and supply of funds and generally feeding inflationary pressures. Under these circumstances, inadequate reliance on fiscal and other policies to help contain inflationary pressures contributed to successive periods of fairly sharp upward interest rate movements. These movements were not fully reversed during the comparatively moderate recessions of the ten-year span.

Another factor of importance has been the growing sensitivity of professional investors to prospects of changes in the government's fiscal position, or in Federal Reserve policy, as forces affecting the markets. This heightened responsiveness in the market means that some market participants try to make at once most of the adjustment in their portfolios that might be expected to become desirable.

Inflationary psychology has also been important in intensifying interest rate rises at times during recent years. As explained previously, expectations of a rising price level tend to increase the demand for funds while limiting amounts lenders are willing to place in fixed income investments. Sharp rises in interest rates, coupled with rising prices of inflation hedges such as stocks and land, are manifestations of a reluctance to lend associated with inflationary psychology. The relationship of anti-inflationary monetary policy to interest rates and inflationary attitudes is double-edged. Such a policy may be associated with relatively large rises in interest rates because of the prevalence of these attitudes. On the other hand, since a policy of restraint has the effect of modifying the public's expectations, such a policy will help to temper pressures on interest rates related to expectations of a rising price level.

In summary, the restoration of flexibility to monetary policy has permitted fluctuations in economic activity and market conditions to be reflected to a greater extent in cyclical movements of interest rates. In the postwar years before 1951, when the Federal Reserve was in effect maintaining an interest rate ceiling, upswings in economic activity and the demand for funds were not reflected in interest rate movements, and demand pressures resulted more in price increases. In the past decade of flexible monetary policy, the range of interest rate variations associated with shifts in credit demands, while not large in longer-run historical perspective, has been wide enough to occasion comment and discussion, especially in the light of the preceding decade and a half of low and relatively stable interest rates.

Upward interest rate movements will tend to be smaller when fiscal and monetary policies both are helping to limit credit demands and to encourage the flow of savings. But whether interest rate changes are small or not, they are important under free and flexible market conditions, as signals of the trend in credit markets and credit policy, and as integral parts of a market mechanism that adjusts effectively to each new situation.

Flexible Rates and Securities Markets

While the interest rate movements associated with inflationary pressures in the past decade have taken place over fairly sustained periods, these upswings have been the cumulative effect of much less dramatic changes in prices and yields on securities in day-to-day trading. It is these very short-term changes that are most closely related to the performance of the securities markets. Hence, an evaluation of the danger that interest rate movements might disrupt these markets should focus on the magnitude and implications of the day-to-day changes associated with the longer term upswings in interest rates. On this phase of the question, it is assumed that the expression "to disrupt the market" means to create a situation in which trading in securities would be severely curtailed, because price declines and yield advances, rather than helping to clear the market of outstanding sell orders, would be leading to accelerated selling and a drying up of demand.

The very short-term changes in price and yield behavior typically consist of variations in both directions, the net resultant of which may be seen in retrospect as a clearly defined upward or downward sweep. This may be illustrated in terms of the sustained advance in yields on long-term government bonds that occurred from their cyclical low in April 1958 to their high in early January 1960.

Over this period of about 20 months, the average yield on bonds due in more than 10 years rose from 3.05 percent to 4.44 percent, or 139 basis points. This advance did not occur evenly; indeed, much of the rise, particularly in its early phase, was concentrated within fairly brief intervals. It is worth noting, however, that on only one-sixth of the 428 trading days of the whole period from mid-April 1958 to early January 1960 did the yield average show an advance of more than 2 basis points, that is of 2/100 of a percentage point. On only one-twelfth of the 428 days did average yields rise more than 3 basis points. On the other hand, on three-fourths of the trading sessions, daily variations in long-term yields were less than 2 basis points. Stated in terms of price change, the cyclical adjustment of 1 2/5 points in yields was associated with daily variations in prices that were generally less than $3.33 per $1,000 of securities, that is, less than one-third of one per cent.[2]

On some trading days, to be sure, price and yield changes were significantly larger. Thus, over one weekend in mid-July 1958, re-

---

[2]On a 25-year, 3 1/2 percent bond, a change of 2 basis points in yield represents a change of about $3,300 for $1,000,000 of securities.

flecting the impact of an international political crisis in the Middle East on an already disturbed market, long-term yields advanced 9 basis points.[3] On a few other occasions that summer average yields rose as much as 5 or 6 basis points and on two days in October average yields declined about 7 basis points.

Although disturbed market conditions are likely to be associated with sharp changes in prices and yields, it does not follow that larger-than-usual changes in quotations necessarily represent some degree of market unsettlement. In any freely functioning market, temporary imbalances inevitably develop from time to time between the supply that enters the market and the demand that arises to absorb it. If prices are unable to adjust flexibly in response to these gaps, perhaps because of institutional rigidities or of attempts to support the market, there will be increased danger either of a drying up of trading or of breakdown in the market mechanism.

Day-to-day changes in yields in the market for Government securities are likely to attract more attention at times of rapid economic transition. Changes in prices and yields at such times are significantly influenced by expectations of participants in this market. When a major turnaround in economic activity appears to be taking place, for instance, reappraisals as to the outlook for interest rates are likely to cause market participants to adjust their positions or to alter the timing or the maturity area of their purchases in response. These actions and attitudes have the effect of accelerating the yield adjustments that are already in process at such times.

The size of initial yield adjustments at cyclical turns, presumed or actual, depends in part on the extent to which active traders revise their expectations and the firmness with which they hold their revised views. Uncertainty, or the possibility that expectations may not be borne out by events, is always present in a securities market. Risks associated with uncertainty are necessarily assumed by those who engage in the positioning of securities in the hope of experiencing capital gains. Losses incurred from such speculative positioning do not reflect any failure of the securities markets to function properly.

Erroneous expectations that are widely enough held to influence the direction of securities prices, or overreactions to other developments affecting prices, are ordinarily corrected promptly by the securities market itself. Only rarely would such a situation

---

[3]Briefly in July 1958, when an international crisis coincided with continued liquidation of speculative positions and the approach of a large Treasury financing, the Federal Reserve found it necessary to enter the market for the purpose of correcting disorderly conditions.

justify official intervention--assuming that such intervention could be based on a knowledge superior to that of the market concerning sustainable price and yield levels and relationships. Experience over a number of years suggests that the occasional emergence of erroneous expectations in the securities market has not been such as to limit significantly the flexible use of monetary policy as a means of countering economic instability.

On the contrary, uncertainties as to market prices for certain types of assets reinforce the effectiveness of countercyclical monetary policy. Holders of longer term Government bonds in particular have come to recognize that such securities, while generally continuously marketable, are not shiftable into an assured amount of cash at all times before maturity. In other words, debt instruments of differing maturity vary in degree of liquidity. Moreover, the facility with which longer term government debt may be converted into money diminishes with the build-up of inflationary pressures. Such differences and variations in liquidity of longer maturities of debt serve as a countercyclical force, and do not imply any impairment of market functioning.

The foregoing discussion of relationships between cyclical movements in interest rates and performance of securities markets has been concerned with short-term changes in prices and yields that may occur within the course of a major cyclical upswing. There remains the question as to whether the level to which interest rates move itself poses a threat to the proper functioning of the securities markets.

When yields on longer term bonds reach levels that represent new peaks within the recent experience of market participants, expectations of further rise may lessen and the possibility of a decline in rates may acquire increased importance in the minds of participants. At such a point, some investors will begin to readjust their portfolios in the direction of larger holdings of long-term securities and some other investors who had been on the sidelines, so to speak, will be drawn into the market, thus tending to change the relation between market supply and demand and contributing to a reversal in the movement of market rates. Apart from effects stemming from such influences as notions of "normal" interest rate levels or technical tax considerations, absolute levels of interest rates in themselves appear to have had little influence on the functioning of the securities markets in recent years.

Potential Sources of Security Market Disruption

During the ten-year period since early 1951, in which yields on securities have been free to reflect the full interplay of supply and demand, the performance of the securities markets has been broadly satisfactory. Intervals of market unsettlement have been infrequent and brief and the markets generally have cleared effective buy and sell orders with reasonable promptness. With the government securities market playing a central role, yield developments in the centralized securities markets have been closely linked. Changes in yields in particular markets, therefore, have reflected the conditions in the economy as a whole with respect to the supply of and demand for funds and not merely the specific pressures acting on the particular market.

That the markets have continued to perform satisfactorily, and without serious disruption even in periods of rapid economic expansion, has reflected the fact that comparatively moderate advances in interest rates in day-to-day trading have served to attract buying and to discourage selling. Markets for most issues of government securities have been kept continuous because professional traders and dealers have been willing to take positions in the securities traded. Investors have generally been willing to put available funds into new issues whenever these issues have offered returns that compared favorably with yields on alternative opportunities for investment.

While the securities markets have performed reasonably well in the past several years, it should be recognized that certain conditions, if permitted to develop, might at some point lead to a serious disruption of the markets. Essentially such conditions might well emerge if the public, i.e., investors, savers, lenders, and borrowers, were to lose confidence in the ability of the government to contain inflationary pressures. Should inflationary expectations become pervasive, even sharp advances in interest rates might be unable to reduce sufficiently a developing imbalance between supply and demand in markets for funds. The risk of disruption of the securities markets becomes greater when the federal government runs a heavy budget deficit at a time when strong business and consumer demands for goods and services are exerting pressure on available resources. Under such conditions the combined impact of private and public demands for funds may severely test the capacity of the financial mechanism.

Debt management policies may also subject the securities markets to unusual strain if the Treasury is unable over a period of time to issue enough longer term securities to counter the effects of the passage of time on the maturity of existing debt. Such a build-up in the size and frequency of the Treasury's need to refinance maturing debt would result in the concentration of the government's debt in short maturities. In such circumstances Treasury refinancing, by contributing to a condition of redundant liquidity, could complicate the task of monetary policy.

The strength of the securities markets depends basically on the stability of the economy. In an economic climate in which decision-makers are confident that inflationary pressures will be effectively countered by appropriate Federal financial policies--including fiscal measures, debt management, and monetary policy, they may be expected to continue to respond to interest rate movements in a way that contributes both to stability of the economy and to proper functioning of the securities markets.

QUESTION VI

In what ways does the existence of a national debt of approximately the present size, composition, and ownership distribution, assist and in what way does it hamper the effectiveness of monetary policy?

ANSWER VI

Summary

On balance, a national debt of the present size, composition, and ownership distribution neither "assists" nor "hampers" to any significant extent the effectiveness of monetary policy. The existence of the debt obliges the Federal Reserve System, however, to adapt its policy actions to compensate for influences that result from shifts in the composition and ownership of the debt.[1]

In an important respect, the existence of a large public debt might be said to assist the monetary authorities. A standardized, riskless public debt, in a wide range of maturities and owned by all types of investors, is a powerful force for the transmission from one area to another of financial impulses set in motion by monetary policy or by the interplay of market forces themselves. The size of the debt, its wide ownership both within and outside the commercial banking system, and the active market in which it is traded enable

---

[1] It should be clear that the question and this statement distinguish sharply between the outstanding debt and surpluses or deficits which arise from current fiscal policies. Substantial changes in the size of the debt in a short period raise many important problems for monetary policy, and for economic stability generally, which are not treated here.

the Federal Reserve to rely principally upon impersonal operations in short-term Government securities. By supplying or absorbing reserves in relatively small amounts through its open market operations in these securities, the Federal Reserve is able to exert workable control over the aggregate volume of bank reserves.

The transferability of the marketable public debt, and the extent to which at least shorter maturities may substitute for cash, does influence the formulation of monetary policy, however. In particular, the tendency during periods of credit restraint and rising interest rates for shorter-term Government securities to be substituted for money in many portfolios, leads to increased velocity of money. This in turn requires continuous study of financial flows in assessing whether any given monetary policy is having the desired effect. Moreover, to some extent the present composition of the debt forces the Treasury to be "in the market" more often than would be desirable from the point of view of monetary policy. This does not necessarily "hamper the effectiveness of monetary policy," in the words of the question, but it does at times make the execution of policy more difficult.

The Shiftability of Public Debt

U.S. Government securities are more liquid than other obligations of comparable maturities, because of both their freedom from credit risk and the breadth of the market in which they may be traded. The size of the public debt relative to the total of all debt, the fact that some Government securities are held by many types of investing institutions, and the fact that Government securities normally may be bought or sold in large quantities, have made these obligations the principal medium for portfolio adjustments. Through purchases or sales of Governments, the impact of shifts in the pattern of the flow of funds through the financial markets may be "cushioned" for the individual institutions directly affected.

The monetary authorities, accordingly, can apply varying degrees of pressure upon the commercial banks without creating unduly severe localized pressure upon the credit structure. Such regulation, shaped by means of orderly market processes, normally requires substantial transfer of short-term government debt among commercial banks and between banks and other financial institutions and investors. In other industrial countries that still lack such a broad and active market for highly liquid and widely held money market instruments, central banks usually rely on changes in reserve requirements or rediscount quotas to achieve similar effects or, in some instances, resort to moral suasion or even to direct controls. In this country, the existence of a large number of independent banks would make application of detailed regulation exceedingly cumbersome and perhaps impracticable. A broad national market for Government securities provides an adjustment mechanism that avoids resort to these methods.

On the other hand, the size and distribution of the public debt has conditioning effects on central bank policy. Because of the relative ease of transfer of Government obligations, and the extent to which at least shorter maturities may substitute for cash, monetary policy actions might be partly offset through changes in the ownership of the debt that influence the velocity of money. Monetary policy must accordingly be formulated to allow for this influence in order to achieve the desired effects on the ultimate availability of money and credit.

Execution of monetary policy has been further complicated in recent years by structural shifts in the ownership and maturity of the debt that have resulted from the passage of time and from debt management policies. Frequent debt management operations have on balance handicapped the conduct of monetary policy, particularly as to timing, thereby lessening its effectiveness to some degree. These recent problems are not, however, inherent in a debt of the present size; in part they have reflected stresses growing out of the sizable expansion and restructuring of debt of all types.

The following sections briefly describe the major ways in which the debt influences the formulation of monetary policy, first under a restrictive monetary policy and then under a policy of ease.

Effects of the Debt on Monetary Restraint

When interest rates are rising in a situation of increasing credit demands and limitations on credit supplies, the relative attractiveness of money versus interest-bearing liquidity instruments falls while the implicit cost of holding money increases. The resulting shifts in ownership and maturity structure of the debt exert an influence on the impact of monetary policy. Periods of most rapid economic expansion, in the intermediate phase of the cycle following recovery from recession, are typically periods of most active demands for credit of all types. Commercial banks as a group may respond to loan demands either with new funds supplied to them by (or with the acquiescence of) the Federal Reserve System or with funds derived from shifting assets to nonbank holders. Other financial intermediaries are similarly able to add to their inflows of funds from other sources by liquidating Government securities.

In recent business expansions, the periods of heaviest credit demands have coincided with periods of largest net cash accumulations by business corporations and by other nonfinancial institutions and individuals. These nonbank sources of credit usually employ a large part of their surplus funds to purchase U.S. Government securities from commercial banks and other financial intermediaries. In this way, funds for net credit expansion are provided in a manner that is reflected in the monetary statistics as an increase in the velocity of money rather than as an increase in the money supply itself.

In most postwar experience, this process has principally involved transactions in short-term public debt, although when prices of bonds were pegged, Government securities of any maturity were equally liquid and served the purpose. On the other hand, if the Treasury had not provided the commercial banks and other institutions with a supply of marketable short-term obligations which could be used to adjust for current cash flows, the market probably would have generated instruments to perform the function. It is questionable, however, whether such paper could ever be as liquid and shiftable as short-term U.S. Treasury securities.

Another part of the role of the short-term Treasury debt in periods of monetary restraint, in addition to facilitating shifts of funds between banks, financial intermediaries, and others, is the movement of short-term debt among investors which does not involve net selling by financial intermediaries. Typically, a large business corporation (or state fund, municipal fund, etc.) will attempt to operate on minimum cash balances. Cash flows are usually projected in advance, and unexpected changes are provided for through alterations in holdings of short-term Government securities. Over a period of seasonal cash drain and return flow, for example, a large corporation may hold an almost constant cash balance, while the total of its cash and short-term Governments swings frequently and substantially. The great bulk of such flows of funds remains within nonbank sectors, so that cash losses by one firm, industry, or region are ultimately offset by gains elsewhere that provide the cash to purchase the short-term securities being sold by the ultimate losers of funds.

In periods of economic expansion, short-term Government securities have thus increasingly replaced cash in the balance sheets of these institutions for all purposes except near-term transactions requirements, with a resulting increase in the velocity of money. A fluctuating portfolio of short-term Government securities permits the same amount of money--or even a smaller amount as efficiency in cash management increases--to support an expanding volume of transactions.

The net effect of all this upon the effectiveness of restrictive monetary policy is to require, in policy formulation, consideration of the availability of the entire range of liquid assets in determining the appropriate amount of the particular liquid asset--money--over which monetary policy has the most direct influence. When there is a huge public debt heavily concentrated in shorter maturities, changes in the volume of commercial bank credit and the money supply may not be as reliable measures of the effects being achieved by monetary policy as in different circumstances.

During periods of monetary restraint in recent years, changes in the maturity structure of the public debt have been such as to shorten the average maturity. This has added directly to the supply of money substitutes and, in general, to the liquidity of the economy. Such maturity shortening has come about not as a matter of intentional debt management policy, but because of the difficulties involved in selling intermediate- and longer-term obligations during periods of credit restraint and, typically, rising interest rates. Recently, the interest rate ceiling on Treasury bonds has further complicated the Treasury's debt management problem.

Another problem of debt composition that has been troublesome in periods of monetary restraint is the management of the large volume of nonmarketable debt. Attrition of savings bonds increases as yields on competitive investments rise. This requires current financings through marketable issues to cover the reduction in nonmarketable debt, and places additional demand on the money market. The fact that savings bonds, being redeemable on demand, tend to take on the characteristics of short-term debt in periods of rising business activity works at odds with what may be desirable from a monetary policy standpoint.

The purely technical problems of managing a debt of the present size tend to make execution of a policy of monetary restraint more difficult, especially with regard to timing, but also from the standpoint of restrictiveness per se. At and around periods in which the Treasury is conducting a major financing, the Federal Reserve System is obliged, by the risk of upsetting that financing, to avoid overt policy actions or changes in the availability of credit and money. A debt of the present size and distribution of maturities necessarily involves frequent, large Treasury debt operations. As a consequence, the Federal Reserve System periodically, and sometimes for rather lengthy periods, finds itself restrained from taking policy actions that it otherwise might have taken.

Effect of the Debt on Monetary Policy at Time of Monetary Ease

In periods when monetary policies are directed at easy availability of credit and money, reserves supplied to the commercial banks are employed to bid short-term Government securities away from other investors, as well as to service their customers' loan requirements. As a result, the money supply probably responds more promptly to reserve availability because of the existence of a large volume of such securities than it would if the banks were required to rely solely upon the extension of bank loans. Commercial bank demand for short-term Governments in periods of monetary ease has helped to drive short-term rates quickly and significantly lower. Purchases of short-term Governments enable the banks to rebuild their secondary reserve liquidity assets from the low point to which they have been driven in the preceding phase of the business cycle, in preparation for servicing customer credit requirements once the economy again begins to turn upward.

Medium- and long-term interest rates also decline in response both to decreased credit demands and the increased availability of bank credit. As short-term rates reach low levels and demands fall off, banks, as well as other investors, become more inclined to add medium- and longer-term securities to their portfolios. The Treasury at times may take advantage of the lower rates and increased demands to increase their offerings of longer-term securities. To some degree, this may tend to limit the reduction in long-term interest rates and the stimulating effect of lower rates. Since, however, lessened Treasury borrowing in the short-term market would tend to lower rates in that sector and thus encourage shifting of lenders into longer-term issues, the net effect on the average level of rates would be minimized and that on the rate structure would probably not be great enough to interfere with policy objectives. If such debt management shifts were very large and repeated, however, they might have material effects.

During business recessions, attainment of the goals of monetary policy is assisted by the fact that all maturities of Government securities become relatively liquid. When prices of securities are rising, it is easy to dispose of them without risk of loss, and this tends to offset the effect on liquidity of debt lengthening. Reduction in liquidity later, as interest rates start rising and prices of securities start declining is, of course, an essential part of the monetary policy.

In concluding, it should be noted that the size, structure, and ownership of the public debt are but a few of the numerous elements in the total financial and institutional framework to which Federal Reserve policy is adapted. Any effort to treat a single component of an interlocking process as an independent force contains elements of artificiality. The national debt is an important part, but only one part, of the entire complex and continuously changing debt structure in the United States, and thus of the financial environment in which Federal Reserve policy is shaped and becomes effective.

QUESTION VII

Are changes in the velocity of money an important impediment to the effectiveness of monetary policy? Have they been an important impediment at any time in the post-accord period? Are there any actions that the monetary authorities can take to influence velocity directly, aside from taking changes in velocity into account in decisions relating to the customary credit control instruments?

ANSWER VII

Summary

Changes in velocity--at least in the short run--are reflections of the economy's adaptation to changes in credit conditions. Rising credit demands tend to be accompanied by increasing borrowing costs, particularly if monetary restraints are needed to contain inflationary pressures. Consequent increases in interest rates induce borrowers to economize on the use of cash balances in order to limit the amounts they will have to raise in credit markets, and at the same time induce holders of idle cash balances to avail themselves of the increased rates available from investment of these funds.

Such responses, which are reflected in rising velocity, are indications that monetary policy is becoming effective, and are not necessarily impediments to policy. Admittedly, if changes in velocity were erratic and large, they might complicate the formulation of appropriate monetary policy, but the changes that have occurred in post-accord cycles have been consonant with fluctuations in economic activity and sufficiently gradual to distribute the pressures of monetary restraints throughout the economy without disruption of financial markets.

Money and Other Liquidity Instruments

The cyclical and other short-term fluctuations in velocity, superimposed on what clearly appears to be a postwar upward trend, are among the many given facts which monetary authorities must consider in determining the proper degree of pressure on, or stimulation of, growth in the money supply required to achieve the objectives set at any given point of time. Like all statistical measures that relate flows and stocks, variations in income velocity may reflect changes in either or both of its determinants--the stock of money and the flow of expenditure.[1]

In modern society, money performs at least two distinct functions, serving as a liquid store of value as well as a means of payment. Any changes in the extent to which a given money stock is used for either or both of these functions, therefore, will be reflected in statistical measures of velocity. Such changes may result in the long run from institutional and technological developments that lead to a speeding up of the payments flow, thus reducing the need for cash balances in relation to a given volume of payments. This is, by and large, a one-way process, resulting in a gradually increasing efficiency of money in its function as a means of payment.

Money is unique in the sense that it alone serves as a generally accepted means of payment (although the total volume of settlements calling for money can be reduced by a variety of offsetting devices). On the other hand, the function of money as a liquid store of value, held to provide for emergencies and for other purposes, can be fulfilled by a variety of substitutes.

Economic units, including Government units, usually distribute their holdings of liquid assets in such a way as to balance the income

---

[1]Two interrelated velocity concepts are used in monetary analysis. The first, income velocity, by relating expenditures for final products to the stock of money $\left[\dfrac{GNP}{M}\right]$, disregards the layering of payments for intermediate products, transfer payments, and payments flows arising from transactions in existing assets. The second, transactions velocity $\left[\dfrac{T}{M}\right.$, but actually measured as $\left.\dfrac{\text{Debits}}{\text{Demand Deposits}}\right]$, encompasses all types of payments made through the medium of demand deposits, irrespective of their economic significance.

Both measures have well-known conceptual and statistical limitations. Since the end of World War II, the two measures of velocity have moved in roughly parallel fashion. Neither the ratio of non-GNP payments to final purchases nor the porportion of currency to demand deposits has fluctuated widely.

Admittedly, each statistical measure of velocity has its advantages. The following discussion focuses on income velocity, which is directly related to the concept of liquidity that is of considerable importance in monetary analysis. Either of the two over-all velocity measures constitutes an oversimplification. In particular, differential changes in various segments of the economy or among types of payments flows are not given explicit recognition when only aggregate national ratios are used.

from such assets (after costs incurred in their investment) against possible losses and inconvenience arising from their conversion into cash. Clearly, current and anticipated fluctuations in interest rates for money market instruments are a key element in determining at any given time the proportion of total liquidity that will be kept in the form of demand deposits. Thus, fluctuations in velocity reflect the composite effect of forces arising from the two main functions performed by money.

The initial policy actions of the monetary authorities affect the reserve positions of member banks, resulting in marginal changes in the availability of credit. These changes, along with other factors, lead to fluctuations in interest rates, which, in turn, lead to shifts between money and the assets that perform some money functions. In periods of monetary restraint, rising interest rates induce a restructuring of liquidity reserves in favor of nonmoney assets, thus shifting some part of money balances previously held for liquidity purposes into active use. This process is reflected in a rising cyclical velocity of money.

Velocity in the Long Run

Some of the apprehensions with respect to the potentially neutralizing influence of changes in velocity can be traced to the failure to distinguish between cyclical and long-run elements (see Chart VII-1).

Throughout the postwar period--before as well as after the accord--the trend of velocity has been upward. It was interrupted only by three mild cyclical declines, corresponding to the three moderate recessions since the end of World War II, and by a short and very mild decline that followed the economic upsurge after the outbreak of war in Korea.[2] The peak in velocity reached during each cyclical upswing has been consistently well above the previous peak, and the declines that have occurred on the downswings have in all cases been considerably smaller than the preceding advances.

This longer run rise over the entire postwar period is traceable largely to the overhang of money supply stemming from war financing (and from the preceding years of depression) and to institutional developments which have tended to widen the range of other available liquidity instruments and to improve their marketability. Velocity also declined in the 1930's, as the forces of depression reduced the use of money while the volume was maintained or increased. As the chart shows, only in recent years has monetary velocity approached the rate that generally prevailed in the 1920's.

---

[2]The only two other post-World War II declines, in the fourth quarter of 1949 and in the third quarter of 1959, reflected the slowing down of business activity caused by steel strikes.

As the volume of payments has expanded along with economic activity in the postwar period, some business firms (as well as households and governments) found that available cash was sufficient to meet their increased cash outflows; others tended to hold to a minimum the additions to cash for transactions purposes. At the same time, the justification for holding money for precautionary motives has been reduced not only by the greater stability of the postwar economy, but also because various transactor groups have come to regard a wide range of interest-earning assets as an alternative to cash balances.

Treasury bills, commercial paper, savings-type deposits, and various other liquid assets are convertible into money at virtually no risk of loss. The attractiveness of such assets rises with the level of interest rates. Once acquainted with these media, however, some business firms and government units, as well as individuals, have continued to use them even when interest rates have declined. This practice is likely to continue in the future, unless interest rates decline to very low levels that are expected to prevail long enough to justify abandoning the arrangements which have been set up.

The practice of investing temporary excess balances in the money market was, of course, widespread among industrial corporations in the 1920's before it fell into almost complete disuse as a result of the depression and the war. The subsequent upward trend in velocity (see Chart VII-1) thus reflects in part the resumption by more and more firms of policies analogous to those abandoned during the long period of excess liquidity. As a result, cash ratios of nonbank corporations, state and local governments, and of various other nonbank institutions have tended to decline, though at varying rates, in the post-accord years.

Developments in the consumer sector, where incomes have risen rapidly and tend to fluctuate less, have had analogous effects on velocity. Several factors have combined to limit the need or incentive to increase cash balances. Various means of making purchases without immediate payment, such as charge accounts and credit cards, came to be widely used, and forms of interest-earning asset holdings (savings accounts) were well publicized and tailored to meet a variety of needs. At the same time, more and more contingencies could be met without requiring immediate use of cash reserves.

Thus, structural developments in the financial sphere, including changes in the amount, composition, and distribution of the public debt, have resulted in the long-run decline of money as a fraction of total liquid assets since World War II. They have given renewed emphasis to the fact that money has two dimensions, supply and velocity. By facilitating shifts between money and a whole array

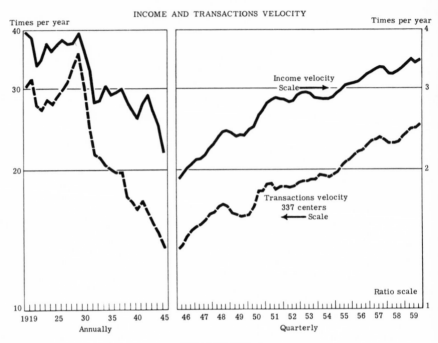

CHART VII-1

of assets of varying degrees of liquidity, the further development of financial markets has permitted a more intensive utilization of the money supply.

It is uncertain to what extent, in the years to come, various money market instruments and such assets as time and savings deposits will continue to displace money in meeting liquidity needs and thus tend to increase velocity of demand deposits. But, surely, a much larger proportion of the total money supply is now used for transactions needs, and less as a liquid store of value, than at any time since the 1920's. Further long-run gains in velocity arising from possibilities of economizing on cash balances may well be more moderate, therefore, than since the end of World War II.[3]

Velocity Swings Over the Cycle

Short-term fluctuations in velocity could be an important impediment to monetary policy and to economic stability if they were erratic. The occurrence of such fluctuations would, indeed, suggest that shifts between money and near-moneys respond to unpredictable influences rather than primarily to changes in economic conditions. This, however, is not the case.

The timing of short-term changes in velocity has generally been closely parallel to that of cyclical fluctuations in over-all economic activity. During the downturn, as incomes decline, the desire to increase liquidity is great. At the same time, falling interest rates reduce the incentive to minimize cash balances. The money supply does not decline as much as do aggregate transactions, partly because of the desire to maintain liquidity and partly because of monetary policies adopted to combat recession. As inventories are liquidated and debt is reduced, cash positions are gradually restored and velocity tends to fall. In the upswing, velocity rises as enlarged cash balances are drawn on to finance increases in spending. Thus, cyclical variations in velocity result, in the main, from changes in the volume of economic activity, reinforced by rising or declining attractiveness of alternative means for acquiring and maintaining liquidity.

---

[3]The various conceptual and technical limitations attached to the numerator and the denominator in both velocity ratios as usually computed are not discussed here. It should be noted, however, that the expanded role of the federal government has tended to increase statistical measures of income velocity. Treasury deposits are excluded from measurements of the money supply used in the attached chart, while U.S. government expenditures are included in GNP. When federal outlays rise, the numerator of the velocity ratio is increased while the denominator is not affected directly (even though Treasury deposits may in fact be rising or falling). The net effect is to increase the computed measure of income velocity.

Some gains in velocity are undoubtedly not reversible; this has been notably true during the post-World War II period. Moreover, each successive increase in velocity reduces possibilities for further economizing of cash for transaction purposes and/or in the management of liquidity reserves.

In view of the complexities of the modern financial system, continuous adaptations to change present challenges to monetary policy, some of which are more formidable than others. Changes in velocity belong to the category of adjustments within our monetary and credit system which can be fairly easily and rapidly identified. Short-run variations in velocity can be meaningfully interpreted only within a broader framework of analysis encompassing changes in the entire credit and liquidity situation of the economy during a given period.

Velocity and the Working of Monetary Controls

It is sometimes contended that changes in the role of different kinds of financial assets have weakened the ability of monetary authorities to influence effectively the liquidity of the economy, that variations in velocity tend to offset, at least in part, changes in the money supply brought about by the monetary authorities, and that such changes in velocity constitute an "escape hatch" from the pressures the monetary authorities are trying to exert. Credit restraint, it is argued, causes rises in interest rates; these, in turn, lead to shifts of some idle balances into the hands of active users, which increases velocity to an extent that largely frustrates the intent of the restrictive monetary policy. While it is recognized that the effect on total demand of the rise in velocity might perhaps be offset by still further restraint on bank reserve positions, it is alleged that such a policy is not generally feasible because beyond a given point such tightening would disrupt financial markets.

While factors other than responses to monetary policy affect changes in velocity, in the long run as well as cyclically, important forces affecting velocity clearly arise as a reaction to changes in monetary policy. In particular, moves toward restraint, by limiting the availability and raising the cost of additional money, intensify the search for alternatives for money, as well as the desire to economize on cash for transactions purposes.

At any given point of time the proportion of liquid assets that various economic units will want to hold in the form of money (as well as the total volume of liquid assets) will depend on their current operations as well as on expectations as to future level of several economic variables. The supply of each category of alternative liquid assets is responsive to demand. Yet, the degree of liquidity of each category of near-moneys depends on the precise conditions under which they are convertible into money. By operating on bank credit and the money supply--the ultimate source of liquidity--the monetary authorities exert an indirect but fairly effective influence on the entire liquidity structure of the economy.

Even though this influence is pervasive, it is not instantaneous and may involve various lags. Since response usually involves shifts in holder preference between money and other liquid assets, more inclusive liquidity ratios tend to show greater stability than income velocity. The important fact to recognize is that changes in money velocity are not an independent force in the credit situation, but rather mirror the behavior of many complex changes in the liquidity conditions of the entire financial structure and the economy as a whole.

On the surface, increases in velocity in response to tightening Federal Reserve policies, which normally are accompanied by rising short-term rates, may appear as an avoidance of the impact of monetary policy actions. In fact, such increases are a reflection of the speed with which the effect of such actions travels beyond the confines of the banking system. The result--in line with the intent of monetary authorities--is a rearrangement of liquid asset holdings that maximizes the use of the existing stock of money and thus speeds the effects of restraint throughout the economy. Moreover, as is noted in the answer to Question VIII, the rise in interest rates accompanying the increase in velocity itself reinforces monetary restraints.

Changes in velocity, along with other mechanisms built into our monetary system, serve to spread the effects of a flexible monetary policy. An increase in velocity is one of the mechanisms that permit the spending patterns and commitments existing at the point of initial impact of restraint to be honored. Thus, the pressure of added restraint is distributed throughout the economy. Conversely, when policy eases, a mechanism, provided by the financial markets, is needed that will make the ease truly general and that will translate the additional demand for assets by some banks into increases in the money supply. Changes in velocity thus reflect reactions to past actions of the monetary authorities as well as set the stage for the determination of subsequent policy moves.

Had short-run fluctuations in velocity been unexpected and violent, rather than systematic and mild, they might have complicated the formulation of monetary policy appropriate to the particular economic situation. In actual experience, they have been sufficiently gradual to permit the economy to adjust itself to changes in credit conditions. The suggestion that direct measures to stabilize velocity of money (income or transactions) might be required (except perhaps for a small range of fluctuations to allow for adjustment lags) implies that monetary policy cannot rely on the crucial position of money within the liquidity structure and on the play of interest rates to affect the total liquidity of the economy.

Behavior of the holders of liquid assets in the major economic sectors since the accord does not bear out these apprehensions. Moreover, the long and difficult process of eliminating from the economy much of the excess liquidity generated during the depression and war years has gradually reduced ratios of money supply to current output, and thus has made the entire liquidity structure more responsive to monetary policy.

QUESTION VIII

Has the rise in the volume of near-money assets--such as savings deposits, savings and loan shares, and short-term Treasury securities--diminished the importance of the money supply proper, and thereby reduced the effectiveness of monetary policy?

ANSWER VIII

Summary

The long-run rise in the volume of near-money assets, absolutely and in relation to the money supply, has not reduced the effectiveness of monetary policy, for over most of the period interest rates have been free to exercise their allocative function. The diffusion of holdings of liquid assets and their diversification has added to the flexibility of the financial mechanism, but it has not destroyed, or even impaired, the key role of money in the liquidity structure of our economy. The restrictive effects of rising interest rates, and the stimulating effects of declining interest rates, together with certain institutional factors which have tended to limit the substitution between liquid assets and cash balances, have permitted changes in monetary policy to affect the entire liquidity structure.

Shiftability of Government Debt

When banks have abundant holdings of Government securities, as they have had in postwar years, they customarily liquidate substantial portions of their portfolios during periods of credit restraint. This enables them to meet the growing demands for loans that are characteristic accompaniments of the rapid growth in total demand.

So long as income is constant and the nonbank purchases of Government securities are financed by diversions of funds from consumption spending, direct investment spending, or lending to others, a growth in the volume of bank loans would involve merely a rechanneling of funds from one use to another, with no necessary increase in the rate of total spending. Under these circumstances the shifting of government debt out of the commercial banks will not lead to an expansion of total credit except to the extent that nonbank acquisitions of government debt are financed by an increase in savings. Thus, the shifting of Government securities clearly is not an unstabilizing influence operating contrary to the aims of monetary policy.

Some analysts have focused attention on the fourth alternative method by which nonbank acquisition of Government securities may be financed; investors may simply substitute Treasury issues for cash balances without reducing their current spending or lending operations. Such a development is always possible so long as existing cash balances exceed minimum levels needed to maintain current rates of spending. Its likelihood is greater when the banks are selling primarily short-term government debt, such as Treasury bills. These instruments serve well as liquid reserves in place of cash.

To the extent that bank sales of Government securities result merely in the absorption of cash balances without depressing either the spending or the lending of the buyers, the additional spending financed by the growth in bank loans is not offset by greater restraint imposed on other types of spending. In this case, the Federal Reserve's influence over the level of bank credit is effective, but nonbank credit expands through the sale of bank-held government debt to nonbank buyers.

Thus, it is claimed, the existence of a large block of short-term government debt in the hands of banks provides a potential "escape valve" whereby a Federal Reserve policy of credit restraint may be met by a more efficient utilization of the already existing money supply. This process would be manifested by a rising velocity of circulation as the nonbank buyers of government debt economized on their cash holdings without curtailing their current spending or lending to other borrowers. Such a development, with its symptomatic acceleration in monetary velocity, would tend to reduce the effectiveness of maintaining a given quantitative restraint on the level of bank credit and the money supply. A similar activation of cash balances could be achieved through sales of short-term securities by the Treasury directly to nonbank investors.

Financial intermediaries may also resort to the liquidation of short-term government debt when they wish to expand their loans at a rate that exceeds current cash inflows. Again, to the extent that the purchasers of the Treasury issues being liquidated merely use them to substitute for working cash balances, the velocity of circulation of money rises.

In addition, some spending units, such as nonfinancial corporations, may come into a period of monetary restraint holding large amounts of liquid Treasury securities. If such holdings satisfy their liquidity needs, these spending units may be willing to draw down their cash balances in order to finance additional spending without having to resort to borrowing.

In all of these cases the suitability of short-term Treasury securities as liquid reserves may permit an increase in velocity of money that is beyond the direct control of Federal Reserve policies and which must be considered in the determination of the proper rate of growth of bank credit and the money supply. Holdings of longer-term Treasury debt are not generally regarded as presenting so significant a problem for monetary control. This is mainly because most potential purchasers regard longer-term Treasury issues as less liquid than short-term government debt, owing mainly to the greater fluctuations in their market values that reduce their reliability as liquid reserves. The kinds of interest rate adjustments that accompany heavy selling pressures in the markets for longer-term Government securities involve capital losses that many investors, including banks, are somewhat reluctant to take. Such securities can be made liquid, of course, by Federal Reserve purchases and particularly by an established and recognized policy of purchasing at fixed prices, as was the case in postwar years before the accord.

Role of Thrift Institutions

All marketable or redeemable assets are in some degree "liquid" in that they provide a potential source of cash for their holders. However, the liabilities of certain financial intermediaries are, along with Government securities, perhaps the most important near-moneys in the contemporary American economy. Redeemable fixed-value claims, such as deposits at mutual savings banks and savings and loan shares, stand out as the most prominent of the nonmonetary liquid claims against financial intermediaries. The funds acquired by the intermediaries when their claims are issued in return for cash are normally used to extend credit; in the United States, the credit of private financial intermediaries that issue such claims is concentrated heavily in the field of mortgage lending.

A build-up of claims against intermediaries may represent a substitution, by those who acquire them, for other securities, for direct investments, or for cash balances. To the extent that individuals acquire such claims by reducing their current spending or their purchases of securities, lending by intermediaries merely offsets this reduction in spending. To the extent that the growth in the share capital or deposits of thrift institutions represents a substitution of these liquid claims for working cash balances, a greater portion of the money supply is activated and the total volume of nonbank credit and of spending is increased.

It is clear that the growth of nonbank intermediaries which issue fixed-value claims has provided an important additional source of highly liquid assets, one that is accessible to many investors who do not normally participate in the securities markets. Some analysts have argued that a distinction between commercial banks as creators of money and nonbank intermediaries as channelers of savings may be overdrawn. They contend that nonbank intermediaries are also able to "create liquidity" in such a way as to contribute to a rise in the total volume of economic activity without a corresponding rise in bank credit and the money supply, i.e., through a rise in the velocity of money.

This aspect of the argument, too, may be overemphasized, however, because the liquid claims created by these financial institutions are not a substitute for money as a medium of exchange. So long as the quantity of money can be adjusted to compensate for velocity changes, the economy's responsiveness to monetary policy is not impaired, even though liquidity needs may be increasingly met through other types of assets.

Time and savings deposits at commercial banks comprise another form of institutional near-money. Time deposits are usually acquired by depositing currency or by shifting from demand deposits. In both cases, the basis for expanding bank credit is enlarged. In particular, a shift from demand to time and savings accounts at commercial banks allows for an expansion of commercial bank credit (unless the Federal Reserve reduces the availability of bank reserves), because the reserve requirement against time deposits (currently 5 percent) is lower than are the requirements against demand deposits. Shifts of funds from demand deposits to time and savings deposits at commercial banks and acquisition of time deposits for cash may or may not be associated with a reduction in spending or lending on the part of those who acquire the time deposits.

Relation to Monetary Policy

Skepticism has been expressed about the ability to compensate for rising velocity through greater quantitative restrictions on bank credit and the money supply. This skepticism derives from the premise that monetary restraint itself leads to an accelerated sub-

stitution of liquid nonmonetary assets for cash at a rate sufficient
to negate financial restraints. Such a development is conceivable
only under highly limiting assumptions.

Monetary controls will lack force in those situations where the
community is able to finance large increases in the total volume of
credit and transactions out of idle cash balances with little or no
changes in interest rates. If interest rates were so low that holders
of loanable funds as a group were unwilling to lend at any lower
rate, they would hold cash balances in preference to earning assets.
Under such circumstances, a given degree of restraint on bank
credit and the money supply might be counteracted for a period of
time by continuing activation of idle balances.

More relevant for monetary policy is consideration of the kinds
of financial conditions under which substitution of liquid nonmonetary
claims for working cash balances involves a penalty. When inflationary pressures threaten, rising credit demands may lead to a
more active use of the money supply, but they do not permit an
unrestrained expansion of credit. During the economic upswing of
1958-59, for example, there occurred a noticeable rise in the velocity of circulation of money that was undoubtedly accomplished
partly through the substitution of liquid claims for working cash
balances. This development was accompanied by a marked restraint
on financial markets, even though bank credit was permitted to grow
somewhat. The significant increases in interest rates reflected in
part large credit demands, but also in part the fact that holders of
cash were unwilling, without the inducement of rising interest rates,
to economize on their cash balances by substituting liquid claims
for them in sufficient amounts to meet all demands.

Institutional Factors

Aside from the effects of the rise in interest rates, certain institutional factors also operate to limit the degree to which shifts
from cash balances to liquid assets can soften the impact of monetary restraint.

The extent of liquidation of short-term Treasury issues by financial institutions during a period of rising credit demands is limited.
This is because each institution has only limited quantities of these
securities, and because many of them are unwilling or unable to
reduce materially their holdings of liquid assets in order to extend
further loan credit. Since this consideration is taken up in answers
to other questions, it is sufficient to note here that, during the process of shifting short-term Treasury debt to the nonbank sector,
banks and other lending institutions undergo a loss of liquidity which
inhibits their willingness to continue the shifting process as financial pressures mount.

Some savings institutions are restricted in their ability and freedom to offer more attractive rates of return to their shareholders or depositors as credit demands intensify. For example, the portfolios of mutual savings banks and savings and loan associations, concentrated largely in long-term mortgages, are relatively inflexible. That is to say, composition of their portfolios cannot be significantly changed by sales of assets and purchases of others in a short period of time, nor would short-period increments in assets be large enough to effect a significant change in composition.

Hence, a very large rise in the rate of return may be necessary to justify more than a nominal rise in the rates paid to depositors or shareholders which must, of course, be applied to existing as well as to new deposit or share accounts. This limitation on the rise in rates paid on the liquid liabilities of thrift institutions restricts their ability to mobilize funds in a period of tight credit availability. When the period of credit stringency is prolonged, however, these institutions may be able to afford increases in their dividend rates sufficient to activate cash balances remaining idle.

Mutual savings banks in some states are not permitted to pay rates above a specified ceiling. There is considerable evidence that these ceilings have in some cases effectively ruled out rate increases that would otherwise have been offered by these banks, making impossible any further inducements to substitute savings deposits for cash.

The growth of time deposits at commercial banks during periods of financial restraint may also be limited by the ceiling on interest paid on these claims under Federal Reserve Regulation Q. During 1959, the growth in time deposits was quite small compared to previous years, as the 3 percent ceiling interest rate made it difficult for banks to attract time balances in the face of rising returns on other forms of investment.

QUESTION IX

Have shifts of funds by depositors, shareholders, policyholders, etc., between financial institutions perhaps induced by interest rate differentials for savers, presented serious obstacles to the effectiveness of monetary policy at any time in the post-accord period?

ANSWER IX

Summary

Shifts of funds among financial institutions have not presented serious obstacles to the effectiveness of monetary policy in the period since the Treasury-Federal Reserve Accord. Most changes in the structure of savings in this period have been continuations of longer-term trends in savings preferences to which monetary policy has continued to adapt. Large short-run fluctuations have occurred principally in time and savings deposits at commercial banks, but only in late 1956 and early 1957 did these fluctuations impinge to any great extent on policy formulation.

Channels of Influence

The highly developed financial markets of our economy offer savers a great variety of outlets for investments of surplus funds. It is not surprising, therefore, to find shifts over time in public preferences among different types of liquid assets.

For the most part, such shifts have tended to be longer-run adjustments to institutional and structural changes in the economy. In addition to interest rate differentials, geographic differences in rates of population growth, changes in laws affecting various types of financial institutions, and innovations in the development of new and attractive saving forms have also been important in giving rise to long-run changes in the composition of liquid asset holdings.

Shifts among forms of saving are also influenced by the fact that not all savings instruments are completely substitutable for one another, and by the related fact that nominal differences in interest returns may overstate real differences. Moreover, different forms of savings are often "earmarked" for particular purposes. Finally, some savings flows are not within the discretion of beneficiaries to divert, as in the case of industrial pension plans. These aspects of competing savings forms condition and limit the extent of the shifting from institution to institution that will occur in response to short-run changes in interest rate differentials.

While monetary policy is formulated in light of general liquidity of the economy, it is not its function to determine the institutional structure of saving or the composition of investment uses to which savings are put. Monetary policy endeavors to provide cash balances in amounts appropriate to the needs of an economy growing at sustainable rates, and to ensure the sound functioning of the banking system through which cash balances are provided.

Shifts in public preferences as to the composition of financial asset holdings can influence the formulation and execution of monetary policy, nevertheless, to the extent that they significantly affect the public's demands for cash, the liquidity of the economy, or the competitive viability of the commercial banking system. Thus, changes in the composition of savings can bear on monetary policy if they involve transfers of funds between demand deposits and other liquid assets, or if they involve transfers among other liquid assets that influence the rate of turnover in cash balances. Special consideration must be given to fluctuations in one savings form-- time and savings deposits at commercial banks--partly because of the Federal Reserve's statutory responsibility for establishing maximum interest rates that member banks can pay on these deposits, and partly because changes in the volume of these deposits affect member bank reserve positions.

Developments Since 1951

In the period since the Treasury-Federal Reserve Accord in 1951, shifts in savings among institutions that have been most significant from the standpoint of the effectiveness of monetary policy have been the flows of funds into and out of commercial bank time and savings deposits. Cyclical fluctuations in these deposits have been mainly in time deposits, which are held principally by foreign depositors, corporations, and state and local governments. When short-term market yields--particularly those on Treasury bills-- dropped sharply after mid-1953 and again in early 1958, flows of funds into time deposits increased substantially. When market yields on short-term investments rose, as after mid-1954 and again after mid-1958, funds flowed rapidly out of time deposits. The magnitude of time deposit fluctuations has been large--from an increase of about $1.5 billion in 1954 to a small net decline in 1955, and from a rise of $2.5 billion in 1958 to a decline of $2 billion in 1959.

Savings deposits at commercial banks, held mainly by consumers, have generally not fluctuated in response to movements in short-term rates in the money market, although the slowing in growth rate of these deposits in 1955 and again in 1959 suggests that they have some degree of sensitivity to competitive rate movements. The most abrupt rise in savings deposits occurred in early 1957 after an amendment to Regulation Q, effective at the beginning of the year, permitted increases in rates on time and savings deposits at commercial banks for the first time in two decades. It is estimated that consumer holdings of savings deposits, which had increased at a rate of between $1 and $1.5 billion over the first halves of the years from 1951 to 1956, jumped by more than $3 billion in the first half of 1957 and continued to rise at a rapid rate throughout the remainder of the year and throughout 1958.

Shifts into and out of time and savings deposits at commercial banks immediately affect bank reserve positions. Fluctuations in 'time deposits, in particular, to the extent that they represent shifts between these deposits and Treasury bills, immediately affect the market in which Federal Reserve open market operations are usually conducted. The economic consequences of shifts in time deposits have been limited, however. For the most part, they have represented reallocation of liquid asset portfolios with little or no apparent effect on current spending plans of the holders. Nor have the fluctuations impeded management of the open market account in the execution of policy under current directives.[1]

The large shift in consumer holdings of savings deposits that followed the rate increase at the beginning of 1957 was accompanied by a somewhat greater than seasonal decline in consumer holdings of demand deposits and currency.[2] Consumer spending for goods and services continued to increase rapidly in this period, as did the rate at which their cash balances were being used. The pressure of consumer demands was reflected in further increases in consumer prices, and contributed to the continuing need for restraint on monetary expansion.

QUESTION X

Have such financial institutions as commercial banks, insurance companies, savings and loan associations and mutual savings banks managed their portfolios in such a way as to present serious obstacles to the effectiveness of monetary policy at any time in the post-accord period? What is the role of and how effective is the so-called "lock-in" effect (to avoid capital losses) in inhibiting financial institutions from selling off assets to make new extensions of credit?

---

[1]See answer to Question XXII for a more detailed description of recent developments in the area of commercial bank time deposits.
[2]Consumers were at the same time making other changes in their financial asset portfolios--redemption of savings bonds increased and the rate of growth in mutual savings bank deposits and savings and loan shares slowed somewhat--and consumers' incomes were continuing to rise. It seems plausible, nevertheless, that some of the $3 billion rise in savings deposits at commercial banks in the first half of the year was directly associated with the decline in consumer holdings of currency and demand deposits.

ANSWER X

Summary

Monetary policy does not attempt to channel flows of credit to or away from specific uses. Monetary policy is primarily concerned, therefore, with those portfolio decisions of financial institutions that influence the total volume of bank credit and money or the rate of use of money supply. Institutional portfolio changes that can influence the total volume of money or its turnover are (a) those involving sales of assets to the banking system which result in an increase in the money supply, (b) those involving sales of assets to other purchasers which result in activation of idle cash balances, and (c) those involving acquisition of new assets in amounts greater than new savings inflows and therefore resulting in institutional borrowing from banks.

Such portfolio changes need not affect the total supply of bank credit unless the Federal Reserve concomitantly changes the availability of bank reserves. Hence, except for the activation of existing cash balances, portfolio changes by financial institutions need not interfere with the effectiveness of monetary policy. Since flexibility was restored to monetary operations in 1951, policy has been able to keep an effective rein on the availability of bank reserves. Financial institutions other than commercial banks have continued to liquidate Government securities over this period, presumably activating idle balances in the process, but these sales have not been of such a magnitude as to create serious obstacles to the effectiveness of monetary policy.

Portfolio Adjustments Through Sales of U.S. Government Securities

Wartime financing and limitations on private investment opportunities resulted in a major distortion of the portfolios of financial institutions. At the end of World War II, the four major financial groups cited in the question--commercial banks, insurance companies, savings and loan associations, and mutual savings banks-- held more than $111 billion of federal government debt, almost half of the total outstanding. Such holdings represented almost three-fifths of the total assets of these institutions.

Containing this surfeit of liquidity in a period of rising civilian demands for still scarce goods and services would have been a difficult task for monetary authorities under the best of circumstances. Hobbled by the requirement of supporting Government security prices in early postwar years, monetary policy could do little to prevent the transformation of a large part of this institutional liquidity into actively used money. In the four-year period

from the end of 1946 to the end of 1950, these institutions reduced
their holdings of Government securities by $22 billion--$10 billion
more than the reduction in outstanding public debt. Meanwhile, with
other asset holdings rising rapidly, Government securities in institutional portfolios fell from almost three-fifths to less than two-
fifths of the total assets of these institutions, and from almost half
to about two-fifths of the public debt outstanding.

Since the beginning of 1951, or roughly the period in which
monetary policy has been able to operate flexibly in countering
excessive fluctuations in demands for bank credit, institutional
holdings of Government securities have generally continued to decline, but at a much slower pace than in the pre-accord period.
In contrast to the reduction of $22 billion, or one-fifth, in the first
four postwar years, these holdings declined only $9.5 billion, or
one-tenth, over the next nine years.

The difference in pace at which institutions have shifted their
portfolio structure in the post-accord period has reflected many
factors in addition to the flexible application of monetary policy.
Moreover, institutions have differed widely in their response to
changing economic developments and credit policy. In some instances, rapid gains in savings inflows have called for additions
to holdings of cash and Governments in order to maintain required
or desired liquidity positions. Thus, savings and loan associations'
holdings of Government securities increased more than threefold
from 1950 through 1959, almost keeping pace with the rise in their
other asset holdings.

Where liquidity considerations have been less important in
portfolio management, or where other sources of liquidity have
been available, holdings of Government securities have continued
to decline. The contractual nature of much of the income of life
insurance companies--both from policy premiums and debt amorti-
zation--and the large volume of high quality bonds and government-
insured mortgages in their portfolios have apparently reduced the
need of these companies for liquidity reserves in the form of
Government securities, and such holdings have continued to decline
while other investments have increased. At the end of 1959, Government securities accounted for not much more than one-fifteenth of
insurance company assets compared with more than one-fifth in
1950 and about one-sixth in immediate prewar years.

To the extent that sales of Government securities result in
activation of idle cash balances, they contribute to the need for
more restraint on the growth of the money supply during periods
of inflationary pressures than might be required in the absence of
such increases in the rate of money use. Sales of Government
securities by life insurance companies, however, could have con-

tributed only a relatively small amount to the rise in deposit velocity in most years since the accord. The largest annual reduction in Government security holdings was the $1 billion decline in 1956, whereas in the earlier postwar period annual reductions ranged up to almost $3.5 billion in periods of strong credit demands, such as occurred in 1948. In 1959, a year of peak demands for credit when interest rates reached new postwar highs, net liquidation of Government securities by life insurance companies amounted to only $300 million.

The small size of recent portfolio adjustments by life insurance companies is all the more impressive when one takes into consideration the extent to which current investment of life insurance company funds is determined by lending commitments made earlier, often in a quite different economic climate. Forward commitments outstanding represent from two-thirds to three-fourths of the annual gross cash flows of insurance companies. Sharp increases in credit demands accompanying rapid economic recovery cause a drain on insurance company investment resources from several directions: through increased demands for policy loans, withdrawals of funds left under deposit-type arrangements, and a reduced volume of debt prepayments, all occurring at a time when rising interest rates open new and more profitable outlets for investment. Such a conjunction of events probably explains in part the billion dollar decline in insurance company holdings of Government securities in 1956. It is significant to note, however, that insurance companies did not permit forward commitments to rise to so high a level, relative to cash flows, during the upswing in credit demands in the latter half of 1958 and in 1959 as they had in 1956.

Mutual savings banks have also been substantial net sellers of Government securities over the post-accord period, but the amounts sold in any one year have again been relatively small. The largest reduction occurred in 1951 when net sales exceeded $1 billion; in recent years, liquidation has fluctuated between $300 million and $500 million.

The continuing reduction in Government security portfolios by such institutional investors as life insurance companies and mutual savings banks suggests that they are not completely "locked in" by unrealized capital losses on their portfolios. Nevertheless, the moderate size of reductions in recent years also suggests that there are limits on the losses they are willing to take in order to finance new portfolio additions. With total investment portfolios much larger than in earlier postwar years, most financial institutions would have to make fairly large changes in portfolio composition to effect substantial changes in investment income. Markets for seasoned securities, however--even those for Government bonds--cannot absorb a substantial volume of sales offerings in short periods without significant price effects. This sensitivity of bond markets has been an important factor limiting shifts in composition of institutional portfolios in recent years.

Commercial bank portfolios of Government securities have shown swings of much wider amplitude, rising from $5 to $8 billion in years when credit conditions were easing, and declining by as much when monetary restraints limited growth of bank credit during periods of excessive demand. Commercial banks are not as limited in portfolio management by possibilities of losses on securities as are many other institutional investors, in part because a larger proportion of their Government security holdings are short term and therefore not subject to price fluctuations as wide as those on longer-term issues, and in part because losses on security sales can be deducted in full from income for tax purposes. Both factors serve to moderate the influence of the so-called "lock-in" effect on bank portfolio management.

On the other hand, Government securities can be carried on bank balance sheets at cost, i.e., declines in market value need not be recorded until securities are sold. Recognition of losses through security sales might reflect adversely on bank management and, more importantly, might impair capital and surplus accounts, the size of which limit certain bank lending practices. Moreover, many smaller commercial banks are subject to the 30 percent rather than the 52 percent income tax rate, and this reduces their tax incentive for portfolio switching.

On balance, these deterrents appear to exercise a strong degree of influence. A study of bank portfolio practices in one Federal Reserve district during a period of rising interest rates and demands for loans (1959) indicates that a majority of banks did not take full advantage of unrealized capital losses to increase current incomes or reduce tax liabilities.[1] To a major extent, therefore, the large fluctuations in bank holdings of Government securities in recent cycles must reflect changes in portfolios of shorter-term issues or longer-term securities closely approaching redemption dates.

These fluctuations in bank portfolios cannot be considered a major obstacle to monetary policy, however, since such a consequence of restraint can be taken into account in the formulation of policy. The degree of restraint appropriate to particular phases of economic expansion is established not only in terms of the absolute size of the money supply but also in terms of its rate of use.

---

[1] Monthly Review, Federal Reserve Bank of Kansas City (June 1960).

Other Aspects of Institutional Portfolio Management

Financial intermediaries on occasion supplement the funds available to them from savings inflows, debt repayments, and security sales by borrowing from commercial banks and others. For the most part, such arrangements are regarded as temporary accommodations to meet seasonal or other short-term incongruities between cash inflows and loan commitments.

There has been at least one occasion in the post-accord period when the duration of such borrowing has given the impression that short-term banking funds were being utilized by thrift institutions as a substitute for permanent capital to finance long-term investments. The situation that developed in 1955 with respect to mortgage warehousing was soon corrected, however, and this type of bank lending has remained under continuing review, through both regular statistical reporting and the examination of individual banks.

Savings and loan associations have available to them a governmental source of funds which is used not only for seasonal adjustments but also to some extent to accommodate cyclical and long-term needs arising out of lending activities in excess of current savings flows in particular communities. During periods of credit tightness member savings and loan associations have borrowed heavily from the Federal Home Loan Banks to acquire new mortgages and to fulfill commitments. At the end of 1959, outstanding borrowing from the FHLB exceeded $2 billion and had increased during the year by about $800 million.

The FHLB must borrow in capital markets at going rates, and the interest they charge on advances to member associations reflects FHLB borrowing costs. The curbing effect of rising interest rates on FHLB borrowing and advances may not be quickly transmitted to member savings and loan associations, however, if the FHLB follows a practice of making advances for a period without counterbalancing sales of debentures in capital markets. It is to the advantage of associations to continue to borrow even at high interest rates to acquire mortgages, because the funds advanced to mortgage borrowers tend to remain as high interest rate mortgage loans on the associations' books after the associations have retired their debt to the FHLB.

Monetary policy does introduce a corrective element in this process. As interest rates rise in periods of expansion, and as costs of borrowing and advances by the FHLB rise, individual mortgage borrowers at the margin may postpone financing through savings and loan associations. This corrective element does tend to restrain the demand for credit during periods of credit tightness, but the effect on mortgage market responses may have a substantial time lag.

QUESTION XI

To what extent do such factors as changes in liquidity positions, loan-deposit ratios, legal and supervisory standards, etc., operate to affect credit availability in periods of expanding credit demands?

ANSWER XI

Summary

Liquidity requirements, loan-deposit ratios and other limits on investment practices imposed by custom or law on financial institutions may have an important influence upon the availability of credit for particular uses. Except to the extent that they relate to holdings of cash, however, they do not necessarily limit the availability of total credit. The acquisition of liquid assets other than cash by financial institutions in order to meet liquidity standards provides funds which sellers of these assets can reinvest, thereby keeping unchanged the total amount of credit available.

Sales of liquid assets by financial institutions in order to meet expanding credit demands do not necessarily change the total credit supply either. In the process, however, such sales can activate idle cash balances and, in an inflationary situation, this requires greater restraint over the expansion of the volume of money. The existence of liquidity standards can therefore assist monetary policy by slowing the pace and limiting the extent of changes in institutional portfolio structures. Minimum requirements with respect to cash balances, of course, provide an ultimate limit on the extent to which velocity can increase in an expansionary period.

Lenders and borrowers may for a time adjust to increasing credit stringency by economizing in the use of cash balances or by liquidating existing assets in order to finance new investments--financial or physical--that offer higher returns. These adjustments will tend to be self-limiting, however, as the processes of economizing on cash balances and liquidation of existing assets bring portfolio structures closer to the minimum liquidity standards dictated by custom, prudence, or statute.

Not only is this process of liquidating existing assets to provide additional lending capacity ultimately self-limiting, but it is by no means inevitable that such individual adjustments will have the net effect of increasing the over-all availability of credit. While lenders may substitute less liquid assets such as loans, mortgages, or corporate securities for more liquid ones such as U.S. Government securities, these securities--or their equivalent in new issues--must simultaneously be absorbed elsewhere unless a comparable reduction in federal debt is taking place. Such transactions do not constitute a net addition to the pool of loanable funds.

Just as institutional sales of liquid securities do not necessarily increase the availability of credit in the aggregate, so purchases of liquid securities by these institutions would not necessarily diminish or limit growth in the over-all supply of credit. If lenders or investors acquire short-term U.S. Government securities, for example, the sellers of those securities have funds for other uses and there is no decrease in the total supply of credit.

Because transactions in liquid securities do not necessarily change the aggregate availability of credit, such devices as security reserves for banks--or for other financial institutions--are not effective means of controlling the over-all supply of credit in a strong expansionary period, unless there is at the same time an effective control over cash reserves. Security reserves can be effective only in case the following conditions are satisfied: (1) the supply of reserve-eligible securities is limited, (2) required reserves other than securities must be held in cash, and (3) the availability of cash is controlled.

Some increase in over-all credit availability is likely to take place if the process of portfolio shifting is accompanied by rising interest rates which stimulate an increase in savings flows. This should ordinarily be viewed as accomplishing the purposes of monetary policies rather than being in conflict with them.

Alternatively, the rate of turnover of the existing money supply could be accelerated and this increased turnover--unless offset by monetary policy--could have the same effects as expansion in the total availability of credit. Whether this occurs would depend not only on the desire of financial institutions to liquidate existing assets but also upon the willingness of the rest of the community to convert idle demand deposits into less liquid but interest-bearing assets.

The task of monetary authorities in offsetting increased turnover resulting from sales of financial assets might be made more difficult if institutional portfolio adjustments were concentrated in Government securities and were, as a result, having a serious impact on the market for these securities. Consequently, the existence of liquidity standards, by limiting the rapidity and extent to which institutions will change portfolio structure, contributes to the ease and effectiveness with which monetary policy can be executed during periods of expanding credit demands.

How quickly liquidity standards will exert effective restraint depends in part upon the extent to which current levels of liquidity exceed those customarily considered necessary and desirable. Excessive liquidity, such as obtained at the end of World War II, and which included cash balances well in excess of normal requirements, permitted a prolonged period of credit expansion. Much of this excess has been absorbed, however, in financing the rapid rise in private debt over the past 15 years. In postwar cycles, there have been significant increases in institutional liquidity during recessionary phases--although in small amounts relative to the wartime experience--and this liquidity has helped to foster recovery. In succeeding expansionary periods, liquidity has declined, and the trend over the postwar period as a whole has been toward reduced liquidity. The scale of liquidity reductions in expansion periods has been much smaller in recent cycles than earlier, suggesting that in many instances liquidity is approaching minimum requirements. It may be, therefore, that financial institutions, as well as the sectors of the economy dependent on them for financing, are now in a position of being more responsive to monetary restraint.

Commercial banks. For the commercial banking system, primary liquidity and ability to expand credit may be fairly effectively limited by Federal Reserve control over the supply of basic reserves. Secondary liquidity is largely based upon the traditions, standards, and needs of individual banks. From the viewpoint of the individual bank, the impact of limitations on the availability of basic reserves will appear initially in a "squeeze" on its secondary liquidity. It is only after the bank has reached the limit of these secondary reserves that it must resort to other means of reserve adjustment, which in turn limit its ability to lend.[1]

Whether measured in terms of the relation of loans to deposits or by similar ratios, the degree of liquidity varies widely among banks by size classes and geographically. While important significance cannot be attached to any single ratio for the banking system as a whole, there is evidence that individual bank standards with respect to maximum loan-deposit ratios do function to limit expansion of loans or certain other assets. Expansion of total bank credit, however, is ultimately limited by the volume of basic reserves available to the banking system as a whole.

In recent years, during recoveries from recessions, banks have been able to finance loan expansion in large part by liquidation of Government security holdings acquired during preceding periods of credit ease. As monetary policy has moved to restrain excessive growth in demand deposits, further bank loan expansion has increas-

[1]This process is described in more detail in the replies to Questions I and XV.

ingly tended to become subject to limitation because of high loan-deposit ratios, although in successive postwar cycles there has been a tendency to push "ceiling" ratios higher. The limiting effect may persist for a time even after pressures of credit demand have eased, since it may take some time for individual banks to readjust their loan portfolios. The time lag will be longer if loan-deposit ratios have previously been pushed close to ceiling levels during expansionary phases of the cycle.

In attempting to hold their ratios at levels they regard as desirable, banks will often revise their lending policies and standards. Since bank preference for different types of loans varies considerably, these adjustments may at times involve curtailment of lending in less preferred areas while other types may be little affected. The declines in real estate and security loans at city banks in the first half of 1960 undoubtedly reflected such adjustments in loan policies.

Bank supervisory authorities, in contrast, strive to avoid cyclical changes in the criteria which they use in appraising the soundness of bank assets. Supervisory appraisal standards ordinarily function in a way that should not, in itself, alter bank credit availability in periods of expanding credit demands. In practice, bank lending is generally conducted well within established supervisory standards. Banker awareness that loan policies will be reviewed in terms of intrinsic rather than transitory market values of the collateral behind loans, as well as in terms of needs for proper diversification, may moderate the pace of expansion in certain types of loans in periods of rapidly rising credit demands. With a given volume of reserves and deposits, liquidity standards may thus affect the distribution of bank credit--between loans or other assets considered as nonliquid and those deemed to be liquid--but these standards do not necessarily affect the total volume of bank credit.

Life insurance companies. Life insurance companies are not subject to liquidity needs comparable to those of financial institutions having demand liabilities or liabilities of relatively short maturity. The contractual nature of much of the income of life insurance companies and the actuarial basis of much of their liabilities minimize the need for large reserves of liquid assets.

During the war, when life insurance resources expanded and the supply of investments other than U.S. Government securities was limited, life insurance companies greatly expanded their holdings of Government securities. In the early postwar years, when prices of Government securities were supported by the Federal Reserve and when other long-term credit demands were large, these institutions rapidly shifted their assets. This process, except to the extent that it was offset by other Federal Reserve operations or by reduction in the public debt out of budgetary surplus, in effect added greatly to the over-all liquidity of the economy because it added to the supply of basic reserves available to the banks.

After the discontinuance of rigid Federal Reserve support of the market in 1951, life insurance companies continued to reduce their holdings of U.S. Government securities, but at a slower pace. As a consequence, over the postwar period as a whole there has been a substantial and fairly persistent decline--to the lowest level since 1933--in the ratio of Government securities and cash to total assets of life insurance companies.

Liquidity problems of insurance companies have arisen primarily from occasional disparities between their cash inflows and the outflow of investment funds committed earlier. Under these conditions, insurance companies have made temporary adjustments by borrowing from banks, by warehousing mortgages and by accelerating liquid asset reductions. They have also tended to reduce their willingness to commit loan funds in advance and have markedly changed the composition of new commitments made. Commitments have shifted away from investment areas where interest rates can have only limited response to rising credit demands, such as Government-underwritten mortgages, and more funds have been committed to areas where rates are more flexible, such as business securities.

Legal and supervisory standards, as they apply to insurance companies, vary somewhat from one state to another, but they are mainly concerned with the quality of long-term investments. As a result of the requirement that private investments meet certain standards of quality, the lowering of the ratio of cash and Governments to total assets may have been at a slower rate than if these standards had not existed, but the effect does not appear to have been a significant determinant of insurance company investment behavior.

Other institutions. Savings and loan associations and mutual savings banks channel most of their flows of savings into the mortgage market. Mutual savings banks confine their credit extensions for the most part to deposit inflows and the proceeds of liquidation of Government securities. Savings and loan associations may supplement savings inflows by borrowing from the Federal Home Loan Banks.

Willingness to borrow from the FHLB becomes subject to restraint as the FHLB pays higher rates on its debentures in tight capital markets and increases its rate on advances to member savings and loan associations. This does not necessarily mean an increase in over-all credit. Funds borrowed by FHLB must be obtained in the market and thus are diverted from other uses, except to the extent that they may cause an increase in bank credit and the money supply that would not otherwise have occurred. Likewise, an increase in the liquidity position of savings associations does not necessarily cause a decrease in the total volume of credit outstanding.

Member savings and loan associations are required to maintain a liquidity reserve of cash and U.S. Government securities amounting to 6 percent of share capital. In addition, the Federal Home Loan Bank Board has, from time to time, restricted advances to associations when credit demand was excessive. The Home Loan Banks are required to keep liquid reserves against deposits made with them by member associations. In December 1955, the Federal Home Loan Bank Board increased the liquidity requirements of the Banks to 75 percent of members' deposits with the Banks, from the former requirement of 20 percent. The Board also required that the Home Loan Banks establish a new liquidity reserve to accommodate some unanticipated demands for advances. These requirements undoubtedly slowed the rate of increase in conventional mortgage lending, which was no larger in 1956 than in 1955, though they probably had no effect on total credit extended by savings institutions; this is determined by the amount of savings placed with them.

QUESTION XII

To what extent is the Federal Reserve concerned with the level of bank earnings and the adequacy of bank capital; what powers and actions are available for the Federal Reserve to utilize if it wishes to affect such magnitudes?

ANSWER XII

Summary

In addition to its primary function of regulating bank credit and the money supply, the Federal Reserve also has certain statutory responsibilities for maintaining a sound banking system through supervision of its member banks. Although actions taken in discharging these functions are designed and carried out in the interest of the public at large rather than particular groups, these actions influence bank earnings, which in turn affect the ability of banks to maintain adequate capital. The System's concern for bank earnings or bank capital derives from their relevance to the System's responsibilities for maintaining a financial structure that is sound and conducive to economic growth.

Banks must have adequate capital in order that they may assume the reasonable risks and provide the credit essential for growth of the economy. Long-term growth in the money supply, too, requires that banks have adequate capital as well as sufficient reserves. The ability of commercial banks to perform these functions effectively in a growing economy is perhaps the most relevant test of adequacy of earnings and capital. Adequate earnings are essential to build up capital funds through internal accumulation or through sales of new stock.

Actions taken by the Federal Reserve which may influence the level of bank earnings or the adequacy of bank capital must be consistent with the Federal Reserve's primary responsibility for regulating bank credit and the money supply. Under the provisions of the Federal Reserve Act, all Federal Reserve monetary policy actions must have regard to their effects on the general credit situation of the country, the accommodation of commerce and business, and prevention of injurious credit expansion or contraction. Under the Employment Act of 1946, they must also have regard to the objectives of maximum employment, production and purchasing power. Any assumption by the Federal Reserve of a direct concern for the level of bank earnings might at times involve inconsistencies with these main responsibilities.

In order that banks may maintain adequate capital to meet the economy's growth needs, gradual increases in their capital funds are needed. Some adequate level of earnings is necessary for this, although increases in bank earnings do not necessarily or automatically result in improvements in bank capital positions.

Retained earnings have been the principal source of additions to bank capital in the postwar period, although this method of increasing capital is a slow process. The alternative method of increasing capital, however, through the sale of additional stock, is also largely dependent on past and prospective earnings. The ratio of capital to assets of member banks declined sharply in the 1930's and early 1940's, and the slow growth during the postwar period has not been adequate to restore earlier levels.

Economic Functions of Bank Capital

The capital funds of a commercial bank have long been visualized as fulfilling a duty to depositors, to afford them a cushion of protection against losses. Since the advent of Federal deposit insurance, this cushion serves in part as protection to the government as well as to depositors not fully covered by insurance.

This function of bank capital has focused attention on the relation between total capital funds and risk exposure. Ratios of capital funds to risk assets are frequently employed as rough indicators of the adequacy of a bank's capital from the depositors' viewpoint.

Another point of view is that of the economy at large which needs a properly functioning credit mechanism. If commercial banks are to contribute to growth and prosperity, they must be prepared to take reasonable risks in meeting the credit needs of legitimate borrowers. A good banker is an expert in identifying sound and constructive risk-taking as distinguished from risk-taking that is speculative or otherwise undesirable. But, in order to contribute to economic growth by sound risk-taking, the bank must have adequate capital against the possibility that losses may develop. Only in this way can it be prepared to finance enterprises that may involve some reasonable but socially desirable degree of risk.

Furthermore, when a borrower runs into adverse circumstances, the banker needs to appraise the situation and determine whether it will be best to require liquidation or to extend further time or credit for working out the problem. It would be undesirable if a shortage of capital made it impossible for the bank to take the risks that a further extension--even if judged sound--would involve. In time of recession, when a significant proportion of a bank's borrowers may have such problems at the same time, the bank should be able to use its best judgment in deciding its policy with respect to each borrower. A stronger capital position enables bankers to adhere to more uniform lending standards during the different phases of the business cycle.

The optimal functioning of the banking system in the interest of the broader economy, therefore, can only be achieved if each banker is able to make decisions based on his best judgment of the position of the credit applicant and that of the economy. He ought not to be inhibited in this by any shortage of capital and consequent inability of the bank to carry the risks that would otherwise be acceptable.

Powers Relating to Capital Adequacy

Under the Federal Reserve Act, adequate capital is one of the requirements for admission of state banks to membership in the System. The Act states:

> No applying bank shall be admitted to membership unless it possesses capital stock and surplus which, in the judgment of the Board of Governors of the Federal Reserve System, are adequate in relation to the character and condition of its assets and to its existing and prospective deposit liabilities and other corporate responsibilities.

Various other provisions of the Federal Reserve Act and the National Banking Act are designed to protect capital adequacy. Member banks are prohibited from paying dividends out of capital; they can be paid only out of current and accumulated earnings. Member banks may not reduce their capital without the consent of the appropriate supervisory authority, and if a member bank's capital becomes impaired, the deficiency must be made up within a stated time; otherwise the bank can be expelled from membership in the case of state member banks or forced into liquidation in the case of national banks.

In addition to these specific legal provisions relating to capital funds, Federal Reserve authorities have certain supervisory functions over member bank operations which indirectly have a bearing on capital adequacy.[1] A regulation of the Board of Governors prescribes adequate capital as one of the conditions of continuing membership for state member banks. Periodic examinations of individual banks are conducted to ascertain the degree of risk inherent in bank assets and other facts bearing on the condition of banks.

Bank supervision embraces a wide variety of functions. Some are technical, relating mainly to operations and compliance with banking laws and regulations. In a more significant sense, however, supervision is concerned with broader questions such as the composition of assets, lending and investing policies, competency of management, risk exposure and adequacy of capital funds. The primary objective is to help maintain a system of individual banks, each financially sound and always in a position to meet its liabilities.

There is no single standard or formula for measuring adequacy of capital that is applicable to all banks. No two banks are exactly alike with respect to the quality and composition of assets, structure of liabilities, and competency of management. Capital adequacy can be determined only by analyzing these and other relevant information for each individual bank.

Powers Relating to Earnings

The powers of the Federal Reserve that affect bank earnings fall into two main categories: those related to bank supervisory functions and those related to monetary policy actions.

As to the supervisory function, it is frequently said that supervisory criticisms have an important effect in inhibiting bank ac-

---

[1]In practice, Federal Reserve supervisory functions relate mainly to the operation of state member banks. Primary responsibility for supervising the operations of national banks is vested in the Comptroller of the Currency.

quisitions of risky assets that would ordinarily tend to promise higher interest yields than items involving less risk. In this sense, standards of the Federal Reserve and of other bank supervisory agencies may affect bank earnings. Supervisory policies of these kinds, however, are not influenced by any purpose or desire to affect bank earnings.

Related to the supervisory function is the authority of the Board of Governors to regulate the rates of interest paid on time and savings deposits. Such payments obviously affect bank costs and earnings.

Bank supervisory agencies, both federal and state, also have important powers relating to the chartering of new banks or permitting banks to open new branches. Decisions in these fields (made primarily by agencies other than the Federal Reserve) are often influenced by considerations of bank earnings. In order to open a new banking office, the supervisory authority ordinarily requires a showing that there are reasonable prospects of adequate earnings.

With respect to Federal Reserve actions in the field of monetary policy, the choice of instruments used in implementing policy affects bank earnings. The proper exercise of monetary policy, however, ordinarily calls for the use of certain instruments under a given set of conditions--regardless of the effects on bank earnings. If bank earnings were considered as an important basis for such decisions, this could interfere with the effective use of the instruments of monetary policy.

A special problem as to the effect of monetary instruments arises in connection with changes in reserve requirements. Given a certain volume of funds to be supplied to the banking system, a lowering of reserve requirements tends to increase bank earnings as compared with the effect of Federal Reserve open market purchases of Government securities. A higher percentage reserve requirement increases the amount of assets held in nonearning form, and thus tends to reduce bank earnings, while a low percentage requirement permits a larger proportion of bank resources to be held as earning assets and tends to increase earnings. Requirements should never be so high as to prevent banks from earning enough to enable them to maintain an adequate capital position.

The level of reserve requirements that member banks are required to hold with the Federal Reserve will also affect, in the long run, the attractiveness of membership in the Federal Reserve System, and national chartering as against state chartering, in the case of both existing and newly formed banks.

Finally, it may be pointed out that Federal Reserve policies affect interest rates and that the level of interest rates affects bank earnings. Theoretically, bank earnings would be increased by a rise in the general level of interest rates. At the same time, a policy that results in higher interest rates could affect bank earnings adversely by restricting the ability of banks to expand credit and by reducing the prices of securities they may wish to sell to make loans. Because the economic effects of changes in the level of interest rates so far transcend any possible importance of bank earnings, however, no conscientious monetary authority would ever exert its influence in the direction of higher interest rates for the purpose of increasing bank earnings. The Federal Reserve has not been influenced, in taking actions that might affect the level of interest rates, by the effect on bank earnings.

QUESTION XIII

What criteria are used in determining the instrument mix to be utilized to achieve policy objectives under varying circumstances? That is, what factors are weighed in determining the extent to which relative reliance should be placed upon changes in discount policy, open market operations, reserve requirements, and margin requirements to achieve a given change in credit conditions?

ANSWER XIII

Summary

There are no criteria which can be said to be utilized especially for the purpose of determining the relative reliance which is placed upon changes in discount policy, open market operations, reserve requirements, or other instruments. The combination of instruments brought to bear on a particular credit situation is the result of an effort to employ each of the instruments as effectively as possible. Thus, rather than setting forth specific criteria which are used to determine the "instrument mix," the following reply discusses how different instruments, or combinations of instruments, are, in fact, employed in making desired adjustments in reserve availability. It suggests that both open market and discount operations are continuously employed as complementary parts of a single policy, while changes in reserve requirements are ordinarily made infrequently for the purpose of absorbing or releasing reserves in response to longer-run developments.

Criteria for Monetary Policy

Monetary policy endeavors to adjust the availability of member bank reserves so as to make the greatest possible contribution to the accomplishment of the broad goal of sustainable economic growth. The System's experience is that the nature and interdependence of available instruments of policy largely determine the instrument mix appropriate to a given economic situation. Intensive use of one particular instrument in pursuit of some secondary objective would almost always detract from the effectiveness with which the primary objective could be accomplished.

It is almost never the case that credit conditions will be affected in exactly the same way by changes in one or another of the basic instruments of policy. In a simple computation of the volume of reserve funds available to the banking system for bank credit expansion, it is true that a specific reduction in reserve requirement would provide the same volume of reserves as the purchase of a corresponding volume of securities in the open market by the System account. However, the effects which follow from the use of one instrument or the other on banks' willingness to lend, on security markets, and on the public generally, may vary considerably.

The effect of a purchase or sale of securities, a change in the discount rate, or a change in reserve requirements, must always be judged in relation to the whole range of economic forces at the time. The choice of the instrument or instruments to be used, and the decision as to intensity of use, flows from an appraisal of the probable effect of current and prospective Federal Reserve operations in the developing economic situation. Primary attention is always focused on those actions that will contribute most effectively to the broad objectives of policy, taking into account the interrelationship among these actions.

Open Market Operations and the Discount Mechanism

Open market operations and discount operations are the two major ways in which the volume of Federal Reserve credit available to the banking system is altered. These operations are essentially complementary. The fact that open market purchases and sales occur frequently, while changes in the discount rate are made at infrequent intervals, obscures to some extent the fact that reserve adjustments take place almost every day through one or both mechanisms and thus both open market policy and discount policy are continuous.

Reserves obtained through borrowing are typically accompanied by a spreading atmosphere of credit restraint, as contrasted with the effect of a corresponding amount of reserves injected by open market operations and appearing in a bank as a normal deposit gain or favorable clearing balance. Administrative restraint exercised by discount officials, together with the reluctance of banks to borrow, make it likely that a bank forced to borrow will in turn begin to search for Federal funds, seek correspondent accommodation, offer securities for sale, sell participations in its more merchantable loans, and/or curtail its direct loan activity. Appraisal of the market atmosphere resulting from these developments is one of the important judgments in the formulation of monetary policy.

When a seasonal demand for reserves may be expected, for example, and an expansive credit climate is desired, the open market account might purchase the full amount of securities necessary to supply the reserves. If an element of credit restraint is desired, however, some or all of the reserve demands might be left to be satisfied via member bank borrowing.

The myriad of payment flows within the banking system are continually creating temporary reserve surpluses in some banks and reserve deficits in others. When a customer suddenly transfers funds, the bank receiving the transfer can be just as unprepared to cope with a reserve influx as is the paying bank with its reserve loss. Accordingly, for varying spans of time, newly shifted reserves may not be fully employed; in the absence of borrowing or some other acquisition of new reserves by the paying bank, the national total of reserves effectively at work may shrink.

Thus, discount policy and open market policy are inevitably integral parts of a single policy. In order to be fully effective, each depends upon and, in a sense, assumes parallel action with respect to the other. For example, a more restrictive open market policy achieves the desired effect on commercial bank loan and investment activity only because reserves alternatively obtained by borrowing are accompanied by restraining effects. Conversely, a restrictive discount policy would be meaningless if reserves were freely available through open market sales to the System account at prices for the securities offered that involve no sacrifice to the seller. In other words, shifts between policies of ease and restraint often do not involve absolute changes in the total amount of reserves available to the banking system, but rather changes in the sources of reserves as between reserve credit made available through open market operations, on the one hand, and loans and advances to member banks, on the other. Hence, in the formulation of policy, discount operations and open market operations are not considered as alternative means of accomplishing a given objective, but are adjusted together, in order for them to contribute effectively to the achievement of the desired objective.

Within this framework, the specific factors weighed in the formation of open market policy are an appraisal of general economic conditions, an assessment of the relation to these conditions of the availability of money and bank credit, and an estimate of the reserve needs that are likely to arise as a result of seasonal and special factors peculiar to the period. Criteria employed in the determination of discount rate changes generally involve the same considerations, combined with attention to the nature and extent of the use being made of the discount privilege and the relation of the existing discount rate to market rates on assets that banks would generally buy or sell in the adjustment of their reserve positions.

Reserve Requirements

Authority to adjust reserve requirements, as an instrument of monetary policy in the United States, was added to System powers in the 1930's, and therefore there has been less experience with its use than with either of the other two major instruments of policy. In fact, the role of reserve requirements as the fulcrum for policy actions related to the volume of bank credit and money, in contrast to their role as a source of liquidity, has only been generally understood and accepted since the 1920's. Even theoretical discussion of changes in reserve percentages as an instrument of policy was very limited until the 1930's. For this reason, there is less factual background and more disagreement as to the conditions under which reserve requirement changes can be used effectively in the accomplishment of the broad objectives of policy.

Apart from technical considerations, there is a widespread feeling that changes in reserve requirements should be made infrequently, because such action constitutes "a change in the rules in the middle of the game," which can present difficult problems of adjustment for many medium- and small-sized banks. Concern over this aspect of reserve requirement changes is not based solely on consideration for the problems created for banks and bankers. The repercussions of sizable changes could be serious for many current and potential borrowers and, in some cases, for whole communities.

A wide variety of possible schemes for adjusting reserve requirements have been considered in this country from time to time, and a number of variations have been employed in other countries. These include special deposit, secondary and supplementary reserve requirements, required liquidity ratios, and other schemes. The specific authority in the Federal Reserve Act to change reserve requirements was originally intended to permit the Federal Reserve to absorb some of the large volume of excess reserves generated in the period from 1933 to 1935, "while they were unused and widely distributed, rather than allow them to become the basis of an excessive credit expansion."[1] This was done in the summer of 1936, when reserve requirements were raised by one-half for all banks and all classes of deposits. In January 1937, a further increase of one-third was announced, which, when completed, brought required reserves to the then authorized maximum of double the basic percentages stated in the law.

Discussion at the time indicates clearly that it was intended and, in fact, assumed that reserve requirements would be maintained at levels higher than the basic percentages prescribed in the law only when injurious credit expansion could not be effectively controlled by open market and discount policy. In view, however, of the manyfold increase in the reserve base that resulted from the large gold inflow in the 1930's and from Federal Reserve purchases of securities in World War II, the higher level of reserve requirements established to absorb these additions to reserves became more generally accepted.

In its most recent action to amend the portion of the Federal Reserve Act which deals with reserve requirements, there was no expressed intention on the part of the Congress that the Board should make special efforts, in using the reserve requirement changes as a monetary instrument, to achieve particular percentages within the ranges specified for the purpose of accomplishing some secondary objective. In the absence of such expressed intention, it seems reasonable to assume that changes in requirements should be limited to those occasions when they can make a positive contribution to the accomplishment of the basic objectives of monetary policy.

In the System's experience, changes in reserve requirements have made their optimum contribution when changes of more than temporary import in the bank reserve situation have been called for. In prewar years, reserve requirements were increased in order to absorb an unnecessarily large volume of excess bank reserves. Postwar increases were applied in an attempt to absorb reserves supplied by Federal Reserve support of Government security prices. Most changes in reserve requirements in recent years have been made in recession periods, when decreases in reserve requirements have been used to supply bank reserves simultaneously to all parts of the economy.

---

[1] E.A. Goldenweiser, "Instruments of Federal Reserve Policy," Banking Studies (Washington: 1941), p. 409.

Regulation of Stock Market Credit

The conditions under which authority has been granted to regulate credit by selective measures, i.e., prescriptions of a minimum equity or a maximum maturity on credit extended for certain specific purposes, have not been such as to lead to the development of criteria which would relate their use to the general instruments of policy. Authority to regulate consumer and real estate credit has been limited to relatively brief wartime situations, when the use of general instruments of policy was circumscribed.

The continuing authority to regulate stock market credit is specifically related in the law to the excessive use of credit for purchasing or carrying securities. It was adopted in part because of the excessive importance that stock market credit had occupied in the country's credit structure.

While bearing directly on the lender, margin requirements put restraint on the borrower and thus dampen demand. A very important aspect of this restraint is the limitation it places on the amount of pyramiding of borrowing that can take place in a rising market as higher prices create higher collateral values and permit more borrowing on the same collateral. The purposes of regulation through margin requirements are to minimize the danger of excessive use of credit in financing stock market speculation and to prevent the recurrence of speculative stock market booms based on credit financing, such as culminated in the price collapse of 1929 and the subsequent severe credit liquidation.

QUESTION XIV

What criteria are utilized in determining when and by how much to alter discount rates? Has the Federal Reserve tried to maintain any particular relationship between discount rates and market interest rates?

ANSWER XIV

Summary

The discount rate derives its significance from the role played by member bank borrowings in the process by which the banking system responds to monetary policies. The discount rate, and the discount facilities of the Federal Reserve banks, complement open market operations in affecting the ability of the banks to extend credit and create deposits.

From the viewpoint of the individual bank, the discount rate is the price paid for a temporary loan of reserve funds from its Federal Reserve Bank. Whether in order to meet its legal reserve requirements, the bank will wish to borrow from this source or, alternatively, borrow elsewhere or dispose of an asset such as Treasury bills will depend in part on the relative costs of these alternative sources of reserves; that is, the relationship of the discount rate to short-term market rates.

From the viewpoint of the effectiveness of monetary policy, it makes an important difference which of these sources banks tend to choose. If banks borrow from each other or sell short-term Treasury securities, bank reserves in the aggregate are not affected; if they borrow from the Reserve Banks, even though each bank borrows only temporarily, additional reserves are drawn into the banking system, providing the basis for credit and monetary expansion.

Changes in discount rates are designed therefore to affect or to restore the margin of preference of member banks as between the various methods of reserve adjustment. Most commonly, changes are designed merely to keep discount rates in line with short-term market rates. Occasionally discount rates may be altered in a way that leads market rates in order to provide a signal to the public that the economic situation and, accordingly, the posture of monetary policy have changed.

Criteria for Rate Changes

As a general rule, the timing of discount rate changes depends upon changes in short-term market rates of interest; that is, market rates on those short-term liquid assets--ranging from the shortest term Treasury bills to Government and other securities of somewhat longer maturity--that banks hold as secondary reserves. Although there is no simple mechanical relationship between the appropriate discount rate and the constellation of existing market rates, discount rate policy is guided by the desirability of preventing so large a differential that member bank borrowing is unduly encouraged or discouraged.

Thus discount rates tend to follow market rates, usually with a lag. There have been periods, however, when discount rates have remained high or low relative to market rates for a considerable span of time. In some instances, the frequency of Treasury financing operations has left few if any opportunities when discount rates could be altered conveniently. In other cases, it was considered that market rates were under the influence of transitory forces and would soon return closer to earlier levels and therefore to discount rates. In addition, it has not been considered necessary to lower discount rates as far as market rates decline in periods of recession and monetary ease; in such periods, member bank borrowings fall to very low levels, and discount rates have little influence on the actions of banks. At times, balance-of-payments considerations may affect the timing and extent of discount rate changes. In so far as discount rates interact with and influence short-term market rates, they have an impact on international short-term capital movements.

A change in discount rates is frequently regarded by the public as an indication of a change in, or a reinforcement of, the direction of existing monetary policy. Possible public reactions to discount rate changes are accordingly taken into account when such changes are being considered. From the viewpoint of monetary policy there are times when it is desirable to utilize a change in discount rates as a signal to the public that the economic situation and the posture of monetary policy have changed. This might call for a change in discount rates in a way that leads rather than follows market rates. Most commonly, however, changes in discount rates are of a routine nature, designed merely to keep discount rates in line with market rates. This guiding principle is based on the role of member bank borrowing in the bank reserve adjustment process.

Discount Function and Bank Reserve Adjustments

As an instrument of monetary policy, the discount rate is only one aspect of the discount function, which in turn is utilized in a complementary manner with open market operations.[1]

Discount rates are prices that member banks pay for a temporary loan of reserves in the form of advances or discounts at Federal Reserve banks. The individual member bank that faces a potential deficiency in its legal reserve position has the immediate choice among (1) borrowing at the Reserve Banks, (2) borrowing elsewhere, as in the Federal funds market, or (3) disposing of assets such as Treasury bills. These short-run reserve adjustments may be followed by more basic adjustments, including curtailment of lending activity.

In periods of credit restraint, open market operations are conducted in a way which leads an increasing number of banks to experience a frequent need to take positive action to maintain their reserves at required levels. In such periods, banks generally are

---

[1]The relationship among the different instruments of monetary policy is discussed in the answer to Question XIII.

faced with rising loan demands, while the reserves being supplied by Federal Reserve open market operations are limited. The actions that individual banks take to avail themselves of the funds for loan expansion (for example, selling U.S. Government securities or drawing down correspondent balances) will unavoidably deprive other banks of reserves. As the latter banks react to such reserve drains and also attempt to expand their own loan portfolios, they in turn take actions that draw reserves from other banks. Each bank that loses reserves in this way faces a reserve adjustment problem and may choose among the three alternatives noted above, unless it has, and is willing to reduce, excess reserves.

How the individual bank decides among these alternatives will depend, in part, on relative costs. The cost of borrowing at the Reserve Bank is measured by the discount rate, although the willingness and ability of banks to borrow at the Reserve banks is also influenced by considerations other than cost.[2] The cost of borrowing Federal funds is, of course, measured by the rate on Federal funds. In periods when bank reserves are under pressure, this rate tends to stay at or only slightly below the discount rate. The cost of adjusting a reserve position by selling securities is measured by the interest earnings foregone--that is, by the current or expected market yields on those types of securities that banks hold as secondary reserves.[3] Treasury bills, other short-term Government obligations, bankers' acceptances, and commercial paper are the main types of secondary reserve assets held by banks; during periods of prolonged credit restraints many banks are likely to draw down most of their secondary reserves, and Government securities with one or more years to maturity may be the relevant asset.

It cannot be assumed that banks will always select the method involving the lowest cost. Other considerations also influence their decisions. For example, reluctance to borrow or Reserve Bank administrative action may discourage borrowing even when discount rates are below the relevant market rates. On the other hand, banks differ in their access to the money market and therefore in their ability to avoid borrowing. Unexpected reserve drains may in some circumstances leave a bank with no alternative but temporary borrowing, even when rate relationships make such a course relatively costly; thus some minimal borrowing is always present, even in recessions when the discount rate is significantly higher than market rates. Nevertheless, the margin of preference of individual banks among the alternative means of reserve adjustment is influenced

---

3In the case of highly temporary needs for funds, the transactions costs involved in selling and rebuying securities might be a relevant cost factor. Tax considerations might also be an influence.

by their costs, in particular by the relationship between the discount rate and market rates.

There are important differences in impact as between member bank borrowing and the other methods of reserve adjustment. When a bank sells securities or borrows Federal funds in order to replenish its reserve balance, it does so at the expense of other banks' reserves (assuming that the Federal Reserve is not a purchaser of securities at the time). Bank reserves in the aggregate are not affected by such transactions. Net credit availability is not affected unless the reserves so obtained would otherwise have remained unused.

On the other hand, when banks increase their discounts at the Reserve Banks, they are drawing additional reserves into the banking system. Each discount or advance is temporary, and the borrowing bank must soon repay. Thus a growing volume of indebtedness to the Reserve Banks makes for an atmosphere of greater restraint on credit expansion than would exist if the same volume of reserves were provided by means of open market operations. In order to help maintain such a restrictive credit policy, the Federal Reserve at times finds it desirable to alter the relationship between discount rates and market rates. This will influence the preference of banks as between discounting and other methods of reserve adjustment; in particular, increases in discount rates will tend to make sales of securities a more advantageous form of adjustment than discounting, from the viewpoint of individual banks.

Discount Rates Over the Credit Cycle

In periods of credit restraint, when loan demands are expanding in relation to credit supplies, market interest rates will be under upward pressure. The rise in market rates will occur not only because business and consumer demands for funds are growing but also because banks will be selling securities to finance loan expansion. In these circumstances, an increasing number of banks will experience drains of reserves and face the alternative of borrowing at the Reserve Banks, borrowing Federal funds, or selling short-term liquid assets in order to avoid deficiencies in legal reserve positions. As market rates on short-term securities rise relative to discount rates, member banks will become more willing to borrow. The number of member banks indebted to Reserve Banks will increase and more of them will renew or repeat their borrowing in successive periods.

In order to help keep the flow of Reserve Bank credit through the discount window under control and to help maintain the restrictive discipline of indebtedness on member bank lending activity, Reserve Bank discount rates are likely to be raised in these circumstances.

Higher discount rates in relation to market rates will not only restrain new borrowing but also encourage repayment of existing debt
to the Reserve Banks.

In a period when monetary policy is attempting to restrain strong
loan demands, short-term market rates are likely to cluster around
the discount rate, but are unlikely to fall very much below the discount rate. If, under these conditions of strong loan demands, discount rates were raised significantly in relation to market rates,
member banks would tend to shift away from borrowing at Reserve
Banks and toward selling short-term securities, in view of the lower
cost of the latter means of reserve adjustment. Such sales by banks
in turn would act to raise short-term interest rates relative to the
discount rate. If market rates once again exceeded the discount
rate, resulting in a tendency toward increased borrowing, a further
rise in the discount rate would be appropriate.

In periods when credit is easing and loan demands are less
pressing, short-term market rates tend to fall below the discount
rate. In these circumstances discount rates may be lowered in order
to reduce the incentive to banks to repay indebtedness to the Reserve Banks and thus encourage banks to utilize a greater portion
of reserve accretions in expanding their loans and investments.
Furthermore, reductions in discount rates may serve to confirm
to the public somewhat more dramatically than concurrent open
market operations that a condition of lessened restraint or greater
ease is being sought by the Federal Reserve.

When short-term market rates are below the discount rate, any
given level of member bank borrowings will be more restrictive than
when market rates are above it. This is so because, with market
rates below the discount rate, member banks have a stronger incentive to repay borrowings. Thus, open market operations will have
to take this tendency into account in working with discount operations
to achieve a given pace of bank credit and monetary expansion. If
the discount rate were low relative to market rates, banks might
have a tendency to increase their borrowings. In order to maintain
a given pace of bank credit and monetary expansion in these circumstances, open market operations would have to be modified
appropriately.

QUESTION XV

Does member bank borrowing act as an escape mechanism through which the banking system can avoid a

restrictive monetary policy? Is there any danger that
it could do so? What criteria are employed in determining the amounts which individual banks (and the
banking system) may borrow from the Reserve Banks?
Are these criteria the same at each Reserve Bank?

ANSWER XV

Summary

Member bank borrowing does not provide an escape mechanism
from a restrictive monetary policy. Its function, rather, is to permit
a gradual and orderly response on the part of banks to the reserve
pressures--some of which could otherwise be fairly abrupt--that
accompany a restrictive policy. A great variety of temporary,
seasonal, and emergency flows of reserves impinge upon banks.
Whenever these prove to be of a size or duration greater than that
expected and prepared for by the banks affected, borrowing from the
Federal Reserve Banks can assist in meeting the developing reserve
pressures pending a more permanent adjustment.

The extent of borrowing both by individual banks and the banking
system is controlled by the operation of three restraining influences: (1) the discount rate, or the cost of borrowing; (2) ingrained
bank reluctance to borrow, or to remain in debt once a borrowing
action is taken; and (3) the exercise of administrative discipline by
Federal Reserve officials.

The latter restraint rests upon a continual review of the experience of each bank borrowing at the Federal Reserve banks.
Relative size, frequency, and duration of borrowings are noted,
and these are related to the apparent trends in the loans, deposits,
and investments of the borrowing bank. Whenever it appears from
such reviews that a borrowing bank may be using Federal Reserve
credit for other than temporary, seasonal, or emergency needs beyond those which can reasonably be met from the bank's own
resources, administrative contacts with the bank are made. Explanations of the circumstances are sought, prospects for future retirement of debt are reviewed and, where appropriate, a positive program
for the adjustment of earning assets is encouraged. The basic guidelines for such administrative action, which are the same for all Federal Reserve banks, consist of a formal regulation on discounting and
a variety of interpretative rulings issued by the Board of Governors
and revised or expanded from time to time as the necessity has arisen.

Discounting in Relation to Individual Bank Needs

Commercial banks are subject to a vast variety of inflows and outflows of funds. Some flows are routine and easily prepared for, while many others are unexpected, of uncertain duration, or too large to be easily met. Each bank pays its depositors upon demand. Accordingly, it must try to forecast the demands of its customers and arrange its own asset holdings to yield cash at the times and in the amounts needed to satisfy the demands upon it. At the same time, it must endeavor to meet the legitimate credit needs of its community and to earn an adequate return for its stockholders. In such circumstances, it is hardly surprising that banks sometimes find the demands upon them exceeding their preparations.

Borrowing from the Federal Reserve banks is one means by which member banks meet unexpected drains, pending a more permanent adjustment. The alternative sources of outside funds to meet unexpected pressure, while varied, are not always conveniently available at the times and in the amounts needed. For example, sales of Federal funds and purchases of U.S. Government securities for same-day payment cease well before the end of each business day, yet subsequent drains upon a bank's reserve balance can develop from late transfers of funds at the order of customers. On other occasions, banks needing cash for a few days will find the volume of available Federal funds fluctuating a good deal from day to day, and as a consequence few can be assured of obtaining all the funds they need from this source. Sale of securities and repurchase after a few days when cash pressures are past is another means of raising temporary funds, but the difference between the "bid" and "asked" prices in the market can make this a relatively expensive source of funds, and the changed tax status of the repurchased issue could be disadvantageous to the bank involved.

For needs of longer duration, such as seasonal swings in loan demand, short-term securities might be liquidated or correspondent banks drawn upon for credit. Correspondent banks, however, are themselves subject to reserve pressures which can occasionally condition the amount of assistance they can extend to other banks. On the other hand, the ability of a bank to build up short-term securities in anticipation of a seasonal concentration of demands depends in part upon the relative size of the peak and off-peak needs of its community. Some seasonal swings are so great that matching them with the acquisition of, say, Treasury bills in the off season would require a bank to constrict its off-peak financing of local businesses and consumers. A difficult aspect of the planning for accommodation of these seasonal swings is the fact that the amounts needed may vary in unexpected fashion from year to year, depending upon such factors as the weather in agricultural areas during the growing season or in resort areas.

Most difficult of all for the banks are the problems that may be associated with localized economic adversities. Crop failures, work stoppages, and the like can produce heavy deposit losses and burgeoning credit needs. Sales of liquid securities by banks caught in such a vise of circumstances may provide some funds, but when demands exceed the proceeds of asset sales that can be effected without undue cost to the bank, there is clear need for some source of funds as an alternative to the curtailing of loans to the hardpressed community.

Restraints upon Discounting

It is to assist in meeting the above types of needs that the discount facility is provided. From published regulations and pronouncements, member banks are aware of the privilege of borrowing to cover temporary, seasonal or emergency needs beyond the bounds which can reasonably be met from their own resources. The use of borrowed funds, however, is intended to be a temporary supplement, and not a substitute for a bank's adaptation of its own asset holdings to the underlying supplies of and demands for credit in its community. Three different influences, singly or in combination, operate to keep member bank borrowings from departing too far from these standards. These are (1) the discount rate, (2) bank reluctance to borrow, and (3) administrative action by discounting officials.

(1) The role of the discount rate in influencing borrowing is discussed elsewhere in these answers. Suffice it to say here that the discount rate represents a cost which banks weigh chiefly in a relative sense. The pertinent comparisons are not only between the discount rate and the yields obtainable from various competing demands for the banks' funds, but, even more importantly, the discount rate and the cost of alternative sources of funds with which to meet demands. Depending upon the placement of the discount rate in the structure of market rates and the particular alternatives open to each individual bank, the discount rate could be a factor encouraging or discouraging borrowing in any specific case. Rate considerations, however, are not the most important of the influences at work that shape bankers' attitudes towards borrowing.

(2) A second influence conditioning bank borrowing is the widespread reluctance of banks to borrow. The factors contributing to bank reluctance to borrow are several. A common expression is that "it is not sound banking" to rely in any important degree upon borrowing. Reference is made to the fact that banks are already "in debt" to their depositors, with repayment due upon demand, and that it can be imprudent to incur additional debt, of a prior claim nature, to such existing liability. If these are not the views of the banker, he may nonetheless be strongly influenced if he believes that such views are held by his directors or his larger depositors.

Historical experience can contribute to a desire to avoid borrowing on the part of some bank officials. In the 1920's and early 1930's, some of the banks that borrowed to avoid portfolio contraction ultimately failed, with greater loss to their remaining depositors and stockholders than would have occurred had these banks been closed at the first concerted outflow of deposits. The result was a kind of penalty upon the loyalty of customers which was of concern to many conscientious bankers. Finally, a number of bankers over the years have had the experience of being questioned by Federal Reserve discount officials concerning their borrowing, and some bankers particularly sensitive to such inquiries are desirous of avoiding any recurrence.

Reluctance to borrow varies among banks, depending upon the experience and outlook of the management. Moreover, the corporate attitude of each bank also shifts over time, as experiences fade into history and the official family changes. Consequently, bank reluctance to borrow is a highly individualistic brake upon use of the discount window. In most cases, however, it appears to be a deterrent sufficiently strong to prevent any excessive use of discounting.

(3) To identify any excessive use of discounting which may be developing, each Federal Reserve bank undertakes a continuing review of the experience of each borrowing bank. Relative size, duration and frequency of borrowings are noted. Changes in individual bank deposit totals are followed, and trends in the composition and aggregate total of the bank's loans, U.S. Government security holdings, and other earnings assets are analyzed. From reports of the borrowing banks and internal Federal Reserve records, information on these developments is obtained quarterly, semimonthly, weekly, and even daily in some instances.

Whenever it appears from such reviews that a borrowing bank may be using Federal Reserve credit for other than temporary, seasonal, or emergency needs beyond those which can reasonably be met from the bank's own resources, administrative contacts with the bank are made. Administrative contacts may be made by letter, telephone, or personal visit, or by a combination of these approaches. Explanations of the local circumstances and bank policies contributing to the need for borrowing are sought. Prospects for the retirement of borrowing are reviewed, and if no changes in loans or deposits promise to provide enough funds to retire the debt within the bounds of time regarded as appropriate, a positive program for the adjustment of earning assets is encouraged.

Borrowing banks are not in a position to ignore the counsel of Federal Reserve officials. Borrowing is done on the basis of

short-term notes.[1] While it is standard practice for Reserve Banks
to accept without question original notes presented by a member
bank, such notes are collected at maturity by an automatic charge to
the reserve account of the borrowing bank, and successive replacement notes may be accepted or not as the Reserve Bank deems appropriate. In point of fact, even the refusal of renewal requests is
a very rare occurrence (always preceded by a prior warning), because borrowing banks typically endeavor to adjust their operations
within the limits as generally set forth in the published regulations
and more specifically interpreted in the administrative contacts by
System officials.

A variety of procedures currently serve to keep discount administration relatively homogeneous among the various Federal
Reserve banks. The basic guidelines for discount policy are set
forth in a formal regulation (Regulation A) issued by the Board of
Governors pursuant to authority conveyed by the Federal Reserve
Act. Over the years a variety of interpretations have been issued by
the Board concerning various parts of the Regulation, and these
have been published in the Federal Reserve Bulletin and summarized
in the Board's Published Interpretations. This material is available to
member banks as well as Federal Reserve banks, making it easier for
each to understand the intended scope and limitations of discounting.

The conformity of each Reserve Bank to these standards in its
discount administration is tested by the examiners of the Board of
Governors in its annual examination of each Federal Reserve bank.
More informally, the presidents of the Reserve Banks often discuss
and compare discount experience during their attendance at meetings of the Federal Open Market Committee and of the Conference
of Presidents. Finally, the discount officers of the various Reserve
Banks meet from time to time to discuss common problems and
compare discount practices.

The uniformity of discount administration gained by these steps
cannot be measured with any degree of precision. A comparative
analysis of borrowing statistics for the various Federal Reserve

---

[1]Most current bank borrowing is accomplished by notes secured
by the pledge of U.S. Government securities. As a standard operating
practice, all Federal Reserve banks limit the maturity of such notes
to fifteen days or less. Exceptions to this general practice, which
have been rare in recent years, may take several forms: Under the
law, banks may borrow for periods of up to three months on collateral notes secured by U.S. Government obligations or eligible customer paper, or for periods of up to four months at a higher rate if
the notes are secured by ineligible assets. Member banks may rediscount eligible customer paper for the remaining life of the customer note within certain maturity limits set by law.

districts is not by itself an adequate basis for arriving at broad conclusions as to the uniformity among districts in the administration
of the discount window. Allowances must be made for basic differences in geography, economic organization, and banking structure
among the twelve districts. Statistics based on administrative action
are also an inadequate basis for policy comparisons. Identical policies pursued may result in different statistical results merely because of a difference in procedures developed at the various Banks
for making such contacts and in the timing of these contracts.

QUESTION XVI

To what extent is member bank borrowing limited by
the cost of borrowing and to what extent by reluctance
to borrow and by "policing"? What are the major administrative problems involved in policing the discount
window? Does the Federal Reserve discount rate function
as a "penalty" rate? Should it so function? What are
the arguments for and against a mechanical tie between
the Treasury bill rate and the discount rate, as in
Canada?

ANSWER XVI

Summary

To the extent that comparisons can be made, it appears that the
most widespread restraining influence upon borrowing is the traditional reluctance of banks to be in debt. "Policing" actions by
Federal Reserve officials directly involve only a minority of borrowing banks, although it seems likely that the effect of any administrative contact continues for some time and spreads beyond the
particular bank involved. Within broad limits, cost changes do not
appear to produce any overpowering response in the volume of bank
borrowing. In particular, the capacity of a low rate to invite borrowing is limited; however, the modest increments to reserves that
result from marginal, rate-induced borrowings are believed to exercise some influence upon market atmosphere and rate levels.

In the "policing" of the discount window, probably the most
persistent problem is one of communication--that is, the conveying
of a correct and uniform understanding of the appropriate usage of

the discount mechanism. A second problem encountered from time to time is the tendency for bankers to be somewhat optimistic as to the likely duration of unexpected reserve drains and hence sometimes to be slow in adjusting thereto. Bank adjustment may also be inhibited in some cases by the size of capital losses which will be realized if securities are sold to retire debt. Federal Reserve officials must be alert in such instances to encourage the appropriate degree of asset adjustment without undue delay.

With the other restraints upon borrowing which are operative in the American banking system, the discount rate does not, and need not, serve solely as a "penalty" rate. Nor is there necessity for a stable rate relationship such as might be sought through tying the discount rate to the Treasury bill rate. For that matter, the variety of asset positions maintained by the uniquely large number of banks in this country makes it a practical impossibility for any one rate, at any reasonable level, to be a "penalty" rate for all banks and at all times. The monetary authorities can utilize discretionary changes in the Federal Reserve discount rate to exercise a gentle, across-the-board influence on bank borrowing decisions in coordination with the use of other and more powerful tools of flexible credit and monetary policy.

In addition, discount rate changes also are a focus of attention within the financial community. This characteristic, some believe, can lead to occasional distortions or perversities of borrower response. The evidence reviewed, however, does not indicate any dominance of this type of perverse reaction.

Difficulties in Distinguishing Borrowing Restraints

Any detailed comparisons of the restraints upon borrowing that are exercised by the discount rate, by bank reluctance to borrow, and by discount administration, respectively, must be undertaken with some caution. The results of these differing restraints are blended together in the final consideration by a bank as to whether or not it should apply for credit at a Reserve Bank. Perhaps not even the banker himself will always be able to say which factor was the most important in the decision by his management or board of directors.[1]

Moreover, as times and bank personnel change, the relative power of each of the three restraining influences also changes. For example, the comparative strengths of the various restraints on borrowing will vary with the fluctuations in general business and financial activity. In such fluctuations, it is not only the current

[1]This answer should be read in conjunction with the answers to Questions XIV and XV.

state of affairs that may moderate the influence of one restraint as against another, but also the changing expectations of bankers and the market regarding the future course of business and credit. As an illustration, the cost of borrowing compared with the alternative cost of selling securities should appear less onerous if the banker anticipates an early decline in credit demands (and hence a rise in securities prices) than if he looks forward to a sustained period of increasing credit pressure.

These considerations are not the only ones affecting bank borrowing in terms of changing business and credit demands. When business expands, the increased flow of payments and the heightened interest of deposit owners in economizing on cash produces a greater number of unexpected pressures upon banks, and thus multiplies the number of occasions when bankers must make decisions concerning borrowing or alternative action. Even if the proportion of such decisions made in favor of borrowing were to remain the same, the number and amount of borrowings within the banking system would rise. Such developments must not be mistaken for a basic shift in the application of one or more of the three restrictive influences on borrowing. This has sometimes happened, for example, with respect to Federal Reserve "policing" actions. Such administrative actions are far more numerous in periods of prosperity than in recessions, primarily because of more instances of extended bank borrowing.

The above cautions should make it clear that a purely statistical review of the record of bank borrowing is an uncertain means of determining causes and effects. There are instances, however, that can be cited in which the directions of influence of the three types of restraint on borrowing are sufficiently at odds to give some idea of the relative order of strength attaching to each at the time. It is in this frame of reference that the following evidence is cited.

Discount Rate as a Deterrent

With respect to the discount rate as a deterrent cost of borrowing, the most relevant comparison is with the costs of alternative sources of ready funds. Comparison of such costs with the changing amounts of funds borrowed does not suggest that there is a powerful borrowing response to changing cost considerations. For example, during the first and fourth quarters of 1959 the yields on three-month Treasury bills, the shortest term and most marketable type of Treasury debt, averaged appreciably higher than the discount rate, while in the second and third quarters this rate relationship was reversed (Table XVI-1). Yet the proportion of banks borrowing was not far different in these periods.

Furthermore, the average amount borrowed in the second quarter exceeded that for the first quarter, and the amount borrowed in the

TABLE XVI-1

Comparison of Discount Rate, Treasury Bill
Yield, Amount of Borrowings and Number
of Borrowing Banks, Quarterly, 1956-59

Year and Quarter	Average discount rate, N.Y.F.R. Bk. (percent)	Average market yield, 3-month Treasury bills (percent)	Average borrowing from F.R. Bks. (millions of dollars)	Proportion of member banks borrowing[1] (percent)
1956	2.77	2.62	831.2	15.9
1	2.50	2.33	866.3	16.3
2	2.72	2.57	933.3	17.1
3	2.85	2.58	809.3	15.6
4	3.00	3.03	715.7	14.7
1957	3.11	3.23	836.8	17.2
1	3.00	3.10	627.0	16.4
2	3.00	3.14	975.0	18.9
3	3.21	3.35	970.0	16.4
4	3.24	3.30	775.0	17.1
1958	2.16	1.78	293.9	15.9
1	2.68	1.76	277.0	15.4
2	1.84	.96	130.3	n.a.
3	1.80	1.68	279.0	n.a.
4	2.30	2.69	489.3	16.4
1959	3.36	3.37	798.8	20.3
1	2.64	2.77	555.3	19.4
2	3.18	3.00	788.0	21.6
3	3.61	3.54	955.7	20.6
4	4.00	4.23	896.3	19.7

n.a. - not available.
Details may not average to totals because of rounding.

1Number of banks borrowing at any time in the quarter as a proportion of all member banks. Annual figures are averages of quarterly totals.

third quarter exceeded that for the fourth, a pattern in contradiction to that suggested by rate relationships alone. Over a longer time span, bill rates averaged below the discount rate for almost all of 1956, and then above the discount rate for most of 1957, yet the borrowing averaged about the same in both years.

The pertinence of such comparisons is reduced by the growing prosperity and credit restraint which were characteristic of 1956-57 and of 1959. In addition, the rate margin noted--between the discount rate and the three-month Treasury bill rate--may have become increasingly inapplicable to borrowing decisions in 1957 and again in 1959 because of the reduced bill holdings of banks.

A comparison of amount and cost of borrowing which is free of some of these uncertainties can be made with respect to the year 1952. In the period 1950-52, a corporate excess profits tax was in effect which provided a strong inducement to expanded bank borrowing. A survey of 1950 and 1951 bank experience revealed that one-fifth to one-fourth of insured commercial banks were subject to this tax (Table XVI-2). Moreover, the proportion of banks subject to excess profits tax ranged upward from three-tenths to two-fifths among bank size groups with total capital accounts of $250,000 or more, the size range which included most Federal Reserve member banks. A provision of this tax allowed a proportion of average borrowing to be counted as capital in computing the rate of return to be exempt from the excess profits tax levy. Technicalities aside, the practical effect for a bank in the excess profits tax bracket was that by borrowing at the 1.75 percent discount rate then prevailing it could earn as much as a 2 percent after-tax gain on such debt, even if the proceeds of the loan were allowed to lie idle.[2] In effect, in such cases a negative discount rate existed.

Given such a striking incentive to borrow, discounts and advances at the Federal Reserve banks rose sharply during 1951 and 1952 to a peak reserve-period average of approximately $2 billion near the end of the latter year. Part of this increase may be attributed to factors other than tax considerations, for the rise started from the depressed borrowing levels immediately following the cessation of Federal Reserve support of the Government securities market and was quickened by the growing business boom of 1951-53. On the other hand, the rise might have been retarded somewhat by the lack of familiarity on the part of some banks with the discount process.

---

[2]For banks allowed a 12 percent return upon invested capital under the law. For illustrative applications of this excess profits tax, see Donald C. Miller, "Corporate Taxation and Methods of Corporate Financing," American Economic Review (December 1952).

TABLE XVI-2

Excess Profits Taxes Incurred By
Insured Commercial Banks on Taxable
Income, By Size of Bank, 1950 and 1951

Size of bank (Total capital accounts, June 30, 1951)	Number of insured commercial banks	Percentage of banks in each size group incurring excess profits taxes	
		1950	1951
$4,000,000 and over	[1] 284	35	33
$750,000 - 3,999,999	1,384	33	30
$250,000 - 749,999	3,877	41	37
Under $250,000	7,868	16	12
Total	[1] 13,413	25	21

[1]Data for banks with total capital accounts of $4 million and over do not include estimates for 5 nonrespondent banks, 16 banks with preferred stock or capital notes or debentures, and one atypical bank. These exclusions are reflected in the "total" data. Data for the other size groups are estimates for all insured banks in each group.

SOURCE: Federal Reserve Bulletin, June 1952, p. 604.

Even with this marked tax incentive to borrowing, the number of borrowing banks remained in the minority. Also, the total amount borrowed remained less than 10 percent of aggregate reserve balances and only one-third higher than the peaks of borrowing reached in subsequent years of high-level business activity in which no such rate advantage obtained. Such evidence suggests that, while the discount rate has undoubtedly had marginal significance in decisions to borrow or not to borrow, the capacity of a relatively low rate to invite borrowing is limited by other influences.

The modest increments to reserves that can result from marginal rate-induced borrowings undoubtedly exercise some influence upon market atmosphere and rate levels (as is discussed in greater detail below), but the point of note in the present section is the fact that rate-induced changes in borrowed reserves are likely to be small in volume relative either to total reserve balances or to the capacity of open market operations to offset them if desired.

Relative Effectiveness of the Tradition Against Borrowing

Available information suggests that the most widespread current restraining influence on borrowing is the traditional bank reluctance to be in debt. This consideration is expressed again and again by bankers who habitually do not borrow from their Reserve Banks. The number involved is large. During the average quarter of 1959, four out of five member banks did not borrow from the Federal Reserve (Table XVI-1). This proportion is only modestly smaller than that for 1957, the latest previous year of strong credit demands, although it is appreciably below the quarterly average for the recession year of 1958.

Here again, other factors may be contributing to the size of this group of nonborrowers. A good many banks are located in areas with such gradual or predictable financial movements that needs to borrow rarely arise. Other small banks regard the act of borrowing and attendant close calculation of reserve positions as more costly in management time and interest outlay than the value lost by leaving an uninvested excess reserve balance to cover unexpected drains.

Still other banks find it cheaper or otherwise preferable to cover borrowing needs as they arise by purchases of Federal funds or obtaining accommodation from a correspondent. Many of the banks that use these other avenues of accommodation also borrow from the Federal Reserve at one time or another. The chief exceptions are those country banks that sell loan participations without recourse to their city correspondents. Thus, they accommodate their larger customers and at the same time avoid the need to show any formal liability for borrowed funds on their financial statement.

When full allowance is made for these possibilities, the preponderance of banks that do not borrow from the Federal Reserve remains sufficiently large to suggest a strong, widespread, and persistent desire to avoid borrowing within much of the banking structure. Furthermore, such desire also appears to exist in milder degree in the minds of many occasional borrowers whose preference not to borrow is sometimes overridden by circumstance.

Deterrent Effects of Discount Administration

The restraint exercised by voluntary banker reluctance to borrow is complemented by the administrative limitation of borrowing performed by the Federal Reserve banks. "Policing" actions by Federal Reserve discount officials directly involve only a minority of borrowing banks, which are in turn a minority of the banks in the System. On the surface, therefore, administrative actions are not nearly as pervasive an influence as bank tradition against borrowing.

The proportion of banks contacted in this connection during the course of a year varies from a minor to a moderate fraction of the total number of banks borrowing, and depends upon the number of extended borrowing cases generated by the underlying credit climate of the period. These contacts come whenever a member bank is deemed to be departing from the standards for borrowing established in Regulation A. The number of contacts with any one bank may be one or several, depending upon the complexity of its reserve problems and the progress made in a program of appropriate asset adjustment, if any is needed.

Any one or a series of contacts continues to have an effect on the individual bank involved and also spreads well beyond the particular instance. News of an administrative contact tends to be passed along to other banks, creating a broadened awareness that Federal Reserve credit is intended for limited purposes. Member banks naturally desire to avoid criticism from the Reserve Bank, and accordingly the majority of borrowing banks are interested in operating within limits acceptable to discount officials. All told, the restraining influence of policing by discount officials appears to be substantial, but much less pervasive than bank reluctance to borrow. Administrative action, nevertheless, reinforces this reluctance and also tends to limit the amount and duration of borrowing which does occur.

Problems of Discount Administration

In undertaking the administrative limitation of borrowing, Federal Reserve officials experience a variety of problems. Probably the most persistent problem in this area is one of communication-- that is, the conveying of a correct understanding of the appropriate usage of the discount mechanism. Concerning the tradition against borrowing, a variety of experiences have conditioned individual banker views toward borrowing. For example, many banks are not familiar with the discount mechanism. For nearly two decades before 1950, only minor use was made of rediscounting because of the ready availability of reserves from other sources. Even in the 1950's, the majority of banks were not ordinarily borrowers. The Federal Reserve System itself has changed the emphasis placed upon borrowing as compared with these earlier decades, and the latest revision of the Board's Regulation A on the subject, issued in 1955, was considerably more explicit than its predecessors on the standards of appropriate borrowing.

As a result of these changes, discount officials of the Reserve Banks meet widely varying attitudes in contacting member banks. Sometimes the problem is not too liberal bank resort to the discount window but the reverse, a tendency to respond too restrictively to any hint of Federal Reserve criticism. Repeated contacts are sometimes necessary before communication and an appropriate understanding can be established between the discount officer and the member bank.

A second type of problem that can arise in discount administration involves banker expectations. There is some tendency for banks to regard unexpected reserve pressures as temporary, in the absence of knowledge to the contrary. When cash positions are short, borrowing may be undertaken to cushion such pressures until their likely duration becomes clearer.

Hopeful anticipations of some turn in reserve drains may occasionally persist beyond the point of realistic appraisal. It is the responsibility of discount officials to discuss such cases and suggest appropriate reconsideration of prospects. Such instances become more numerous during periods of monetary restraint when growing demands for funds and more attractive investment outlets may generate subtle drains upon bank deposit totals of a more lasting nature than the bank immediately detects. Oftentimes bank adjustment to one reserve drain has only begun when a second and third round of pressures have developed from added loan requests or successive declines in deposits. Such compounding of drains can occasionally lead to a substantial span of indebtedness, as disposals of the bank's earning assets run behind needs for funds.

A final difficulty worthy of mention is the size of realized capital losses that can result for banks faced with the necessity of selling securities to adjust to reserve pressures in the advanced stages of a period of credit expansion. If interest rates have moved up considerably, the price depreciation below book value can be substantial on intermediate- and longer-term securities acquired during preceding periods of credit ease.

If securities are sold, the offset to earnings in the year of sale can be large, and may conceivably even extend to a temporary reduction in total capital accounts. Banks are understandably reluctant to realize such losses. The Federal Reserve System, furthermore, is concerned with the maintenance of adequate bank capital cushions to support deposit liabilities. A decline in prices of existing assets, however, is one of the mechanisms by which a restrictive monetary policy slows bank credit expansion. In these periods, discount officials must be careful not to let bank borrowing extend to the point of dulling the restraint on bank lending that stems from declines in prices of bank investments.

The Discount Rate as a "Penalty" Rate

While administrative contacts are experienced only by banks that rely unduly on the discount mechanism, the prevailing discount rate is a factor known to all members and applicable uniformly to each. It may or may not be a "penalty" rate, depending upon the bank being considered and the particular bank assets or liabilities to which borrowing is being related. Over the longer run, the basic source of funds for an individual bank is the deposits which it can attract and maintain. For a bank which has previously gained loanable funds by deposit increase, the discount rate charged on borrowings usually represents a step-up from the marginal out-of-pocket costs of obtaining and servicing increases in deposits. In this broad view, borrowing appears as a relatively expensive source of funds.

To measure the theoretical profitability of borrowing, an alternative comparison may be made between the discount rate and the net return to be gained from earning assets in which borrowed funds might be invested. In most circumstances, both the loans and the securities in the typical bank's portfolio are likely to yield a gross return higher than the prevailing discount rate. But certain partially offsetting expenses must be recognized. Acquisition and servicing costs are usually nominal for securities, but they can bulk quite large in the case of some types of loans. In addition, the prudent banker also makes some allowance for the risks of loss which he is assuming, both for default of payment at maturity and for possible depreciation of market value in the case of sale before maturity. The end results of such balancing of considerations are not always easy to foresee. In most situations, it is likely that the net return available on most components of a bank's loan and investment portfolio would equal or exceed the discount rate.

It should be pointed out, however, that these opportunity cost considerations are of a longer-run nature, and may recede into the background in the circumstances in which a bank is deciding whether to borrow. At such a point, a bank usually would not have sufficient time to meet its need for funds by attracting additional deposits. On the other hand, if it raises funds by borrowing, both its own reluctance and the attitude of Federal Reserve discount officials would prevent it from keeping the borrowed funds long enough to take advantage in any dependable way of the long-run average net rates of return available on loans and investments. When under immediate reserve pressure, a bank's alternatives to borrowing from the Federal Reserve are only those assets and alternative borrowing possibilities which can generate cash on short notice. To the extent that a bank in such a situation is considering the cost of borrowing, its practical comparisons are with the rates, charges, and net current yields associated with its alternative sources of liquidity. Against some of these sources, the discount rate will sometimes appear as a "penalty" rate; against others, it will not.

Obviously, it costs more to borrow than to draw down any excess reserve balance or any excess deposit with a correspondent bank.

In addition, the discount rate is ordinarily the practical ceiling for Federal funds quotations, and hence borrowing from the Federal Reserve banks is usually at least as expensive as, and often more costly than, resort to the Federal funds market. On the other hand, the alternative of borrowing from correspondent banks usually carries an interest cost equal to or higher than the discount rate. The fact that borrowing from correspondents also may involve other indirect costs (e.g., pressure for increased interbank deposit balances) tends to make this source more expensive than borrowing from Federal Reserve banks.

Finally, a bank may also raise funds by selling its liquid earning assets, such as Treasury bills, commercial paper, or other Government or private issues of the shortest maturity owned. In this area of "money market" earning assets, rate relationships are close and changes come frequently. For example, in the eight years, 1952-59, the discount rate averaged above the market rate on three-month Treasury bills in twenty quarters but below in twelve quarters, with this relationship shifting seven different times.

It should be noted that the yields on money market assets have tended to fluctuate more than the discount rate. Consequently, the relative cost of selling such assets as compared with discounting is likely to be greater during periods of credit restraint than during credit ease. Indeed, the market rates on such assets often fall below the discount rate during easiest credit periods. Among other factors, the greater fluctuations in money market asset yields reflect the tendency for such assets to be the residual assets in bank portfolios, and hence to be disposed of as other needs materialize during periods of credit expansion. As a consequence, in the later stages of credit growth, more and more banks may have disposed of all (or all except some irreducible minimum) of their "money market" assets. For banks denuded of such easily disposable assets, the alternative to borrowing may then become the sale of intermediate-term Treasury notes and bonds. Such sales may well involve sacrifices in return larger than the discount rate.

The foregoing discussion should make it clear that the discount rate as administered in the United States is not a "penalty" rate for all banks or at all times. Furthermore, within the domestic institutional structure there are limits as to the extent of any "penalty" margin which could be maintained during periods of strong credit demand. As credit pressures mount and market rates move higher relative to the discount rate, a larger number of marginal borrowing decisions tend to be resolved in favor of borrowing. Such decisions result in the inflow of modest increments of reserves to the credit markets, thereby moderating in some degree the supply pressures contributing to the rise in market rates. Other Federal Reserve actions intended to restrain bank credit expansion of course take into account the reserve effects of increased member bank borrowing, and look to the various restraints attending such borrowing to assist in promoting the desired degree of restraint upon over-all bank credit growth.

The attributes of the discount rate as a cost, which have been outlined in this answer, have led the Federal Reserve System to utilize the discount rate as a tool of flexible monetary policy. Ingrained banker reluctance to borrow is slow to change, and the initiative in such changes rests with the individual banks. Discount administration is controlled by the Federal Reserve, but it is impractical to attempt to make important countercyclical changes in the promulgation or enforcement of appropriate borrowing standards. A change in the discount rate represents the only across-the-board action which the Federal Reserve System can take with a view to generally affecting bank borrowing decisions.

At times when banks appear overcautious in borrowing, and as a result are tending to tighten credit availability more rapidly than underlying economic conditions and the level of the aggregate reserve base warrant, holding down the discount rate in the face of rising market rates can serve to ease the "penalty," or widen the "benefit," to be considered in future bank borrowing decisions. The reverse is true in periods of overborrowing. Such widening or narrowing of rate margins is a way of influencing banking decisions. The discount rate is in fact an important complement to open market operations in the execution of flexible credit and monetary policy.

Tying the Discount Rate to the Treasury Bill Rate

Discount rate changes are typically the most overt of all central banking policy actions and involve difficult judgments as to the appropriate timing and degree of action. Rate changes exercise not only a cost effect upon the banking system, but also a psychological effect upon observers of financial affairs everywhere.

With the aim of avoiding the difficult judgments as to when to change discount rates and by how much and of minimizing psychological impacts, measures have been proposed to tie the discount rate to some independently determined market rate, such as the three-month Treasury bill rate. Among the central banks of the major industrial nations, one--The Bank of Canada--has adopted the system of a "tied" discount rate. The applicability of such a device depends, of course, upon the characteristics of the national financial structure, which can vary widely from country to country. Whatever the virtues of the tied rate in other environments, this kind of device would have both advantages and disadvantages under the present United States monetary system. The more important are reviewed below under the general headings: (a) cost effects and (b) signal effects.

Cost effects. The most obvious advantage claimed for setting the discount rate at a specified margin above, say, the average auction rate on 91-day Treasury bills (as in Canada) is that it would provide a relatively constant differential between the cost of borrowing from the central bank and the cost of bank adjustment by disposition of Treasury bills.[3] A stable "penalty" for borrowing would thus be automatically maintained, since the yields on most other money market instruments move more or less in sympathy with the rates on Treasury bills. The advantage that particularly appeals to some proponents of the device is that it would enable the central bank to continue a "penalty" relationship without overt action during periods when market rates were moving upward.

On the other side of the argument, there are times when the central bank may deem it advantageous to be able to alter the relative cost involved in borrowing. As was pointed out earlier, the two major restraints upon borrowing other than relative cost-- the tradition against borrowing, and Federal Reserve administrative standards--are not easily modified by the monetary authorities. If shifting economic conditions made it important to encourage a change in bank willingness to borrow, a change in the discount rate relative to market rates would be the one quick and direct means of doing so.

Even if a stable "penalty" rate for each instance of borrowing were to be desired, simply tying the discount rate to a focal money market rate would not necessarily accomplish that purpose. Ideally, the rate relationship should be established with those instruments which represent the alternative source of liquidity for banks that are prospective borrowers.[4] But such alternative sources of funds are

---

[3]Certain transitory exceptions to this statement are conceivable (e.g., when a rapid rise in market bill yields occurs between the weekly auctions), but they are not likely to happen with sufficient frequency to alter the general analysis presented here.

Alternative proposals might suggest that the discount rate be established at a level equal to, or even below, the Treasury bill rate or some other market rate. Because historical experience and conventional argument have been in terms of a "penalty" margin of the discount rate over the bill rate, the discussion in this section is cast in those terms. The basic import of the various pro and con arguments, however, is believed to apply regardless of the size or the sign of the rate margin specified, inasmuch as they flow from the rigidity of the "tied" rate relationship.

[4]The text discussion is phrased in terms of banks, for in the United States the primary borrowers from the central bank are its

(Footnote continued on following page)

not the same for all banks and at all times. This point applies with
particular force to the U.S. banking system, which is unique in its
large number of banks. Thus what might be a "penalty" cost for
one bank might well be a profitable borrowing rate for another.[5]

In the United States, accommodation of reserve pressures pending bank adjustment via sales of money market instruments is not
the only role of the discount window. It is also intended to be available to assist banks in meeting seasonal or other temporary needs
for funds beyond the dimensions which can reasonably be met by
use of their own resources, and in meeting emergency demands of
extended duration which may arise from national, regional, or local
difficulties. These borrowing needs arise less frequently and less
generally than do those associated with money market adjustments,

---

(Footnote 4 continued from previous page)
member commercial banks. In some other banking systems, such
as in Canada and Great Britain, central bank credit is extended
primarily or exclusively through loans to securities dealers. In such
circumstances, the question of appropriate rate relationships may be
answered differently. In the case of central bank loans to dealers
specializing in a narrow range of securities, an interest rate tied to
the market rate on a major category of such assets is likely to produce a more stable influence on the cost than could be true for a
"tied" rate charged to banks, which typically handle a much wider
range of earning assets.

[5]The choice of the auction rate on 91-day Treasury bills as the
base for the discount rate would pose a particular problem. In recent years such bill rates have moved through wide temporary and
seasonal swings which were largely unrelated to the degree of pressure prevailing in the banking system. This experience reflects the
growing importance in the bill market of nonbanking institutions,
particularly industrial corporations. At the end of 1959, for example,
reporting commercial banks in the Treasury Survey of Ownership
held only 12 percent of all Treasury bills outstanding. (Treasury
Bulletin, March 1960, p. 49.)

In Canada, by way of contrast, the proportion of Treasury bills
held by chartered banks on December 30, 1959, was 35 percent,
although this higher percentage reflects in part the fact that Canadian
banks have agreed to a secondary reserve requirement which involves
holding as much as 7 percent of their deposits in bills. (Statistical
Summary, The Bank of Canada (January 1960), pp. 18-19.)

Insofar as the United States is concerned, in periods of credit
ease bank holdings of Treasury bills tend to increase in importance,
but in such periods bank reliance upon borrowing also becomes in-
consequential. Heavy bank borrowing periods tend to coincide with
periods of minimum bank position in the bill market.

but they are nonetheless important in our system with its large number of independent banks that are small enough to be dependent upon the economic fortunes of local areas. So long as the central bank is to retain a uniform discount rate, not differentiating among borrowers, the logical course is to establish the discount rate at whatever level appears the best compromise between the cost considerations of money market adjustment and those appropriate to necessitous seasonal or emergency assistance.

In the U.S. banking system, a "penalty" discount rate is not as important as in other countries for the functioning of an effective discount mechanism. Major reasons for this are the well-established banker tradition against borrowing and Reserve Bank discouragement of extended borrowing by member banks. With such restraints operative, decisions concerning the discount rate may be shaped in part by noncost considerations. Prominent among these is the "signal effect" of discount rate changes.

Signal effect. When discretionary changes are made in the discount rate, the announcement of the change itself is likely to have consequences beyond its direct effect on member bank borrowing. On occasion, such an announcement is the first clear indication of a change in monetary policy.

It is sometimes said that because of the attention attracted by discretionary rate changes, there is some risk of an exaggerated public reaction to such changes. Focus of attention on shifts in the discount rate could lead to an underemphasis upon the many more fundamental supply and demand influences flowing through credit markets. At the extreme, some segments of public opinion might under certain conditions come to believe that other market rates were set or controlled by the manipulations of the discount rate. Such a view might lead to ill-considered opposition to discount rate action that would be desirable on general economic grounds. Tying of the discount rate to the bill rate has been proposed as a means of avoiding or minimizing the "signal effect" risks.

Elimination of the signal effects of discount rate changes would deprive the monetary authority of a tool which can sometimes be useful in implementing its policy. A discretionary discount rate change is probably the most widely publicized step that a central bank can take. Yet for all its attention-catching nature, it has little or no immediate effect on the available supply of bank reserves. In this respect the discount rate is a useful complement to the other major tools of credit policy.

A problem sometimes raised in connection with discretionary rate changes is that of perverse market response. It is argued that a discount rate increase would be taken by individuals and businesses as an authoritative confirmation of a developing business boom, and accordingly would stimulate additional demands for credit in anticipation of higher prices and greater credit restraint in the future. Seriously destabilizing results upon the volume of credit extended would not, however, be likely to occur unless borrowers reacted perversely to discount rate changes and lenders did not. As a matter of practice, a variety of reactions is ordinarily apparent among both borrowers and lenders, and this variety of reaction in itself makes for stability. In addition, lenders ordinarily are more closely attuned to financial developments than are borrowers, and hence are more likely than borrowers to perceive the portents of a rate change and to act on the basis of such knowledge in credit contracts.

A search of the record for evidences of perverse market response to discount rate changes is undertaken in the following answer. No significant perverse response is detected. In all likelihood, the many other factors underlying business decisions to borrow or not to borrow--and bank decisions to lend or not to lend-- were of sufficient importance to outweigh any specific destabilizing response to Federal Reserve action.

QUESTION XVII

What is your view regarding the statement that a rise in the discount rate actually increases demands for credit by business firms, because it generates expectations that business will be good and money tighter in the future?

ANSWER XVII

Summary

While many business decisions are greatly influenced by expectations as to prospective economic and financial developments, there seems little logical or statistical support for the supposition that a rise in the discount rate would increase business demand for credit. The primary factor in a company's decision to accelerate or initiate expansion plans is more likely to be the economic outlook for its own industry and/or products. The relation between a rise in the discount rate and the prospect of good business for a given industry must appear indirect, at best, to most businessmen. At some times, a rise in interest rates may bring acceleration of borrowing plans that are already well under way, but it would likely stimulate the hasty initiation of entirely new plans.

In recent years, changes in other money rates have generally preceded changes in the discount rate. Thus, businessmen who consider money rates a "leading indicator" would have found the clues they sought in these other rates. Empiric evidence available on business borrowing in recent years does not support the view that business demands for credit increase when the discount rate is raised.

It seems extremely doubtful that businessmen generally view Federal Reserve action with respect to the discount rate as an indicator of the prospective course of economic and credit conditions, or that they actually increase their demands for credit following a rise in the discount rate.

Most discount rate changes in recent years have followed, rather than led, changes in other money rates. Thus, if there are businessmen who look to money markets for clues to prospective economic developments, they would find such clues sooner in rates other than the discount rate. Those who look to current money markets for clues to the prospective cost of their own future borrowing would also find such clues earlier in other rates. A change in the discount rate usually serves to confirm the evidence already at hand and to add an indication that the Federal Reserve considers it advisable to restrict or expand, as the case may be, the availability of additional bank credit. On some occasions, perhaps when actions to counteract seasonal or special factors may have obscured the basic intent of current open market operations, a change in the discount rate has clarified the situation by indicating that Federal Reserve policy has changed.

A rise in the discount rate may induce some business firms to advance the timing of borrowing they had planned to do at a somewhat later date, but this shift in timing, even when it does occur, does not augment business credit demands except in the very short run. Moreover, it takes time to arrange new borrowing, especially long-term borrowing in the capital markets. The only businesses able to step in quickly, fearing that rates will go even higher, are those whose expenditure plans have already been made and whose credit arrangements are practically completed, or those who have credit lines.

The circumstances are likely to be rare when very many businessmen would feel that the relationship between prospective business conditions and current changes in discount rates is so direct that a rise would induce them to borrow contingently or to initiate outlays they had not previously intended to make. Cost of credit, as mentioned earlier, is only one of a number of factors that enter into business decisions to undertake outlays that require outside financing. Evidence that the cost of such financing may be in a rising trend seems at least as likely to result in a re-examination of the urgency of any project that is in the initial planning stage, though it may result in an acceleration of plans that are further along.

Neither is there reason for businessmen to assume that, once the discount rate has been increasing for some time, other rates will continue to rise and that the next change in the discount rate will be another increase. Based on cyclical money market movements in the past, however, it would be reasonable to make this assumption when the increase in the discount rate is the first after a series of declines, as in the spring of 1955 and in the fall of 1958. Some businessmen may view these initial increases as convincing evidence that the tide has turned and that the economy has entered a new phase of expansion. Most businessmen who are aware of the course of discount rate movements are also likely to be knowledgeable about other economic and financial developments, especially those closely related to their own business; their expenditure plans and credit demands are probably more influenced by such developments than by increases in the discount rate per se.

One way to test the validity of the statement that a rise in the discount rate actually increases demands for credit by business firms is to examine changes in business borrowing before and after increases in the discount rate. Such an examination cannot be as conclusive as would be desirable. Apart from the fact that we know only how much credit businesses actually received, rather than how much they were attempting to raise, it is difficult to tell from actual data how much larger or smaller business credit expansion might have been without the rise in the discount rate. Also, the data are customarily subject to wide fluctuations from month to month which reflect the strong influence of seasonal factors in the case of demands for bank loans, and the presence or absence of extremely large security issues in the case of capital market financing.

The attached charts show, for the period since the beginning of 1955, changes in the discount rate of the Federal Reserve Bank of New York and two different measures of business demand for credit. Chart XVII-1 shows changes in business loans at all commercial banks plus public offerings and private placements of corporate security issues for new capital. The sum of these two components is plotted as a three-month moving average in order to moderate

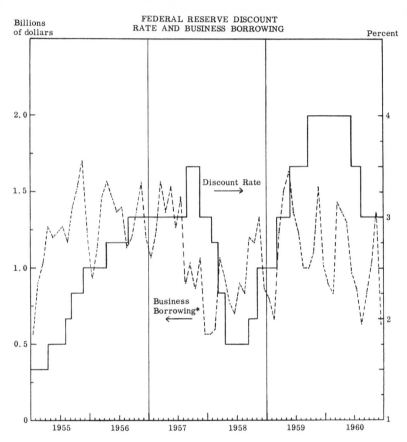

Billions
of dollars

FEDERAL RESERVE DISCOUNT
RATE AND BUSINESS BORROWING

Percent

* Borrowing at banks and in securities markets, 3 month moving average.

CHART XVII-1

the influence of the seasonal and special factors noted above. While the chart shows considerable short-run fluctuation in business borrowing, the general impression conveyed is that initial changes in borrowing have generally preceded, rather than followed, initial changes in the discount rate, and that borrowing has not continued to rise after later increases in the discount rate. The recurrence of the usual seasonal drop in borrowing in late 1959 and early 1960, though the discount rate was the highest in 30 years and a further rise was generally expected, may be worth noting.

Chart XVII-2 measures business credit demand in terms of forthcoming large public offerings of corporate securities.[1] Similar data are not available for privately placed securities nor for business loans at commercial banks. A series on forthcoming issues measures credit demand at a somewhat earlier stage than the actual sale of securities, though not at as early a stage as would be most appropriate for examining the effect of increases in the discount rate on business decisions to borrow.

Chart XVII-2 suggests that there is little relation between changes in the discount rate and registrations of new corporate security issues. The discount rate was raised on six occasions in 1955-56, once in 1957, and five times in 1958-59. On five of these twelve occasions the volume of forthcoming issues rose immediately after the increase in the discount rate; in seven cases it declined.

Broad movements in the volume of forthcoming issues also seem to show no consistent relationship to changes in the discount rate. The volume was generally declining in 1955 while the discount rate was rising, but it showed an upward tendency as the discount rate continued to be increased in 1956. During the 1958-59 period of increase in the discount rate, the volume of forthcoming large public corporate issues was relatively stable at a very low level.

Thus the only recent period when increases in the discount rate appear to have been accompanied by expansion in the prospective volume of public security offerings was the period from March through August of 1956. The increase in financing began during March, after the discount rate had been unchanged at 2 1/2 percent for five months. It appears to have been related to the very large increase in business expenditures for plant and equipment both current and in prospect.

It hardly seems likely that the more optimistic plans for capital outlays could be attributed in any appreciable degree to the earlier

---

[1] The series shown on the chart includes all corporate new capital issues of $15 million and over in registration with the Securities and Exchange Commission at the end of each month.

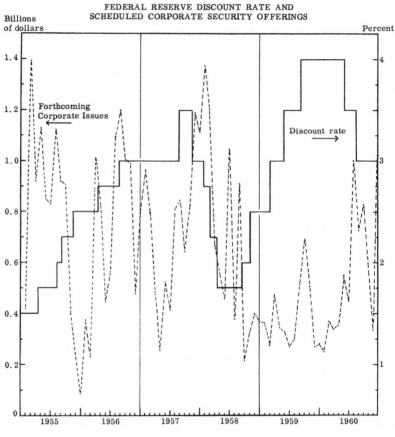

FEDERAL RESERVE DISCOUNT RATE AND
SCHEDULED CORPORATE SECURITY OFFERINGS

Billions
of dollars

Percent

CHART XVII-2

increases in discount rates during 1955. On the other hand, heavy borrowing demands no doubt contributed to the further rise in the discount rate in 1956.

QUESTION XVIII

Do the monetary authorities currently make any effort to accommodate monetary policy to differences in regional economic conditions, particularly in regard to discount policy?

ANSWER XVIII

Summary

Because our credit and money markets are essentially national in character, monetary policy is largely shaped by national rather than regional considerations. The domestic economy is a large free trade area with fixed exchange rates within which there is free movement of funds which affect the credit base. Adjustments in interregional trade are corrected in part by regional changes in price and income levels; in part this adjustment is made through the national credit and money markets.

There is also an expansible supply of interregional bank reserves created by the lending practices of the Reserve Banks; any region has access to additional funds to tide over temporary balance-of-payments difficulties. Monetary policy is designed for the economic welfare of this whole free trade area. The pooling of banking reserves as provided for by the Federal Reserve System results in the movement of a relatively large share of short-term funds through the national market. Thus short-term money rates in any Federal Reserve district are unlikely to remain out of line with the prevailing national market. In fact, all forms of domestic financing are at least marginally sensitive to the influence of a national credit and money market and thereby to national monetary policy.

Since national economic developments are a composite of those taking place regionally, regional considerations are necessarily weighed in assessing the need and consequences of a national monetary policy. The collection and analysis of economic data depicting both regional and national trends provide the basis for better understanding of the relationship of regional to national economic change, as well as for a better informed policy determination.

Representatives of the Reserve Banks not only participate in national policy formulation but also interpret national policy and its objectives to their own communities, thus encouraging a wider public understanding of national decisions and contributing to improved effectiveness of general policy. Policy that is responsive to both national and regional developments and considerations has the merit of being broadly based and therefore more acceptable to public opinion which in the end must approve of it.

In recent years, there have been few circumstances in which it has been deemed desirable to maintain regional differences in discount rates for an extended period. Conditions might arise in the future, however, in which some differentials might be appropriate over fairly extended periods. Administration of the discount window, however, does provide a means of giving account to unusual developments affecting economic conditions within a region that may call for cushioning or stimulation from the monetary side.

Discounting and Open Market Operations

The question of differentials in discount rates among Federal Reserve districts may be clarified by reference to the historical record. From the establishment of the System until about 1922, the discount rate was considered the most important single instrument of monetary regulation. During the 1920's open market operations assumed a more significant role in System policy.

Experience with the open market instrument made it clear that there was a close interrelationship between discount and open market operations. Open market operations were occasionally used to absorb reserves, and at such times, member banks as a group increased their borrowing at the Reserve Banks in order to adjust their reserve positions. This development had a tightening effect on the money market which resulted in conditions calling for increases in Reserve Bank discount rates. When open market operations provided reserves to the market, member banks as a group were enabled to reduce their indebtedness to the Reserve Banks. This resulted in an easing of the money market and in conditions favorable to discount rate reductions.

Open market operations were conducted in both Government securities and bankers' acceptances. Those in Government securities were employed principally to effect major policy shifts, while operations in bankers' acceptances were used primarily to help cover seasonal variations in reserve needs. Many temporary money market variations were covered by discounting, and some banks outside the money markets used discounting for more or less extended periods. In general, attention was directed to the discount rate as a major indicator and instrument of System policy.

The banking crisis of the early thirties together with the large inflow of gold from abroad in the late thirties resulted initially in a liquidation of member bank indebtedness to the Reserve Banks and subsequently in an accumulation by the banks of large excess reserves. This period was followed by a decade dominated by war finance and postwar adjustment problems in which additional reserves needed by the banking system were freely made available through Federal Reserve open market operations in support of Government security yields and prices. Thus, over this period of nearly two decades, member banks had little occasion to obtain discounts or advances from the Federal Reserve banks. For the time being, discount operations were an inactive instrument of monetary policy and the Reserve Bank discount rates, which were generally uniform, had little more than symbolic importance.

Since the Treasury-Federal Reserve Accord in 1951, open market operations and discount policy have again functioned as complementary instruments in influencing changes in credit conditions. In resuming a more active use of discount operations, the System carefully reviewed its entire experience both with regard to the administration of discounts and with regard to determining discount rates. One result of this review was a basic revision of Regulation A of the Board of Governors concerning Reserve Bank discounting for or lending to member banks. The revised regulation restated and clarified the principles that the Reserve Banks had applied historically in discount administration and thus contributed to further evolution of standard practices among the Reserve Banks in administering their discount windows.

Throughout the history of the System the effects on general credit conditions of the use of the interrelated instruments of open market and discount operations have been largely channelled through central money markets. Banks outside the money centers required to make reserve adjustments have done so either by drawing upon balances with correspondents in central markets or by liquidating open market paper in such markets. Banks with more reserves than needed have tended to put these funds to use in central money markets. Banks in outlying areas, unable or not choosing to make adjustments through national markets, have used the discount facilities of the regional Reserve Banks.

Regional Patterns in Rates

In the early years of the System's existence there was some tendency toward uniformity of regional discount rates. Proponents of such uniformity felt this would effect a better adjustment of commercial bank rates over the nation as a whole, as well as improve the interconnections between regional and local credit markets.

In 1921, Senator Harris proposed unsuccessfully to amend the Act to provide for uniform rates and to give the Board sole power to fix them. Nevertheless, during the period 1922-1923,[1] a differential pattern of regional rates was established, which was continued until 1927. In agricultural regions discount rates were higher and less frequently changed than in industrial and financial districts. Rates were uniform for areas in which conditions were essentially similar but differed among areas of varying development in financing requirements and credit conditions.

Discount rates again became uniform for all practical purposes during 1927, when most or all of the districts had the same rate throughout the year and when rate changes made at the several Banks were close together and in the same amount. Whether or not uniform discount rates were desirable was still an unsettled question, however, and opinion differed among Reserve Banks. Differentials existed for some months in 1928 and again in 1929. During the 1930's although some variation in discount rate practice continued, depressed economic activity, generally low credit demands, and the accumulation of excess bank reserves from an inflow of gold from abroad resulted in a tendency toward elimination of discount rate differentials. Since the early 1940's, rates in all districts have been uniform except during relatively short intervals.

The National Character of Credit Markets

Of the total net debt in the nation, about two-fifths is composed of obligations of the federal, state and local governments. Those securities are exchanged in national markets; business is conducted for all sections of the nation at one time and at virtually the same price for any given security. The widespread ownership and convenient liquidity of Government securities have supplied a common denominator to the entire credit system.

Within the private credit sector, practically all residential mortgage financing is affected by national competitive factors, although there remain important regional differences in rates and availability. Much of the credit extended to individuals for consumption purposes also is responsive to national conditions of credit availability. Many farmers seeking real estate credit can

---

[1]A single rate for discounts for all classes of paper was adopted in 1922, in contrast to the earlier practice in which rates varied according to class of paper, maturity, and security.

obtain local accommodation on terms fairly comparable with those offered by national lenders. Corporations place their bonds through distribution channels covering the nation and larger businesses, whose operations may be regional or national in extent, obtain most of their short-term credit from sources which conform to national or industry-wide influences. Federal legislation creating lending authorities and loan guarantee programs has also contributed to rate uniformity.

Of the variety of credit demands, the only forms which appear essentially local are the short- and intermediate-term borrowings by farmers and smaller business. Even these forms of borrowing, however, are not insulated from national market influences. The possibility of taking advantage of some source of funds other than local helps to keep credit charges and terms, after allowance for administrative and risk costs, close to national averages. These local credits are concentrated in the commercial banking system which has access to national pools of funds through selling assets or borrowing.

The short-term money market, particularly since World War II, has undergone marked growth in unity and breadth, and has strengthened its links to the long-term credit markets. Specialization has developed to meet the needs of large classes of borrowers and lenders, and transactions are accomplished rapidly and at low cost. These changes have accompanied the improvements in communications systems and knowledge of markets, together with new provisions for the transfer of funds and other money market instruments.

Financial institutions as a whole have been more integrated into a national system. Thus, interest rates are more closely interrelated and differentials in rates paid have substantially diminished. In the U.S. Government securities market and Federal funds market, business is conducted for a widened variety of customers in increasing volume at nearly uniform interest rates.

At the bank loan counter, the prime rate on commercial loans is now an important aspect of the money market rate structure and follows fairly closely movements of market rates. The prime rate reflects the forces of competition in the open market as well as among banks. Moreover, syndicate lending and more general use of other forms of participated loans have further narrowed rate differentials within the banking system.

Possible Bases for Differentials in Discount Rates or Policy

Although it is recognized that credit and money markets have become predominantly national in scope, discussions of discount policy and discount rates during postwar years have continued to be concerned with whether or not differentials in discount rates are desirable. They have focused particularly on possible bases for discount rate differentials.

Although most of the Reserve districts contain varieties of business interests similar to those in the nation as a whole, at any one point of a business development some parts of the nation may be sluggish while others are reflecting rising or high levels of activity. Over-all levels of activity will include segments of the economy in which resources are underutilized. Moreover, not all sectors will be experiencing the same rates of growth. It has been suggested that a uniform discount rate or discount policy takes inadequate account of these differences.

This suggestion underestimates the variety of economic activity that goes on within each Federal Reserve district. Moreover, the many economic advantages that arise from a single market for goods and services make it clearly inappropriate to consider the use of discount rate differentials or other adaptations of monetary policy that would contribute to regional barriers within the nation.

To the extent that inflationary and deflationary trends operate along industry lines rather than through geographic areas, the experience of a particular producer is probably more closely related to that of other producers in the same industry, wherever located, than to the fortunes of his district neighbors. Consequently, one part of a depressed industry may be located in a district experiencing high levels of activity while another part of the same industry may be in a district that is experiencing a slackening.

In recent years, there have been large internal population shifts within the United States. The principal economic impact of such shifts on areas gaining population is a need for more funds for housing and community facilities--schools, water and sewage works, roads, and the like. Such needs are financed largely in national credit markets. Lower discount rates in expanding areas than in other areas might not enable more of these demands to be met locally and might retard needed inflows of funds from other regions.

Use of lower discount rates to assist underdeveloped areas within the country would assume that the areas contain investment opportunities and that lack of funds is limiting their development. In underdeveloped areas, however, the critical shortage is likely to be either entrepreneurial skill or risk capital on an equity or long-term loan basis, rather than bank credit, which is necessarily short or relatively short in term. Lower discount rates than in other regions would not encourage the necessary flow of risk capital into underdeveloped areas. Neither would they necessarily aid chronically depressed areas, which need more fundamental measures of re-suscitation. Finally, because of the national character of the market for other instruments used by banks in adjusting reserve positions, differential discount rates may not accomplish their intended pur-pose, although they may create technical problems for discount administration.

Rate Changes

Even though long-maintained regional differences in discount rates have not been considered appropriate in recent years, present procedures for establishing rates permit differentials if they become desirable at any time. The discount rate is reviewed every two weeks, at meetings of the boards of directors of the Reserve Banks, as provided by statute. At meetings, the president of the Reserve Bank usually will recommend to his board either a change or con-tinuance of the present rate, and this recommendation is discussed and acted upon by the directors. At times, the board chairman or any other director will open the discussion. In addition to its own views about financial and business developments--local and national, the board of directors has available economic information and analysis furnished by the staff of the Reserve Bank as well as the advice of operating officers engaged in administering policy.

At meetings of the Federal Open Market Committee, where open market policy is formulated, consideration is also given to the relationship of open market operations to discount operations and to other monetary instruments. These discussions are conducted against the background of the national and district-by-district review of banking and business conditions. All of the Reserve Bank presi-dents attend the meetings and contribute to the discussion. In these discussions, members of the Board of Governors may at any time question the appropriateness of existing discount rates.

Discount Administration

The existence of the regional Reserve Banks and the fact that initiative in borrowing lies with the member bank offer assurance that variations in local needs will be recognized. Discount officers take account of the degree of pressure on the reserve positions of individual banks and the reasons for such pressures--distinguishing factors operating in the banking system as a whole from those operating in the individual bank. Appraisal of changing conditions on district levels and their review in relation to national conditions is continuous. Since this procedure permits some adjustment to indivi-dual local situations, monetary authorities have more freedom than would otherwise be the case to determine general credit policy on the basis of national considerations.

Although the discount mechanism is administered uniformly, the regulation provides for modification to meet unusual situations. The foreword to Regulation A governing discounting states in part: "Federal Reserve credit is also available for longer periods when necessary in order to assist member banks in meeting unusual situations, such as may result from national, regional, or local difficulties or from exceptional circumstances involving only particular member banks."

Recent examples of these situations during the postwar period were the hurricane and flood which affected large parts of the Connecticut valley in 1955 and the prolonged droughts in the Midwest in other years. The Reserve Banks gave special consideration to the borrowing needs of banks in the affected areas.

The discount mechanism helps to maintain a continuous availability of bank credit and so to provide a more satisfactory distribution of banking accommodation to the public. The complementary nature of open market operations, in which the initiative lies with the Federal Open Market Committee, and the discount powers, which lie mainly with the Reserve Banks, answers the peculiar needs of the unit banking system for fluidity of funds.

QUESTION XIX

What are the pros and cons of reserve requirements based on the turnover of deposits rather than upon their amount? What are the pros and cons of reserve requirements based on bank assets rather than upon liabilities?

ANSWER XIX

Summary

The principal function of the legal reserve requirement is to serve, along with control over the volume of reserves, as a base for regulating the volume of bank credit and the money supply. The required percentage thus provides the fulcrum for the quantitative regulation of bank credit and money. When total reserves available to the banking system exceed the required reserves by more than a customary margin, expansion in bank loans and investments tends to occur; and on the other hand, when the supply of reserve funds is limited in relation to required reserves, expansion in bank loans and investments is inhibited.

If reserve requirements were based on deposit turnover, changes in total required reserves would reflect changes in the use of money as well as in the amount of money balances held. The distribution of required reserves among individual banks might also be more equitable from some points of view. On the other hand, it may be said that the Federal Reserve System already has ample ability to adjust the reserve position of the banking system in accordance with changes in the use of money, and to consider turnover rates as well as other characteristics in assigning individual banks to reserve classes.

If reserve requirements were based on bank assets, this could lead to a relative lowering of market interest rates on the kinds of paper having the lower requirements. However, assuming that Government securities were the favored class, it is doubtful whether the government would obtain any real net interest saving, and other possible advantages from this form of reserve requirement seem questionable.

Requirements Based on Deposit Turnover

The term "turnover" or "activity" requirements refers to a rule, such as has been proposed by students of banking from time to time, whereby each bank's reserve requirement would be related to its volume of deposit activity rather than only to its volume of deposits. Under one such plan, a part of the bank's reserve requirement, in any given week or month, would be based upon the volume of checks written by the bank's depositors as recorded on its books during a preceding period, while the rest would be determined as a percentage of the bank's deposit liabilities.

In its effects on the banking system, an activity requirement would differ in two main respects from the type of requirement now used. It would cause the total required reserves of all member banks combined to fluctuate in a somewhat different manner than is now the case. It would also distribute required reserves among the individual banks in a different manner.

Bank deposit activity is a rough measure of the volume of money payments that are made in the economy. Fluctuations in the volume of money transfers are directly correlated with movements in total economic activity. Indeed, they are more sensitively correlated with such movements than are fluctuations in the volume of bank deposits.

In general, in periods of prosperity when demands for credit are strong, the rate of deposit turnover increases. That is to say, while pressures of credit demand tend to expand the money supply, the volume of money payments is likely to be increasing even faster. Hence, in such periods, the total required reserves of banks would increase faster under an activity requirement than under the present form of requirements. Stated in another way, with an activity requirement the ratio of total required reserves to deposit balances would automatically rise in periods of prosperity and it would automatically tend to fall in periods of declining business.

As between different banks at the same time, the banks with the higher rates of deposit turnover include most of the largest banks. These banks carry many of the major deposit accounts of large or national businesses, which tend to be more active than the accounts of individuals or of most kinds of small or local businesses. Most of these large banks already have higher requirements than other banks, however, because they are now classified as reserve city or central reserve city banks, for which the present required percentages are higher, although the existing differentials are not based on differences in deposit activity.

Effects on total reserve requirement of all banks. One argument in favor of basing reserve requirements upon deposit activity is that under the present system, large changes in the use of money in the economy are not reflected in any change in total reserve requirements. With an activity requirement, changes in the use of money as well as changes in the total amount of money balances held would be reflected in required reserves.

To perform their function most effectively, it may be argued, reserved requirements should reflect the demand for money in both of its main functions, (1) as a store of value and (2) as a medium of exchange. The member banks and the Reserve Banks would thus be put on notice by changes in the demand for reserves whenever a change in the use of money occurs as well as when there is a change in its volume.

The automatic movements of an activity reserve requirement could not be expected to obviate the need for continuous operations and policy modifications by the Federal Open Market Committee and other Federal Reserve policy-determining groups in accordance with economic developments and credit demands. However, these automatic movements would ordinarily reduce somewhat the magnitude of the specific Federal Reserve actions needed.

Distribution of reserve requirements among individual banks. An activity requirement would result in differentials among banks in their ratios of reserve requirements to deposits. These differentials could be viewed as a more appropriate method of distributing the total volume of required reserves than the present system which classifies banks into broad groups, especially if it is assumed that banks holding the more active deposits ought to be more limited in their credit-granting ability than banks with deposits that are relatively inactive.

The well-established distinction between demand and time deposits for reserve requirement purposes reflects such a principle as to rate of use. Similar differences in rate of use exist between different demand deposit accounts. Through an activity requirement, allowance would be made for such differences and a given deposit would have the same requirement regardless of the bank in which it might be located.

Under the present arrangement, in which the reserve requirements for central reserve and reserve city banks are higher than for country banks, something of the same effect is achieved, because the city banks tend to be those that have higher rates of deposit turnover. However, there are quite a number of exceptions where banks with high activity are now classified as country banks, or vice versa.

Arguments against adoption of an activity reserve requirement. The function of the reserve requirement, in monetary regulation, is to serve as a fulcrum so that the monetary authority, with its ability to vary the total reserves of the banking system, can thereby regulate the volume of bank credit and deposits. For this purpose, no great importance attached to the manner in which the reserve requirements are determined, as long as the authority is able to learn, with reasonable accuracy, the amount of reserves required at any given time and the amount actually held, and is able to vary this relationship by means of open market operations (or other actions) when that seems desirable.

The volume of money payments in the economy is indeed of great importance in determining whether monetary restraint or an expansionary influence is needed. An "activity requirement" would seem to have the advantage of causing changes in the volume of payments automatically to affect the reserve position of banks in a restraining or expansionary direction. However, the Federal Reserve already can, and does, take into account such changes in the volume of payments when it is making its policy decisions. It takes them into account explicitly when it considers data on payments and implicitly when it uses data on the many kinds of economic activity which affect the volume of payments. Thus, even though instruments of monetary control themselves relate to the volume of money and credit rather than to activity, the effects can be about the same as if the instruments were directly based on deposit activity.

Under these circumstances, the question arises whether an activity requirement would have advantages such as to justify the very considerable effort that would be required to substitute it for the present system.

The introduction of an activity reserve requirement would involve substantial administrative complications. The basic matter of requiring banks to ascertain and report the total amount of their debits to deposit accounts does not in itself seem serious; these figures can readily be determined as a by-product of a bank's ordinary bookkeeping operations. There would be various other problems, however. The novelty and strangeness of the system would involve revision of established practices and concepts. The relating of reserve requirements to the volume of deposits, as done now, has the advantage of being familiar and customary, and is generally accepted.

A difficulty of application may arise because some types of moderate-sized businesses develop an extremely large volume of receipts and payments in relation to the amount of their deposit balances. It might be desirable to provide some special exception for the banks handling accounts of such businesses. Moreover, there are various possibilities whereby a bank, with cooperation from its customers, could avoid the full effect of an activity requirement. Hence, the problems associated with initiating and administering an activity requirement would seem numerous and difficult.

Another problem is that of a time lag. An activity requirement would need to be based on the bank's activity for some period in the past, rather than for merely the latest week or month. Because of the effects of seasonal fluctuation in activity, it might be best to base the requirement upon the bank's total volume of debits for the preceding 12-month period. This would seem to introduce a time lag. However, it might not be serious, because sharp downturns in general business activity have been accompanied by sharp reductions in deposit turnover, which have generally, in turn, caused the 12-month average also to follow rather promptly.

Requirements Based on Bank Assets

As pointed out at the beginning of this reply, the function of reserve requirements now is to provide a fulcrum for the quantitative regulation of bank credit and money. With this as the purpose, the question arises whether basing the requirements on banks' assets, rather than on their volume of deposits (or deposit activity), might be a more effective regulative instrument.

Basing a reserve requirement upon a bank's total assets would not have any special advantage over using the bank's total deposit liabilities; the possible advantage of a requirement based on assets would lie in the ability to be selective in providing different treatment for different kinds of assets. Theoretically, such selectivity could be carried to any desired degree of detail, but the following discussion will relate to a system based on the distinction between holdings of U.S. Government securities and other kinds of earning assets.[1]

There are several kinds of situations in which it might be desired to restrain especially the expansion of bank assets other than Government securities, and in which this kind of selectivity might therefore seem useful. First, such a situation might arise in time of war or national emergency if it became necessary to limit the expansion of bank credit to the amounts needed by the government. Second, in other periods when monetary restraint is necessary, an instrument of this kind could be used to make it more attractive for banks to hold Government securities, as against liquidating them in order to expand other assets.

The main effects of such an instrument may be summarized as follows: It would cause a new differential between the interest rates on Government securities enjoying a special reduced reserve requirement and the interest rates on other types of assets. If this were accompanied by a rise in the level of interest rates on assets other than these Government securities, it could help to restrain the growth of such other credit. However, the widened differential would also tend to cause a gradual shifting of such assets from banks to other lenders. Because of this, it is unlikely that any effective control over the total amount of credit extended to nongovernmental borrowers would be achieved, except during an initial temporary period when the instrument was first introduced.

To indicate the effects more clearly, let us assume a requirement of 10 percent against Government securities and 20 percent against other loans and investments, and assume also that of the amounts that the bank lends or invests, no part will remain on deposit at this bank. If the bank had $10 million of excess reserves and wanted to use this amount to buy Government securities, it could buy about $9.1 million; the remaining $0.9 million of reserves would become the required 10 percent to be held against this asset. If the bank

---

[1]It should be noted that if it were desired to establish other classifications of assets to be favored (or the reserve) through the use of an asset reserve mechanism, numerous administrative problems would need to be solved, such as those of defining the classes of credit to be favored or restrained, determining the classification of particular assets, and establishing equitable relationships between banks and other lenders.

wished instead to acquire other loans or investments with these excess reserves, only about $8.3 million could be bought; the 20 percent reserve requirement on these assets would be $1.7 million. Thus, with the funds needed for this $8.3 million investment, it could have bought $9.1 million of Governments.

Under the present system of reserves against deposits, a bank with excess reserves of $10 million could increase earning assets of any kind by that amount, assuming that none of the proceeds were left on deposit. Shifts from one type of asset to another can be made on a dollar for dollar basis.

Under an asset reserve system as outlined above, the bank would prefer Governments to other earning assets until the yield on the latter exceeded that on Governments by enough to compensate for the difference in reserve requirements. This refers, of course, to the net yield after making allowance for risk factors and servicing costs, giving consideration also to any customer relationships of the bank that might be involved (including, where applicable, a borrower's willingness to leave part of the proceeds of his loan on deposit in this bank).

Hence, in view of the importance of banks in the market for Government securities, there would undoubtedly develop a new relationship between the interest rates on Government securities (or on those classes enjoying the reduced reserve requirement) and the rates in other credit markets in which banks participate. That is, there would have to be an extra differential in addition to the previous customary spread between rates on Governments and other rates.

Some intangible factors might further cause a bank to hold, for liquidity purposes, somewhat more Governments than would otherwise be indicated; it is not clear whether these effects would be quantitatively significant. First, in case of a reserve loss from deposit outflow, the bank would no longer have an automatic reduction in required reserves, as it has now. Second, banks often regard holdings of Governments as "insurance" that they will be able to meet customer borrowing needs, and they would need to be prepared to liquidate more than $1 million of Governments for each million of loan expansion.

Effects on government financing. In considering the pros and cons of this kind of regulation, we must first consider whether it would provide an assured market for the amount of securities that the government might need to sell, or whether the government would merely gain an interest rate advantage, enabling it to do its financing at lower rates (relative to other rates in the market) than it would otherwise have to pay. The latter would seem to be the case. Under the example cited, it is true that the banking system as a whole would be enabled to expand its holdings in the favored class of securities by about twice as much as the expansion that would be possible in other assets, but each individual bank's investment would be limited by its own reserve position at the time. The bank would still prefer other assets if the yield differential became big enough--that is, if the yield on other assets were higher by enough to compensate for the reserve requirement against them. Furthermore, the government might not obtain any real net interest saving from the relatively lower interest rates on its securities.

Effects on credit markets. Although the ability of banks to acquire loans and investments, other than items in the exempted class, would indeed be limited by the higher reserve requirement against them, total credit expansion in the economy might not be effectively limited by this requirement. This is because, with a sufficient credit demand from private borrowers, nonbank investors might gradually be lured by the interest differential into switching out of Government securities (which banks could absorb) and into items that the banks wanted to dispose of. While other investors could hardly extend regular commercial loans like a bank, they could take other loans or securities that would normally be held by banks. Mortgage loans and perhaps some kinds of open market paper would tend to flow to other lenders rather than to banks; and large businesses might replace bank borrowings with bond issues or with loans from savings institutions. Any such shift could only occur under the pull of interest rate differentials.

An arrangement of this kind would tend to cause substantially all of the favored (Government) issues to go into bank portfolios, if the total amount outstanding were not too great. Because of the special advantage of these securities to banks and the consequent willingness of banks to buy them on a lower yield basis, they would become relatively unattractive to all other classes of investors. Incidentally, for the longer run, such an insulation of a large share of government debt outstanding could be quite harmful to the functioning of Government securities markets.

As a result of these processes, the purposes of adopting an asset reserve system, intended to provide a better control over expansion of the money supply through bank acquisitions of assets other than Government securities, might be frustrated. The main effect, instead, might be that of gradually shifting many of these credits from banks to other lenders, rather than achieving the desired control over either the total amount of such credits or the total volume of bank assets and the money supply.

QUESTION XX

Does the existence of nonmember banks represent a serious source of escape from monetary controls and perhaps lead to an unhealthy competitive situation between member and nonmember banks?

ANSWER XX

Summary

Differences in reserve requirements between member and nonmember banks give nonmember banks a competitive advantage that tends to weaken their incentive to join the Federal Reserve System and provides an inducement for member banks to withdraw from the Federal Reserve System. This problem is not general, but there are areas of the country in which it exists.

The fact that nonmember banks are not subject to the same reserve requirements as member banks is a source of some escape from monetary controls. However, as long as nonmember bank deposits represent such a small percentage of the deposits of all banks, the existence of nonmember banks and of varying reserve requirements presents no serious problems in this respect.

Relation to Monetary Controls

Present statutory reserve requirements are different for central reserve city member banks, reserve city member banks, and country member banks; requirements for nonmember banks are different and vary among the states. Consequently, the volume of deposits that can be supported by a given volume of reserves varies not only with respect to the category of the member banks which hold them but even more importantly with respect to whether they are held by a member or a nonmember bank.

The reserve requirements of nonmember banks are usually less stringent than those of member banks, and both types of banks frequently compete for the same business and the same customer. The difference in reserve requirements gives nonmember banks a competitive advantage that tends to weaken their incentive to join the Federal Reserve System. Similarly, it provides an inducement for member banks to withdraw from the Federal Reserve System.

Differences between member and nonmember bank reserve requirements are competitively disadvantageous to member banks not only because of lower percentage reserve requirements prescribed in some states, but also because of differences in the composition of reserves. Member banks are required to hold their reserves against deposits in the form of balances with Federal Reserve banks or in allowable cash. Balances with other banks are a deduction item in the computation of net demand deposits subject to reserves and therefore affect required reserves only to a fractional degree.

Nonmember banks, on the other hand, may hold their reserves in the form of vault cash, balances due from other commercial banks and, in some states, certain amounts of securities of the United States, state governments, or other political subdivisions. In one state, there are no legal reserve requirements.

Only the vault cash of nonmember banks, which amounts on the average to about 2.3 percent of their total deposits, is a fully effective reserve in a monetary and credit sense, i.e., in limiting the availability of money and credit. It absorbs basic reserve funds, most of which must be obtained directly or indirectly from the Federal Reserve.

The reserves of nonmember banks consist largely of balances on deposit with correspondent banks. The maintenance of such balances does not restrict credit and monetary expansion for the banking system as a whole, except to the extent that the correspondent banks hold reserves against these deposits in the form of vault cash or of balances at the Federal Reserve banks. For the most part, such nonmember bank reserve balances are available for lending by their correspondent banks and thus may contribute to the process of multiple credit expansion on the basis of a given amount of basic reserves--balances with the Federal Reserve banks and cash in vault.

Reserves consisting of securities, permitted in some states, are not an effective general restraint on the expansion of money and credit because they are not immobilized assets; on the contrary, they are earning assets which reflect credit expansion. A reserve requirement in the form of specified securities, e.g., United States Government securities, may limit the amount of nonmember bank funds which can be invested in private loans and other types of securities but may not restrict an expansion of total credit or the money supply, unless the available supply of the reserve-eligible securities is sufficiently limited.

Even though there is no direct limitation on credit expansion by nonmember banks, as they expand loans they are likely to lose deposits to member banks, which in turn are required to immobilize a significant fraction of such deposits in the form of reserves. In addition, an adverse clearing balance in itself will restrict nonmember bank expansion.

Competitive Consequences

At the present time, about one-half of the banks in the country are not members of the Federal Reserve System, but these banks are smaller on the average than member banks and hold only 16 percent of the total deposits of the country. Thus, the nonmember reserve requirements affect only a small proportion of total deposits of all commercial banks. Nonmember banks, however, are distributed unevenly throughout the country. In relative importance their total deposits vary from approximately 5 percent of total deposits of all commercial banks in the Federal Reserve District of New York to approximately 35 percent in the Federal Reserve District of St. Louis. Thus, although the problem is not general, it is of consequence in some areas.

Problems arising from the existence of nonmember banks have long been recognized by Federal Reserve authorities and by other students of banking. It has been suggested that identical reserve requirements might be applied to all commercial banks in the country. Such identical requirements might be considered analogous to the federal regulations that have been maintained on stock market credit. These regulations have applied to nonmember as well as member banks and other lenders and have been administered with the cooperation of state bank supervisors.

For reasons of established practice, uniform reserve requirements could be administered by state banking departments. Approximately half of the states have already enacted legislation which would permit state authorities to vary reserve requirements of nonmember banks in a degree consistent with changes made in reserve requirements of member banks. There remain, however, important differences in the types of assets that can be counted as reserves.

TABLE XX - I

Total Deposits And Number Of Commercial Banks In U.S.
December 31, 1959

Federal Reserve District	Total	Member	Nonmember	Percent of total in District	
				Member	Nonmember
Deposits (In millions of dollars)					
Boston	9,103	7,799	1,304	85.7	14.3
New York	47,824	45,435	2,389	95.0	5.0
Philadelphia	11,081	9,312	1,769	84.0	16.0
Cleveland	16,748	14,783	1,965	88.3	11.7
Richmond	11,865	8,442	3,423	71.2	28.8
Atlanta	14,759	10,566	4,193	71.6	28.4
Chicago	34,728	28,291	6,437	81.5	18.5
St. Louis	10,334	6,774	3,560	65.6	34.4
Minneapolis	7,060	4,824	2,236	68.3	31.7
Kansas City	11,135	8,483	2,652	76.2	23.8
Dallas	12,807	10,670	2,137	83.3	16.7
San Francisco	32,459	29,299	3,160	90.3	9.7
Total	219,903	184,678	35,225	84.0	16.0
Number of Banks					
Boston	421	277	144	65.8	34.2
New York	601	508	93	84.5	15.5
Philadelphia	656	499	157	76.1	23.9
Cleveland	939	572	367	60.9	39.1
Richmond	957	447	510	46.7	53.3
Atlanta	1,348	403	945	29.9	70.1
Chicago	2,468	1,005	1,463	40.7	59.3
St. Louis	1,477	488	989	33.0	67.0
Minneapolis	1,301	477	824	36.7	63.3
Kansas City	1,808	755	1,053	41.8	58.2
Dallas	1,119	633	486	56.6	43.4
San Francisco	379	165	214	43.5	56.5
Total	13,474	6,229	7,245	46.2	53.8

QUESTION XXI

To what extent are U.S. monetary policies influenced
by such international considerations as interest rates
abroad, the U.S. balance-of-payments position on current
account, the direction of long-term international lending,
and shifts by foreigners between their holdings of bank
deposits, Government securities and gold?

ANSWER XXI

Summary

External developments that may affect demand and supply factors
in this country necessarily enter into assessments of the domestic
situation with which monetary policy has to deal at any given
moment. Moreover, attention must always be paid to factors influencing the balance of payments between this country and the rest
of the world, and, in particular, to developments which evidence,
or could lead to, a shaking of confidence, at home or abroad, in the
stability of the dollar.

To maintain this confidence, the government, and also those who
guide private actions, must follow policies that will contribute to the
maintenance of reasonable equilibrium in the balance of payments,
or facilitate a return to equilibrium. While considerations related to
the international transactions of the United States do not change the
underlying objectives of monetary policy, which are to contribute to
the maintenance of U.S. financial stability and to sustainable growth
in the U.S. economy, they do at times have a bearing on the choice
of actions to be taken. Monetary policies designed to contribute to
achievement of the domestic objectives can contribute to achievement
of the external objective also. This they do chiefly by giving time and
opportunity for adjustment mechanisms here and abroad to bring the
long-run balance on current international transactions into line with
the long-run balance of international capital transactions and grants.
Fluctuations in the balance of payments due to moderate cyclical
forces here and abroad do not create enduring problems of balance-
of-payments adjustment. Fluctuations due to minor disturbances of
confidence may present troublesome problems, but such problems
should be surmountable if underlying economic and financial conditions are making for improvement in the long-run balance.

The strong reserve position of the United States and its demonstrated past record of flexibility in monetary policies are important

assets in maintaining confidence in the dollar in the event of temporary adoption of policies appropriate for dealing with a recession at a time when the balance of payments is in deficit.

During most of the postwar period, the effects of relationships between interest rates here and abroad have not been such as to be significant factors in the determination of U.S. monetary policy. International capital movements are influenced by many factors besides interest rates. The problem that was posed for the Federal Reserve by the outflows of liquid capital in 1960 was not of halting all such outflows, but rather of doing its part to minimize the speculative disturbances associated with the capital outflows.

Assessment of Current Economic Situation

Exports and imports of goods and services by the United States are each equivalent to about 5 percent of the Gross National Product and amount to slightly more than expenditures for new residential construction in the United States. Thus, demand conditions abroad, international competitive pressures in markets for manufactured goods, and supply conditions for internationally traded materials and foodstuffs all influence demand and supply conditions in this country.

The relative importance of external influences is not measurable simply by the volume of trade actually consummated. While exports and imports have direct effects on domestic output and income, external events also exert indirect effects on U.S. business investment and production plans and on U.S. business inventory policies, through market price developments and the general climate of business expectations.

For example, during the 1953-54 recession in the United States, economic activity in Europe was expanding rapidly and sensitive commodity prices were accordingly stronger than many had expected them to be. Undoubtedly the economic situation abroad contributed to early recovery in the United States, not only through the increase in U.S. exports that actually occurred in 1954, but also through indirect effects of the kinds that have been mentioned.

Again, in the spring of 1959 it was becoming evident that a general upturn in economic activity in other industrial countries was under way. By the autumn it was clear that foreign demand for U.S. products had risen. At the same time, the world supply position for many raw materials and foodstuffs was not as tight as it had been in 1955 at a corresponding point of time in the U.S. business cycle.

Such facts and judgments as these, about foreign developments that may influence demand and supply factors in this country, need to be integrated with the mass of facts and judgments about purely domestic developments in arriving at decisions of monetary policy. External developments, therefore, may be said to influence monetary policy in the sense that, through their effects upon the U.S. economy, they continually modify the situation with which monetary policy has to deal.

The state of the balance of payments of the United States with other countries is itself an important feature of the general economic picture. In assessing the forces acting on the balance of payments, account must be taken of demand and supply conditions abroad as well as in this country, both as to goods and services and as to capital and credit. Developments which evidence, or could lead to, a shaking of confidence, at home or abroad, in the stability of the dollar will always call for careful attention.

Bearing of the Balance of Payments on Monetary Policy

Developments in the balance of payments between the United States and the rest of the world may help or hinder the achievement of stability and growth in this country. For this reason, the choice of actions to be taken in pursuing the underlying objectives of monetary policy--to contribute to the maintenance of U.S. financial stability and to sustainable growth in the U.S. economy--may be influenced at times by considerations related directly to the international transactions of the United States.

A deficit in our over-all balance of payments represents a failure of our exports of goods and services to match the total flow of dollar claims being placed at the disposal of the rest of the world through imports, net lending and investment, and government grants and private donations. A deficit so defined is evidenced by accumulation by the rest of the world of liquid dollar assets and gold from transactions with the United States. Foreign purchases of gold from the United States reduce our gold reserves, and foreign net acquisitions of dollars increase our liabilities in such forms as bank deposits, Treasury bills, and other lqiuid assets owned by foreigners.

Persistent large deficits in the balance of payments could pose a threat to financial stability in the United States, by raising doubts not only abroad but also in this country about our ability to maintain the exchange value of the dollar in terms of gold. Flight from the dollar into goods, foreign currencies, and gold, motivated by fear of dollar devaluation or of the institution of exchange controls, would disrupt in manifold ways the orderly processes of growth. It is important to prevent such threats to financial stability.

The limit on the extent to which U.S. payments deficits generated by current transactions and ordinary capital transactions can continue is not subject to precise specification. U.S. gold reserves are large. More importantly, the U.S. dollar is an international reserve currency--that is to say, foreign monetary authorities want to hold dollars as part of their reserves. During the eleven years from the end of 1949 to the end of 1960, foreign monetary authorities increased their gold holdings by more than $11 billion (nearly $7.5 billion of which came from the United States) and their short-term dollar holdings by about $7.5 billion. In addition, foreign commercial banks and others increased their short-term dollar holdings by $4 billion.

To retain the advantages of having a currency that is used for international reserves and to guard against possibilities of a flight from the dollar, it is essential that confidence in the dollar be maintained. Three things are important in this connection.

First, as our gold reserves exist for the purpose of being available to cover temporary deficits in the balance of payments, it is essential that they always be readily available for that purpose.

Second, it must be clear to all observers that policies are being followed that will maintain reasonable equilibrium in the underlying elements of the balance of payments, or facilitate a return toward equilibrium whenever large deficits in the balance of payments emerge for whatever reason. Private policies as to pricing and other competitive actions enter into the question, and also government policies, including those of the monetary authorities.

Third, when outflow of short-term capital for any reason become so heavy as to create a large deficit in the balance of payments and accordingly lead to a sizable drain on U.S. gold reserves, the problem arises of how to prevent the generation of unjustified apprehensions that might cause a snowballing of the capital outflows and the gold drain.

With respect to monetary policy, actions aimed at contributing to domestic financial stability and sustainable growth during times of strong pressures of demand clearly help at the same time to minimize deficits in the balance of payments. During times of slack demand, dilemmas may be posed for monetary policy. For example, toward the end of 1960 when rising unemployment and declining output justified the Federal Reserve's policy of credit ease and might have justified further lowering of interest rates, consideration had to be given in the choice of actions to the effects of low interest rates, along with other factors, upon capital outflows, the gold drain, and confidence in the stability of the dollar.

Adjustment of the Balance of Payments

The implications for U.S. monetary policy of a deficit in the balance of payments depend upon the forces that have given rise to the deficit. The large balance-of-payments deficits of 1958, 1959, and 1960 reflected four main sets of forces, two of them more enduring than the others. First, the postwar economic and financial reconstruction of other industrial countries made them again important competitors of the United States in markets here and abroad. Second, during the postwar period the United States assumed heavy international responsibilities, one indication of which is the annual expenditure abroad of $3 billion to support U.S. military forces. Third, imports were stimulated by rapid U.S. recovery from the 1957-58 recession while exports were curtailed by the lag in European recovery and by international readjustments in some other foreign markets, as in Latin America. Fourth, while exports rose strongly after mid-1959 and imports fell off, large amounts of short-term capital, both U.S. and foreign, moved from the United States to foreign countries in 1960.

Cyclical forces here and abroad are constantly affecting the balance of payments. Although their effects may be felt in one direction or another for extended periods, forces that are eventually reversed do not create enduring problems of balance-of-payments adjustment. Fortunately, the international reserve position of the United States can absorb the impacts of such forces. The more difficult problems of long-run adjustment in the balance of payments relate to those parts of the disequilibrium that are caused by deeper-lying shifts in the international competitive situation or by actions taken by the government in response to noneconomic considerations.

Solutions to this problem lie partly outside the province of the monetary authorities. The contribution that monetary policy can make is to foster credit conditions conducive to over-all price stability in the United States in a manner that will permit adjustment mechanisms here and abroad to function. Our deficit is the surplus of the rest of the world, and rising international reserves in other countries permit relaxation and dismantling of controls on international trade and give governments and central banks greater leeway in allowing or encouraging expansion of demand. In the United States, meanwhile, the spur of foreign competition forces American producers to make their goods more saleable both here and abroad. Fundamental adjustments such as these are essential to the establishment and maintenance of equilibrium in our international balance of payments.

Policy in a U.S. Recession

The process of adjustment of the balance of payments may extend through more than one cycle of expansion and contraction in foreign demand for U.S. exports and through more than one cycle (perhaps differently timed) of recovery and recession in the United States.

Existence of a balance-of-payments deficit at the time of a recession should not divert the monetary authorities of the United
States from following policies otherwise appropriate in such a situation. What is needed for long-run adjustment of the U.S. balance of
payments is not deflation, but avoidance of inflation, continuing expansion of our productive resources, and an effective response by
the U.S. economy to competitive pressures and opportunities.

The ability of the Federal Reserve and other agencies of the
government to follow appropriate policies in a recession without
major disturbance of confidence in the U.S. dollar rests on two factors. First, as has been noted above, the international reserve position of the United States is strong enough to absorb considerable
drains of gold or accretions of liabilities. Second, and equally important, the record of the past has demonstrated that the adoption
of appropriate policies in a recession does not mean abandoning
either the objective of avoiding inflation or the aim of achieving
reasonable equilibrium in the balance of payments.

If, despite such facts as these, private capital outflows initially
stimulated by differences in credit conditions here and abroad lead
to a sizable drain on U.S. gold reserves, and if the capital outflows
and the gold drain create a minor disturbance of confidence, the
monetary authorities may be faced with troublesome problems in
reconciling the domestic and external objectives. But when underlying economic and financial conditions are making for improvement
in the long-run balance of our international transactions, such
problems should be surmountable.

Interest Rates, Capital Movements, and Gold

Cyclical changes in the relative strength of demands for goods
here and abroad are often accompanied by corresponding shifts in the
relative strength of demand for capital and by opposite shifts in the
availability of liquid funds. Changes in international capital movements that result from these shifts are influenced by many factors,
including relative interest rates in various countries. Speculative
forces at times play an important role.

In the postwar years before 1960, changes in the balance-of-
payments surplus or deficit of the United States were determined
less by changes in capital movements than by changes in transactions in goods and services. The change from an over-all deficit
of $1.2 billion in 1955 to a surplus of $500 million in 1957, and the
subsequent change to a deficit of $3.8 billion in 1959, were both
dominated by changes in exports and imports of goods and services.
Exports increased by nearly $7 billion and then declined by about
$3.5 billion. Imports increased by $3 billion from 1955 to 1957, and
by a further $2.5 billion from 1957 to 1959. In contrast, the net

outflow of U.S. private capital increased only by $2 billion from 1955 to 1957, and then decreased by about $1 billion. Changes in the net inflow of foreign long-term investment in private U.S. enterprises and securities were still smaller. Changes in the flow of foreign funds into and out of dollar liquid assets are discussed later; these do not affect the balance-of-payments surplus or deficit as here defined.

A restrictive monetary policy makes its most important contribution to restoring equilibrium in the balance of payments through its effects on exports and imports. In the short run, however, it may also influence capital movements in a way that will help to minimize an over-all deficit. Since the end of 1958, when most European countries restored external convertibility of their currencies, international flows of liquid funds have been larger than they were in the earlier postwar years, and the potential influence of credit conditions and interest rates in various countries upon international payments balances has increased correspondingly.

The $1 billion decline in private U.S. capital outflow from 1957 to 1959 and the increase in inflow of foreign long-term capital served as partial offsets to the $6 billion shrinkage at that time in the goods and services export surplus. It is perhaps significant that this alteration of the net capital flow occurred mainly from 1958 to 1959, at a time when U.S. interest rates were rising and interest rates in several major European countries were declining. Interest rate changes may at times have appreciable effects on international capital movements. The changes in net capital flow from 1957 or 1958 to 1959, shown in the accompanying table, were due, however, only in minor part to interest rate changes in the United States and other leading financial markets.

During 1960, when the goods and services export surplus expanded significantly, an increase again occurred in private capital outflow. In this instance, the year-to-year shift in capital movements was fully as large as the improvement in the current account, and the increase in net exports from the first half to the second half of 1960 was more than offset by increased capital outflow. The widening of short-term interest rate differentials after mid-1960 between the United States and some European countries played a large role in this development, by attracting short-term investments abroad. But it would be a serious oversimplification to lay stress solely on short-term rate differentials. In addition, loans and credits to borrowers abroad were stimulated by the increasing availability of funds in the United States. At the same time, prospects of capital gains on both equity and fixed-income securities abroad attracted movements of funds, and speculation on currency values was an additional influence of considerable importance. As estimates given in the table show, a large amount of capital outflow in 1960 took forms not identifiable from the available statistical reports.

In 1958 and 1959, as well as in 1960, the shifts in some of the types of capital movements listed in the table had not represented responses to current changes in interest rate differentials. Most foreign purchases of U.S. private long-term securities in recent years have been in common stocks rather than in interest-bearing securities, and most of the U.S. purchases of foreign long-term securities other than those newly issued have been purchases of stocks. In addition, changes in the outflow of direct investment in subsidiaries or branches abroad of U.S. corporations are determined primarily by business opportunities and plans.

Net outflows of U.S. bank loans to foreign borrowers are affected to some extent by money market conditions in the United States, and offerings of foreign and international institutions' securities in U.S. markets are at times significantly affected by absolute and relative levels of interest rates here. While influences such as these did affect the outflow of bank loans and of capital raised by new issues in recent years, other forces played an important role in the 1958 increase in outflow and in the reduction from 1958 to 1959, as well as in the new increase in 1960.

For example, the foreign demand for U.S. bank loans originates to a considerable extent in countries without highly organized money markets, and this demand for credit varies with changes in the trade or in the balance of payments of the borrowing countries. The decline in U.S. purchases of newly issued foreign securities after the spring of 1958 reflected partly the timing of new issues in this market by the International Bank for Reconstruction and Development, and this timing was apparently influenced by interest rate changes. But offerings by other foreign issuers remained about as large in 1959 as in 1958, despite the rise in U.S. rates. Canadian borrowings in the United States, which generally provide a considerable part of the new foreign issues, were evidently influenced by the level of Canadian interest rates relative to U.S. rates, and Canadian rates rose even more than U.S. rates from 1958 to 1959. In 1960, however, new Canadian issues in this country fell off, despite a continuation of relatively high interest rates in Canada.

There has been omitted from the discussion thus far one important category of capital transactions. These are the transactions within the U.S. market that do not contribute to the over-all surplus or deficit as commonly defined; they reflect decisions as to the forms in which accretions to foreign liquid assets will be held.

In 1958 the total addition to foreign and international institutions' liquid dollar assets plus purchases of gold from the United States was $3.5 billion, and in 1959 it was $3.8 billion, apart from a $1.4 billion addition to International Monetary Fund holdings through the additional U.S. subscription made that year. In 1958, $2.3 billion of the total was taken in gold and $1.2 billion in dollar liquid assets of various types. In 1959, U.S. transfers of gold to foreign countries and international institutions were $1.1 billion, the increase in special noninterest-bearing notes held by the IMF was $1.3 billion, and foreign and international institutions' holdings of other dollar liquid assets increased $2.8 billion.

Interest rate increases in the United States and declines in other leading financial markets had only a minor effect on the magnitude of the total increase in gold and dollar liquid assets. This magnitude was determined by the over-all surplus in the balance of payments of the rest of the world with the United States. Even in the distribution of total foreign gains between gold and liquid dollar assets, with gold a smaller part in 1959 than in 1958 and dollar assets a larger part, interest rate changes played only a minor role.[1]

The distribution of foreign asset gains between gold and dollars is determined by two sets of decisions, in only one of which relative interest rates play any part. Foreign commercial banks and others may be induced by interest rate differentials (in excess of costs of covering foreign exchange risks) to make short-term investments in the United States. Insofar as this happens, their purchase of dollars in foreign exchange markets for this purpose are balanced by sales of dollars by others, including foreign central banks. Thus, given an over-all U.S. balance-of-payments deficit during a particular period, additional purchases of interest-bearing dollar assets for foreign nonofficial accounts ordinary mean, in the first instance, smaller accretions to foreign official dollar holdings than would otherwise have occurred.

Some foreign monetary authorities hold their reserves mainly in gold, some mainly in dollars, and others in both forms. These practices of central banks with respect to the choice between dollar assets and gold, while differing from country to country, have shown no significant tendency to vary in response to changes in interest yields available on dollar assets.

Thus, the direct effect of interest rate differentials on movements of foreign funds into or out of dollar assets is limited almost exclusively to private transactions.[2] A movement of foreign private

---

[1]Although relative rates on time deposits and Treasury bills had the effect of creating a preference for the former in 1958 and for the latter in 1959, such shifts between types of dollar assets have no effect on the distribution of foreign asset gains between gold and dollars.

[2]Official holders of dollars do, of course, make shifts from one type of dollar asset to another in response to relative interest rates on the different types. See preceding footnote.

funds into dollar assets, accompanied by reduction in foreign official gains of reserves, may then lead indirectly to reduction in foreign official purchases of gold.

The final outcome as to foreign acquisitions of gold from the United States depends not only on the extent to which private short-term investments in the United States are influenced by interest rate changes, and on the reserve policies of the foreign countries from which the funds move, but also on all other elements in the balance of payments and on the country-by-country pattern of surpluses or deficits. In 1959, for example, gold purchases from the United States were much smaller than in 1958 largely because countries that customarily convert reserve gains into gold had much smaller increases in their official reserves in 1959 than in 1958; these reductions in reserve gains were only in part the result of movements of foreign private short-term investments in response to interest rate changes.

In 1960, foreign private holdings of dollar liquid assets increased much less than in 1959. After July, the rise in total U.S. short-term liabilities to foreign commercial banks and other private persons gave place to a decline. Like the 1960 movements of U.S. short-term capital and movements of unidentified capital, this net outflow of foreign private funds in the latter part of 1960 responded to a variety of forces associated with the strength of demands abroad for goods and for liquid capital, including the pull of interest rates, and also in part to speculative influences. Despite great improvement in the goods and services export surplus, the outflows of foreign and U.S. private funds resulted in large additions to foreign official reserves. Net purchases of gold from the United States amounted to $1.7 billion in 1960.

To sum up, certain types of international capital movements affecting the surplus or deficit in the over-all balance of payments are responsive to changes in the relation between U.S. and European interest rates, but others are not. Furthermore, the disposition by the rest of the world of its liquid asset accretions as between gold and dollar assets depends to a great extent on factors other than interest rate relationships.

Gold movements reflect the whole state of the U.S. balance of payments, the country-by-country pattern of foreign balance-of-payments surpluses or deficits, and prevailing practices with respect to holding reserves in dollars. Responses of capital movements to interest rate changes alone cannot match in ultimate importance to various influences that affect for better or for worse the competitive position of the United States and the maintenance of confidence in the stability of the dollar.

TABLE XXI - 1

Net Flows of Private Capital
(In millions of dollars)

	Calendar Years			Halfyears, 1960	
	1957	1958	1959	1st	2nd p.
A. Outflows affecting the surplus or deficit in the balance of payments[1]					
New issues less redemptions:					
International institutions	171	350	- 2	80	- 2
Canada	205	328	382	163	6
Other	42	192	150	86	114
Short-term (net), including bank loans	258	306	89	215	1,013
Long-term bank loans (net)[2]	335	188	183	+ 54	95
Subtotal	1,011	1,364	802	598	1,226
U.S. direct investments (net)	2,058	1,094	1,310	566	975
Other long-term (net)[3]	106	386	189	65	92
Foreign direct and portfolio investments other than U.S. Govt. securities (net) (inflow,-)	- 361	- 24	- 548	- 337	10
Subtotal	1,803	1,456	951	294	1,077
Total	2,814	2,820	1,753	892	2,303
Estimate of capital unrecorded [4] (inflow,-)	- 250	100	- 300	450	- 950
B. Increase in foreign private short-term dollar assets[5]	282	226	1,126	449	- 478

p. = preliminary

[1]I.e., excluding recorded foreign movements into or out of dollar liquid assets (U.S. short-term liabilities and U.S. Government securities). The only item in the first part of the table reflecting recorded changes in foreign assets in U.S. is "foreign direct and portfolio investments..." Other items reflect changes in U.S. private assets abroad. The estimate of "capital unrecorded" necessarily refers to both foreign and U.S. capital.

[2]Change in long-term claims on foreigners reported by banks in the United States, "mainly loans with an original maturity of more than one year" (Federal Reserve Bulletin).

[3]Mainly net purchases of outstanding foreign securities. Derived by deducting "long-term bank loans (net)" from the Department of Commerce balance-of-payments item "U.S. private capital, other long-term (net)."

[4]Very rough estimates based on the assumption that year-to-year variations in the balance on unrecorded transactions are due chiefly to unrecorded capital transactions.

[5]Change (increase,+) in short-term liabilities to foreign countries, excluding official accounts, reported by banks in the United States (Federal Reserve Bulletin).

Source: Department of Commerce balance-of-payments data, except as indicated in footnotes.

QUESTION XXII

What are the repercussions of interest rate regulations on time deposits with respect to the competitive position of the various financial intermediaries, flows of domestic funds, and the composition of foreign holdings of dollar assets?

ANSWER XXII

Summary

The competitive position of commercial banks has been affected by the regulation of interest they could pay on time and savings deposits in that at times they have not been able to match rates paid by other intermediaries or available in the market in periods of high interest rates. The flows of domestic funds and the composition of foreign dollar assets may have been affected, though in degrees that can be assessed only roughly.

Regulation, however, has not been the only factor checking rate increases. An appreciable proportion of insured commercial banks paid rates under the ceilings permitted by regulation in higher interest rate periods such as mid-1956 through the third quarter of 1957, and in the second half of 1959 through the first quarter of 1960.

To some extent commercial banks may have been reluctant to raise rates paid on time and savings deposits to the level permitted by regulation, even when market interest rates went up, because of the prohibition on the payment of interest on demand deposits. Banks prefer not to "compete with themselves." The extent to which banks would have posted higher rates if the regulatory ceilings had permitted them to do so, or in the absence of regulation, is thus conjectural. Moreover, because of other services available, some depositors find it convenient to keep their savings on deposit at commercial banks and will do so even at a lower interest return. Many other factors have caused shifts in competitive relationships and new directions in the flow of funds.

Interest rates have unquestionably been used aggressively as a competitive device by various savings intermediaries, including commercial banks themselves. Savers have also become more conscious of other alternatives such as investment in marketable U.S. Government obligations. The result of these influences, however, is probably concentrated on the outlets used for financial saving; the effect on the total amount of saving is far from evident.

The clearest case in which regulation of rates on time and saving deposits has influenced the employment of funds is that of foreign-owned dollar assets. Some foreign owners of dollars appear to be quite sensitive to interest rate differentials and to have switched back and forth between time deposits and Treasury bills as rate advantages have alternated. A similar though less clearly marked sensitivity seems to be found in the movements of state and local government liquid investments. Money market commercial banks now are "selling" negotiable time certificates of deposit to domestic corporations, and a market is being maintained in these certificates by at least one dealer.

The flow of funds into savings institutions has changed in pace several times in the last few years; differentials in rates offered clearly have been one of the factors causing these shifts. However, as suggested above, the responsibility for these differentials is only partly regulatory.

Initial Rationale for Regulation

Mandatory regulation of interest paid on time and savings deposits was adopted largely because of the opinion that high rates of interest paid by some commercial banks in the 1920's had contributed to the serious losses they suffered during the depression of the 1930's. The banks that failed or got into financial difficulties during that period were often found to have paid exceptionally high rates for time and savings deposits and to have had vulnerable loan and investment accounts, particularly the latter. A connection seemed to exist between these facts. Deterioration in the quality of assets, brought to light during the depression, seemed to have been related in part to excessive efforts at income maximization during the preceding boom. Active competition among banks led many individual institutions to commit themselves to rates they could not continue to pay while pursuing a prudent loan and investment policy. Factors other than excessive interest payments, of course, accounted for some of the adverse loan and investment experience.

Early Regulatory Experience

The initial regulation of interest rates on time and savings deposits by the Federal Reserve Board in 1933 (Regulation Q) established a blanket 3 percent rate ceiling on time and savings deposits. The regulation, applicable only to member banks of the Federal Reserve System, did not press with any severity on the level of rates that banks were actually paying. In 1935, when this blanket rate ceiling was reduced to $2\frac{1}{2}$ percent, very few banks were forced to decrease the rates they were paying, since voluntary reductions in response to lower levels of market interest rates had already been widely made.

A schedule of maximum time deposit rates by maturities became effective at the beginning of 1936 and at the same time the FDIC initiated a parallel regulation of the rates paid by insured non-member commercial banks. These rates are shown in column 3 of Table XXII-1. The change was principally an adjustment of the regulatory terms to the requirements of the Banking Act of 1935.

TABLE XXII - 1

Interest Rate Ceilings Authorized by Regulation Q

	Oct./31/33 to Jan./31/35	Feb./1/35 to Dec./31/35	Jan./1/36 to Dec./31/56	Jan./1/57 through first quarter 1961
Savings deposits)			(2-1/2	3
Time deposits--initial)			(	
maturity:)			(	
6 months and over)	3	2-1/2	(2-1/2	3
90 days to 6 months)			(2	2-1/2
30 days to 90 days)			(1	1
Under 30 days	(not permitted; defined as demand deposits)			

During the first two decades of Regulation Q, its prescribed maxima were almost always appreciably above the rates banks were actually paying. Although market interest rates moved up slightly in the early postwar period, serious pressure on the regulatory ceilings did not come until 1955, and to an even greater extent in 1956, when stronger demands for credit induced a number of savings institutions to increase the interest rates they offered for funds.

For the first time in two decades, Regulation Q could be said to be limiting the level of rates that might have been paid by some commercial banks. This was not generally true, however, as relatively few insured commercial banks were paying rates at or near the regulatory ceiling when Regulation Q was amended near the end of 1956. The amendment raised permissible rates effective January 1, 1957. During 1957 expanding investment opportunities combined with a variety of other factors stimulated more active promotional efforts by almost all institutions seeking time and savings deposits. Posted rates were increased in many banks and supplementary competitive devices were widely adopted. Advertising, premiums, and more liberal computational methods were used to attract new business.

In the brief recession at the end of 1957 and in early 1958, market rates of interest declined sharply but remained low for only a short time. No appreciable number of commercial banks and only a few competing savings institutions reduced the rates of interest or divi-

dends paid on time and savings deposits and share accounts. Even
the somewhat more volatile rates paid on time certificates of deposit
by money market banks appear to have been maintained at rather
high levels relative to the reduced levels of open market interest
rates. With time deposit rates relatively advantageous to investors,
commercial banks and other savings institutions attracted a large
inflow of funds.

In late 1958 market interest rates once more rose, and in 1959
reached the highest levels of the past 30 years. Because of the
limitations imposed by Regulation Q, however, those commercial
banks that were seeking aggressively to attract or maintain deposits
were unable to follow the rise in market rates by increasing the
rates offered on time and savings deposits. Thus, regulatory rates
had finally come into close touch with the market. The increase of
time deposits was slowed down and in some quarters almost halted.
Savings and loan associations continued to increase materially the
dividend rates they offered, thereby maintaining or enlarging differentials above the rates of interest permitted by Regulation Q.

In recent years time and savings deposits have assumed a position of increased importance in the affairs of commercial banks.
During the past decade they have grown from 28 to 36 percent of
total commercial bank deposits. With a slackening in the growth of
demand deposits, individual banks have increased their endeavors
to attract new funds through time and savings deposits. Some corporate customers, enjoying a strong bargaining position with respect
to their bankers, have induced banks to accept time certificates of
deposit as acceptable compensatory balances. In a few cases these
time certificates have subsequently been discounted below par
through money brokers, thereby providing a higher rate of return to
the purchasers.

More active pursuit of time and savings deposits has raised some
problems of bank liquidity. Funds attracted with only mild competitive efforts probably tend to remain with relative stability in the
institution holding them. Funds obtained as the result of more
vigorous competitive efforts probably are not quite as stable and
should be protected by a wider margin of liquidity.

Economic Background

Regulation Q was promulgated against an economic background
of relatively slack demands for funds and low interest rates. During the 1930's commercial banks reduced the rates they paid on time
and savings deposits considerably below the regulatory ceilings.
Some even refused to accept time deposits, or allowed additions to
be made to savings accounts only by established customers in small
regular amounts.

When the economy passed from the prolonged depression of the 1930's into a state of defense preparation, and then into war, the situation with respect to savings flows changed radically. Federal government borrowing exceeded the entire flow of voluntary saving, and substantial monetary expansion ensued.

During the war period, private competition for savings was not vigorous. With a negligible supply of new mortgages coming into the market, savings and loan associations were moderate in their promotional efforts. While mutual savings banks were not as closely tied by tradition to mortgages as outlets for funds, their promotional activities also tended to be restricted. Savings institutions helped to promote the sale of Treasury savings bonds and increased their own holdings of Government securities.

In the early postwar period, official support of U.S. Government securities prices, and the attendant influence on the yields from other securities, held the earnings of most savings institutions at relatively low levels. In such an environment, promotional efforts on the part of these institutions tended to be restrained. Nevertheless, the increasing demand for mortgage funds and more active borrowing by corporations stimulated greater competitive zeal considerably before this influence was fully reflected in an upward trend of interest rates.

The rise in interest rates following the termination of Federal Reserve support of low market rates on Government securities encouraged more aggressiveness in promoting new saving and in expanding facilities for handling savings funds. The sustained high levels of economic activity and the continuing demands for funds, even during the brief periods of moderate economic recession, supplied even stronger motives to the principal financial intermediaries for vigorous and aggressive pursuit of new savings.

Although investment quality of commercial bank portfolios is generally quite high, appreciable differences in the rates of both gross and net earnings on investments are encountered. Some banks acquired a substantial proportion of their present portfolios in earlier periods of lower rates, while other banks bought the bulk of their present holdings in recent higher rate periods. The turnover of portfolios because of special tax considerations may partly obscure these differences among banks but it would not obliterate them.

Because of variations in earning capacity, the rates that banks can appropriately offer customers on time and savings deposits also vary appreciably. The differences are of a character that cannot be fully matched by a regulatory classification of rates. Many differences among individual banks are more appropriately dealt with on a case-by-case basis.

The prohibition of the payment of interest on demand deposits has also caused banks to hesitate about increasing the rates they offered for time and savings deposits even when room for such increase existed under the regulatory ceilings. In the ever sharpening postwar competition for funds, banks have been aware of the investment alternatives available to those who managed corporate or individual liquidity positions. Aside from perfecting the services offered demand deposit customers, including loan services, little more can be done to lure funds back into demand deposit accounts. When banks raise rates on time and savings deposits, they are in effect "competing with themselves."

Competitive Influences on the Flow of Savings

When the statutory base underlying Regulation Q was first adopted, the commercial and mutual savings banks were the dominant savings institutions. Although some degree of competition prevailed among various types of savings institutions, the competition many commercial bankers felt most keenly came from other banks. Since that time, however, the competititve pattern has changed appreciably. A number of other savings outlets and institutions, all of which lie outside the formal regulatory pattern, have emerged as strong competitors.

The most vigorous and aggressive of these competing savings institutions are unquestionably savings and loan associations. The increased supply of mortgages and the improved earnings from them have permitted associations to increase their dividend rates materially. This improvement in earnings has been particularly marked in some areas of the country such as California, where savings and loan associations live in an environment of such strong demands for funds that they have not only competed vigorously for funds in their own localities, but have advertised nationally and used a variety of other competitive devices to attract money.

Most savings and loan associations have grown faster than the mutual savings banks or commercial banks in the same areas. They are now attracting a larger gross inflow of funds each year than that received by life insurance companies. While savings and loan associations are not subject to a formal regulation limiting the dividend rates paid to shareholders, the federal and state authorities that charter and supervise these institutions provide some check on the level of dividend rates.

Credit unions are a smaller, but nevertheless rapidly growing competitor for savings funds. While these institutions offer a savings outlet to only a limited portion of the population, they have nevertheless grown rapidly and have attracted funds in considerable volume in the locations where they operate. The dividend rates paid by credit unions show considerable dispersion but in general have been slightly higher than the dividends paid by savings and loan associations and considerably higher than rates that commercial banks pay on savings deposits.

In a very broad sense both life insurance companies and pension funds could be viewed as competitive with deposit or share-account type of savings institutions. In practice, however, the buyers of insurance contracts and the holders of pension rights probably do not view these arrangements in many instances as alternatives to, or competitive with, savings accounts.

The securities of the federal government compete for private investment funds. Effective competition is now offered by marketable obligations of the government, and savings bonds have been attractive to investors in some periods. Savings bond interest rates, however, are not directly comparable with rates offered by other savings instruments because of the penalty on redemption before maturity.

The marketable securities of the federal government have recently proved to be effective competitors with time and savings deposits in a variety of ways. The Treasury bill is treated as an alternative to time certificates of deposits by foreign holders of liquid dollar assets, by some state and local governments, and by many corporate treasurers. The section below shows that there has been a reciprocal relationship between the relative rates offered by banks and Treasury bill rates, and the shift of funds into or out of these investment vehicles.

Recently, some holders of savings deposits have also become more aware of the investment merits of intermediate- and longer-term marketable U.S. Government securities and have bought them when attractive yields were available. High-yielding new issues such as the "magic fives" of August 1964 (offered in October 1959) induced appreciable withdrawals of funds from savings accounts. When yields in the secondary market have approached this level, U.S. Government security dealers have received larger numbers of small or odd-lot purchase orders for marketable U.S. bonds. This suggests that when the yield is attractive, individual investment in U.S. Government securities has taken place with increasing frequency even outside the periods of new Treasury offerings.

Corporate equities, and mutual funds composed mainly of corporate equities, have also been effective competitors for savings funds. The capital gains from sharply rising stock market levels and the widespread fear of secular inflation have contributed to their attractiveness. While yields from some equities have sometimes been attractive in comparison with interest rates on time and savings deposits, it does not appear that yield differentials have been a major influence; indeed, the yields on many of the most popular equities have been appreciably below the rates available on time and savings deposits. To a major extent transactions in corporate equities or mutual funds simply represent redistribution of stock ownership in the secondary market. This produces no net inflow of saving into equities. The funds invested by some are merely transferred to others who sell their holdings. The high prices for corporate equities, however, have unquestionably encouraged an increase in the volume of new equity issues and so encouraged some net inflow of funds.

Competititve Position of Time Deposits

Since the re-establishment of a flexible market for U.S. Government securities and the advent of greater fluctuations in yields, a clear cyclical pattern has developed in the movement of time deposits into and out of commercial banks. This movement appears to be dominated by the relative yields available in market instruments, primarily the Treasury bill, and the rates of interest offered by commercial banks on time deposits.

In 1954, when Treasury bill rates dropped sharply, commercial banks quickly gained a large volume of time deposits from foreigners, from state and local governments, and from business corporations. This movement ceased abruptly in 1955 and some loss in deposits was experienced. The pattern of rapid gain quickly emerged again in early 1958 when low Treasury bill rates brought another very large movement of foreign funds, state and local government funds and corporate funds into commercial banks. This inflow, however, ceased abruptly when bill rates started to go up in late 1958 and during 1959. During 1959, in fact, commercial banks suffered a sizable net loss of time funds, presumably to the bill market.

Whether these swings in the acquisition and loss of time deposits would have existed in the absence of an interest rate regulation is not altogether clear. It is worth noting, however, that this movement took place in 1954 and was reversed in 1955 before regulatory rates pressed with any severity on the rates that banks might have normally wished to pay for competitive reasons. Even in the absence of regulation, reciprocal movement probably would take place unless banks adjusted their rates as frequently and as fully as Treasury bill yields changed. Rates have not been adjusted with this degree of frequency.

Competitive Position of Savings Deposits

Passbook savings deposits do not show such a clear cyclical pattern. The movements of savings deposits into commercial banks and into mutual savings banks were not greatly different in 1954 and 1955. A notable fact, however, is that larger gains took place in 1957. During that year many commercial banks, spurred by a higher regulatory ceiling, promoted vigorously the attraction of these funds as a matter of business policy. In the first three quarters of 1958, time deposit gains as well as savings deposit increases continued at an accelerated pace, but then tapered off as savings institutions not restrained by regulatory limits on the rates they paid increased their competitive efforts and offered still higher prices for funds.

Although savings deposits appear to be less responsive to fluctuations in short-term interest rates than are time deposits, the slowdown in the rate of savings deposit growth since early 1959 shows that external competition is exerting more influence. In some areas of the country, commercial banks have lost savings deposits at a time when some competitive institutions have been growing at record rates.

Marketable Time Certificates of Deposit

Some money market commercial banks have long refused to accept time deposits from domestic nonfinancial corporations. Their general feeling seemed to be that to do so would have made one department of their banks competititve with another department. It is evident, however, that many attractive liquidity vehicles are available to nonfinancial domestic corporations, particularly Treasury bills. Recognizing this fact, money market commercial banks early this year began to negotiate time certificates of deposit with domestic corporations in a form that was specially tailored to insure their marketability. One of the dealers in U.S. Government securities "makes" a market in these time deposit certificates. The amount outstanding had already passed the half billion dollar mark by early May 1961. Some of these certificates of deposit appear to have originated as compensatory balances which were then sold by the corporation holding them.

Time Deposits and Foreign Dollar Holdings

The form in which dollar assets are held by foreign central banks or by other foreigners has been influenced by the regulation of time deposit rates. Those dollar funds that foreign governments and central banks do not convert into gold are largely invested in Treasury bills, bankers' acceptances, or time deposits at commercial banks. Foreign central banks often hold a portion of their dollar funds with the Federal Reserve Bank of New York, and the Bank acts as agent for them in the investment of dollar funds. Many foreign central banks and other foreign interests also maintain close banking relationships with one or more of the money market commercial banks.

192   THE FEDERAL RESERVE ANSWERS

Correspondent relationships with foreign customers depend on and require the furnishing of many kinds of banking services. Money market commercial banks expect the maintenance of an adequate deposit balance as a part of the price for these services, just as for their services to domestic customers. A time certificate or deposit is usually viewed as a discharge of a part of the customers' obligation even though interest is paid on such accounts.

Existing tax legislation (Internal Revenue Code, Sec. 861(a)(1)(C) and 881) exempts from taxation the income received by foreign holders from time deposits and bankers' acceptances, but some foreign holders are subject to certain taxes on income received from the securities of the U.S. Government. Thus, yields on U.S. Government securities must be somewhat above the rate paid on time deposits to be competitive with them.

QUESTION XXIII

To what extend are and should bank examination standards be related to and integrated with general monetary policies? For example, are or should standards be eased in periods of recession and tightened in boom periods, along with similar changes in monetary policies? What would be the dangers and advantages of such an integration?

ANSWER XXIII

Summary

The objectives of bank examination and supervision are to keep individual banks in sound condition and to preserve a strong, viable, and competitive commercial banking system. The intrinsic value of assets is considered in the examination and supervisory processes and, basically, the same standards of appraisal are imposed regardless of fluctuations in economic conditions.

Standards designed to be eased in periods of recession and tightened in boom periods, complementing similar changes in monetary policies, could not be applied simultaneously to all banks because of the nature of the examination and supervisory processes. Such shifts of standards might impair the nondiscriminatory characteristics of the examination and supervisory processes, and would likely diminish the contribution of these processes to a strong banking system and a sound economy.

At the outset, it should be made clear that although the terms "bank examination" and "bank supervision" are frequently used interchangeably, in practice bank examination is only one phase of bank supervision. "Bank supervision" in its broader aspects embraces not only examination of banks, but in addition, other important activities performed by banking authorities. Supervision includes, for example, actions taken in the discharge of continuing responsibilities with respect to the organization and chartering of banks, issuance and interpretation of regulations, formulation of corrective requirements based on findings in examinations, permission to merge and establish branches, changes in capital structure or corporate powers, and liquidation and dissolution proceedings if and when banks discontinue operations.

Fundamentally, bank supervision is directed toward the protection of the public interest. In relation to the individual bank, the objective of supervision is to foster the maintenance of each institution in sound and solvent condition and under good management, in order to protect depositors and assure continuation of essential banking services in the community. With respect to all banks, its further objective is to help maintain a banking system that will continuously adapt to the financial needs of a growing economy.

Focusing now upon the more familiar aspect of bank supervision--the visitorial bank examination function--its immediate objectives are to develop information as to the financial condition and soundness of the individual institution, to ascertain its operating policies and practices and whether it is complying with applicable laws and regulations, and to appraise the capabilities and performance of its management in relation to its responsibilities. The bank examiner in the field is primarily a fact-finder and appraiser. His task is to report the facts as found and base his conclusions as to asset quality, capital adequacy, and management performance on those facts.

After reviewing the facts and conclusions reported by the field examiner, the supervisory authority--not the examiner--formulates expressions of supervisory policy and prescribes necessary corrective requirements regarding criticized phases of the banks' affairs. The supervisory authority adjusts expressions of supervisory policy and corrective requirements with respect to individual banks in light of the composite experience derived from the examination and supervision of many banks.

In an economy characterized by periods of nationwide contraction and expansion, the policies of bank supervision need to avoid impeding or deterring individual banks in making necessary adjustments to changing conditions. Insofar as possible, supervisory policies should function so as to facilitate banking adaptations to these changes. It would be both unwise from the standpoint of bank supervision and damaging to the banking system as a whole if bank examination standards and practices should operate so as to increase unnecessarily the pressure for forced liquidation of bank assets at times when financial markets are sensitive to deflationary dangers, or if they were relaxed in boom times when markets are strong and prices of equities and goods are advancing.

In this connection, the Revision in Bank Examination Procedure, or so-called "Uniform Agreement," of the three federal supervisory agencies and the Executive Committee of the National Association of Supervisors of State Banks, adopted in 1938 and amended slightly in 1949, was designed particularly to further the maintenance of economic stability. Through its emphasis upon appraisal of bank assets in terms of intrinsic values, rather than current market values, the Agreement operates to prevent appraisals of bank assets in the examination process from being unduly influenced by transitory market conditions associated with fluctuations in economic activity. It also operates to minimize differences in the approach to the appraisal of bank assets as among examiners of the same or different supervisory agencies.

An attempt to relate and integrate bank examination standards to cyclical movements in the economy other than through the adoption of bank supervisory policies such as those embodied in the "Uniform Agreement" would seem to be neither feasible nor desirable. The frequency with which banks are examined varies as between bank supervisory agencies. All agencies change the sequence of examination from year to year to maintain an element of surprise and to obtain a clearer insight into the patterns of seasonal expansion and liquidation of bank portfolios than that afforded by periodic reports of condition. As a consequence, the intervals between successive examinations of an individual bank may vary from several months to approximately two years.

Any decision to complement changes in monetary policy by applying more rigorous or less rigorous appraisal standards in examinations, therefore, would result in the application of divergent standards of appraisal with respect to the same or similar types of assets in different banks, or over a period of time in the same bank. Such a policy might impair confidence in the nondiscriminatory characteristic of the examination and supervisory process.

In summary, as a general policy, bank examination and supervisory procedures consider the intrinsic value of assets and impose basically the same standards of appraisal regardless of fluctuations in economic conditions. Bank examination standards designed to be eased in periods of recession and tightened in boom periods, to complement similar changes in general monetary policies, would require substantial changes in this established approach to the appraisal process. Such shifts in standards would be extremely difficult to administer, and might not be in the best interests of either the banking system or the bank supervisory function. It is believed that the present supervisory policy based on intrinsic values and designed to maintain banking stability will tend to preserve a strong, viable, and competitive commercial banking system, and that efforts directed toward this end are the most constructive and worthwhile contribution that bank supervision can make in support of monetary policy.

QUESTION XXIV

How important are bank supervisory and examination policies in influencing the portfolio policies of commercial banks and the composition of bank assets? For example, are certain types of loans and investments considered inappropriate for banks, either altogether or beyond specific amounts? Can or should bank examination procedures be designed which facilitate economic growth? For instance, do present examination standards inhibit certain types of loans which could contribute to economic growth? Do they impede the free mobility of credit resources? Can or should they be designed to facilitate credit mobility to encourage its flow to highest priority users?

ANSWER XXIV

Summary

The influence of bank supervisory policies on the portfolio policies of commercial banks cannot be measured quantitatively. Other than for the enforcement of legal restrictions, in reviewing commercial bank assets supervisors and examiners are guided by broad banking principles regarding the quality, collectibility, and diversification of assets in relation to the deposit liabilities, liquidity, and capital adequacy of the particular bank.

It is not the function of bank supervision to attempt, through influence on the banker, to make funds more readily available for particular groups of borrowers or less available for others. The role of bank supervision is not to encourage or discourage banks in assuming credit risks but to apply standards of prudence in assessing credit risks which are taken. Due to the breadth of our markets for investments and loans, the fact that a particular investment or loan may not prudently be acquired by one bank does not mean that it will not be acquired by some other bank or other lender, or that economic growth will suffer.

The nature and extent of the influence of bank supervisory policies on the portfolio policies of commercial banks cannot be measured quantitatively. Moreover, in considering the above questions, a distinction should be made between (1) supervisory influence in preventing banks from acquiring assets which, if acquired, would be in violation of the statutes and regulations, and (2) supervisory influence in restraining banks from making loans or investments which, while within the broad limits of their legal authority, would not be desirable or prudent to acquire in light of their existing asset or liability structure. In this response, primary consideration is given to the second type of influence; also, no attempt is made to differentiate between bank examiners in the field and the follow-up activities by bank supervisory authorities.

Other than for the enforcement of legal restrictions, supervisory and examination activities with respect to the types and quality of commercial bank assets are concerned with the maintenance of solvent banks, a strong and viable banking system, and sound credit conditions. In reviewing the portfolios of banks, supervisors and examiners are guided by the following broad banking principles:

(1) The funds of banks should be invested in assets of good quality which afford reasonable assurance of ultimate collectibility and regularity of income. Moreover, the types of assets acquired need to bear a reasonable relationship with the nature of the business conducted by the bank, the type of customer served, and the locality.

(2) Diversification of bank assets by type and maturity is desirable to avoid undue concentration of risk. Where banks have large concentrations in local extensions of credit, diversification may be afforded through acceptable outside investments.

(3) Because of the special debtor-creditor relationship existing between banks and their depositors, the particular types and maturities of assets held by banks should take into account the nature of their deposit liabilities. That is, the assets of banks (except cash, bank balances, and amounts invested in essential physical facilities) need to have a maturity composition related to the character and composition of their deposit liabilities.

(4) The investment and lending policies of a bank should be formulated with a view to avoiding either continuous or excessive resort to borrowing by the bank.

(5) The capital structure of a bank should be adequate in relation to the character and condition of its assets and to its deposit liabilities and other corporate responsibilities. If a bank becomes under-capitalized, it may be faced with the alternatives of either (a) increasing its capital through the sale of additional shares, or (b) reducing its capital needs by reducing the risk or increasing the liquidity of its assets, or both.

(6) In general, a bank should have sufficient cash and readily marketable assets of high quality and short maturity to provide for current operating requirements and to offset any temporary or highly volatile deposits, whether in demand or time form. All other deposits should be invested in loans and other obligations with maturities so arranged that normal rotation will provide funds for substantial deposit withdrawals and for new loans. Due regard should also be given to maintaining reasonable ability to reinvest at prevailing interest levels in order that a satisfactory average rate of return may be realized over a period of time.

Privately owned banks naturally seek to invest their funds profitably and without abnormal risk of loss. It is not the function of bank supervision to attempt, through influence on the banker, to make funds more readily available for particular groups of borrowers or less available for other groups. In no case is a bank supervisory agency justified in encouraging a bank to undertake unreasonable risks in attempting to meet the credit needs of business, nor in discouraging particular extensions of credit unless such advances involve over-concentrations with respect to that bank, or other unsound banking practices which may contribute to endangering the safety of depositors' funds.

With respect to investment securities, bank supervisors give consideration to the matter of diversification as to industry and maturity, as well as credit quality. Consequently, criticism by supervisors may, to some extent, restrain bankers from making investments which in themselves would be acceptable but when added to the existing portfolio might result in unwarranted concentrations in long-term or medium-grade securities, or poor diversification as to industry or maturity.

Commercial banks, however, are only one of several kinds of purchasers in the market for investment securities, and any effect that commercial bank investment policies might have on issues of such securities is considerably modified by the activities of large members of other investors in these markets. Ordinarily when banks participate in the markets for investment securities it is to attain suitable liquidity, assure appropriate diversification, or obtain income on funds not currently employed in loans. Under the type of banking system in the United States, such participation will usually tend to be subordinated to the banks' primary functions of serving depositors and other types of borrowers.

Although the protection of depositors is a primary concern of supervisors, this does not mean that supervision is directed toward the elimination of all risk. All credit transactions necessarily involve some element of risk. Banks exist as credit institutions with the purpose of meeting the legitimate borrowing needs of the community, locally and at large. The role of bank supervision is not to prevent banks from taking credit risks but to apply standards of prudence in assessing the credit risks which are assumed.

Prudence in lending may tend to inhibit the making of loans by a particular bank in two general kinds of situations: (1) when credit-worthiness of individual loans is either clearly deficient or borderline, and (2) when the loans are individually credit-worthy but would represent undue concentrations of risk for a particular bank. However, if that particular bank does not make the loans in question, it does not necessarily follow that the loans will not be made by some other bank or other lender, or that economic growth would suffer. The correspondent banking system usually provides a reasonably satisfactory means of shifting loans of the second type to some other institution. The first type of loan presents more problems and deserves to be discussed in more detail.

Sound bank management and sound bank supervision, both of which apply similar lending standards, allow considerable latitude for financing the development of new enterprises. The most important requirement in such cases is the character and experience of the management of the new enterprise. Even if the new enterprise can provide relatively little capital, if it has suitable management it usually can obtain enough financing--frequently from banks--to get started on a modest scale and test the merits of the project. Such a modest beginning may be a positive advantage to a new enterprise by helping to limit the size and seriousness of the mistakes that often occur in any pioneering effort. Furthermore, new enterprises are often considerably strengthened by the sound financial and other policies that good bank management, reinforced by good bank supervision, attempts to get borrowers to follow.

Certain kinds of lending activities--certain types of consumer credit, for example--have not been pioneered as directly or as vigorously by banks as by some other lenders, and banks have sometimes tended to enter such fields only after others have developed them. As the principal source of the nation's money supply, it is proper that banks be circumspect about undertaking broad new lines of lending or investing. At relatively early stages of new ventures, it can be a sound division of functions for a finance company, manufacturer, or vendor to supply the specialized experience and some of the basic risk capital, while a bank supplies funds subject to less risk and also encourages the new enterprise to follow tested general principles of management and finance.

Unnecessary restrictions placed by law or supervisory action in the way of the lending process can, in times of depression, delay recovery. At such times bank supervisory agencies are alert to see that unwise or unnecessary restrictions on their part do not impede the revival of the economy. Looking backward, there seems to be good reason to believe that bankers and bank supervisors may have become too deeply concerned in the early 1930's about the collection of loans not considered prime, and unnecessarily rigid in their attitude toward new extensions of credit. The Revision in Bank Examination Procedure, or so-called "Uniform Agreement," of the three federal supervisory agencies and the Executive Committee of the National Association of Supervisors of State Banks (adopted in 1938 and amended slightly in 1949) was designed to further maintenance of economic stability through emphasis upon appraisal of bank assets in terms of intrinsic rather than current market values. It is believed that this agreement would have had a beneficial influence if it has been in effect in the early 1930's. Continued adherence to the principles of the "Uniform Agreement" will contribute to the maintenance of solvent banks, a strong and viable banking system, and the sound credit conditions essential to economic growth.

QUESTION XXV

What are the pros and cons of having the administrative responsibilities for bank examination and supervision remain, as at present, divided among a number of different authorities?

ANSWER XXV

Summary

Complete unification of bank examination and supervisory functions necessarily would have to take place under federal law and under either an existing or newly created federal agency. It presumably would involve termination or significant abridgment of the chartering and supervisory powers of the several states and would present, at least in theory, the following principal disadvantages:

(1) It would require drastic changes in the existing legal structure of commercial banking, as well as in bank examination and supervision;

(2) it would disrupt many existing relationships in the banking structure and in the administrative system of bank examination and supervision; and

(3) it would precipitate controversy on the grounds that it would (a) invade states' rights and be inconsistent with the principles of local self-government; (b) concentrate too much power in the federal government, and in one agency of that government; and (c) destroy essential "checks and balances" and benefits derived from the competitive interplay inherent in the present dual banking structure.

Some of the principal advantages, at least in theory, which might flow from giving a single authority administrative responsibility for bank examination and supervision would be:

(1) It would simplify the banking structure of the United States and the problems of regulating the banking system;

(2) it would eliminate any possible discrimination between different types of commercial banks and eliminate overlapping in the administration, interpretation, and enforcement of various banking laws and regulations;

(3) it would provide greater control over new bank charters, mergers, and establishment of branches; and

(4) it would facilitate mobilization of bank examination and supervisory resources to keep pace with the growth and complexity of commercial bank operations and the banking system as a whole.

In considering possible changes, it is well to bear in mind that our present system of commercial banking and bank supervision, including banks operating under state or federal charters, is the result of an evolutionary process extending over a period of almost one hundred years. There are at present some areas of overlap and duplication in functions essential to the discharge of examination and supervisory responsibilities. The common interests of bank supervisory agencies, however, have produced working arrangements by which much of the seeming duplication in activities is avoided.

There has never been a time in our history when one authority was charged with administrative responsibility for the examination and supervision of all commercial banks. Any proposal to consolidate such responsibility in one body would need to be appraised on the basis of whether the advantages would outweigh the disadvantages enough to warrant disrupting established relationships.

Before reviewing the pros and cons of centralizing administrative responsibilities for bank examination and bank supervision, it is desirable to comment briefly on the types, numbers, and deposits of commercial banks in the United States; the agencies now concerned with the examination and supervision of commercial banks; and the areas of cooperation between such agencies.

At present, from the standpoint of supervisory organizations, there are four classes of banks: national banks, state member banks, state nonmember insured banks, and state nonmember noninsured banks. As of December 31, 1959, there were 13,474 commercial banks in the United States and its territorial possessions operating a total of 23,126 banking offices and having total deposits of $219.9 billion. Of this number, all but 366 commercial banks, operating 408 offices and having deposits of $1.4 billion, were insured. Of the insured banks, 4,542 were national banks, operating 9,515 offices, and 1,688 were state member banks, operating 4,207 offices. These national and state member banks had total deposits of $119.6 and $65.1 billion, respectively, and their combined deposits represented 84 percent of the total deposits of all operating commercial banks. Insured nonmember commercial banks numbered 6,878, operated 8,996 offices, and had total deposits of $33.8 billion.

The authorities having administrative responsibilities for the examination and supervision of the four classes of commercial banks and the general scope of their activities at the present time are as follows:

1. The State Banking Authorities

The direct and primary responsibility for the examination and supervision of all state banks, whether members of the Federal Reserve System or not, and whether insured or not, rests with the supervisory authorities of the 50 states. State banks are chartered by the state, operate under the supervision of state authorities, and, in the event of liquidation, have their activities terminated in accordance with provisions of state law.

The number of examinations of each bank made by the various states varies from one to two annually. Examinations of insured banks usually are made jointly with the Federal Reserve banks or the Federal Deposit Insurance Corporation, depending on whether the particular bank is a member or nonmember insured bank. Non-insured banks are examined independently. Reports of examinations made by the state authorities are made available to the Federal supervisory agencies, and the latter agencies furnish copies of their reports to the state authorities.

2. The Comptroller of the Currency

The Comptroller of the Currency is under the law directly and primarily responsible for the examination and supervision of all national banks. National banks obtain their charters from the Comptroller and are liquidated under the provisions of the National Bank Act, administered by the Comptroller.

National banks are examined at least three times every two years and reports of such examinations are furnished the Federal Reserve banks and made available to the Board of Governors and the Federal Deposit Insurance Corporation.

3. The Federal Reserve System

The Federal Reserve has no direct power with respect to chartering or liquidating banks. Although authorized to examine all member banks, both state and national, as a matter of practice neither the Federal Reserve banks nor the Board of Governors examines national banks, since the Comptroller of the Currency is directly charged with that responsibility under the law.

All state member banks are examined by the Federal Reserve banks on behalf of the Board of Governors by examiners approved by the Board. It is the established policy to make at least one regular examination of each state member bank during each calendar year, with such additional examinations of any particular bank as may be desirable. These examinations usually are made jointly with the state banking authorities and in all jurisdictions reports of one agency are made available to the other.

4. The Federal Deposit Insurance Corporation

The Federal Deposit Insurance Corporation regularly examines all insured state nonmember banks, usually on a joint basis with their respective state authorities. Examination reports are exchanged with state authorities and made available to the interested federal bank supervisory agencies.

Since all member banks are insured, the Federal Deposit Insurance Corporation has access to reports of examinations made by the Comptroller of the Currency and the Federal Reserve banks. The Corporation also is empowered to make special examinations of national banks and state member banks whenever such an examination is necessary to determine the condition of any such bank for insurance purposes. However, such examinations have been infrequent and have been made only in anticipation of financial assistance by the Corporation in a rehabilitation program or where a bank desired to continue as an insured bank after withdrawal from membership in the Federal Reserve System.

Inasmuch as the examination and supervision of the various classes of commercial banks are divided among the different state and federal supervisory authorities, there are unavoidably some areas of overlapping and duplication in functions essential to the discharge of their respective responsibilities. Nevertheless, through arrangement of joint examinations, the waiver of authority to make examinations, and the exchange of reports of examination, much of the seeming duplication of examination and supervisory activities is averted in practice by common interests that result in reasonably close working arrangements among the several authorities.

In addition to the foregoing accommodations, the supervisory authorities also have cooperated in the following respects:

(a) Adoption of generally uniform condition and earnings and dividend reports;

(b) compilation of comprehensive statistical data relating to banking institutions;

(c) standardization of examination reports forms;

(d) adoption of the so-called "Uniform Agreement" with respect to the treatment accorded certain types of assets in reports of examination;

(e) submission of formal reports on the competitive factors involved in mergers and consolidations, as required by statute, and informal clearance with respect to new charters and branches;

(f) exchange of information with respect to criminal violations; and

(g) the joint establishment and operation of the Inter-Agency Bank Examination School for training and developing bank examining personnel.

Furthermore, representatives of the three federal supervisory authorities and the National Association of Supervisors of State Banks also meet on call to discuss and devise mutually acceptable approaches to existing and developing problems in the field of bank examination and supervision. For example, as an outgrowth of these meetings, the federal and state authorities issued a joint statement with respect to bank capitalization, meetings by examiners with boards of directors, problem bank situations, and internal audits and controls of banking institutions, with a view to coordinating practices in these fields of mutual or joint responsibility.

There has never been a time in our history when one authority was charged with administrative responsibility for the examination and supervision of all commercial banks. Since such banks are an integral part of our banking and monetary establishment, as well as a primary source of strength and sustenance for our whole operating and expanding economy, it would seem at first glance that centralization of the examining and supervisory function would be highly desirable and in the public interest. However, it must be borne in mind that complete unification of these functions necessarily would have to take place under federal law and under either an existing federal agency or a newly created one; presumably, this would involve termination or significant abridgment of the chartering and supervisory powers of the several states.

Some of the principal advantages which might be expected, at least in theory, to flow from the centralization of responsibility for bank examination and supervision in a single authority would be:

(1) It would simplify the banking structure of the United States and the problems of regulating the banking system;

(2) it would eliminate any possible discrimination between different types of commercial banks and eliminate overlapping jurisdictions in the administration, interpretation, and enforcement of various banking laws and regulations;

(3) it would provide greater control over the issuance of new bank charters and over applications to merge with or absorb banks and to establish branches. This would facilitate, among other things, determinations as to the lessening of competition or the creation of monopolies in commercial banking;

(4) it would provide a basis for more efficient and economic gathering and processing of banking statistics; and

(5) it would facilitate mobilization of bank examination and supervisory resources to keep pace with the growth and complexity of commercial bank operations and the banking system as a whole, and thereby contribute to a better coordinated, more efficient, and stronger bank supervisory authority.

On the other hand, some of the principal disadvantages, at least in theory, of centralizing responsibility for the examination and supervision of commercial banks in a single authority might be:

(1) It would require drastic changes in the existing legal structure of commercial banking, as well as in bank examination and supervision;

(2) it would disrupt many existing relationships in the banking structure and in the administrative system of bank examination and supervision; and

(3) it would precipitate controversy on the grounds that it would (a) invade states' rights and be inconsistent with the principles of local self-government; (b) concentrate too much power in the federal government, and in one agency of that government; and (c) destroy essential "checks and balances" and benefits derived from the competitive interplay inherent in the present dual banking structure.

It has sometimes been suggested that some of the advantages mentioned above could be obtained if all present federal bank examination and supervisory functions were unified in a single agency, and that this might be done without making any change in the primary authority of the several states. Such a rearrangement of only federal responsibilities would involve less drastic changes in the existing commercial banking structure than would more sweeping proposals for centralization; but it would likely be subject to many of the other disadvantages outlined above.

In considering possible changes, it is well to bear in mind that the present system of commercial banking and bank supervision has evolved over a period of almost a hundred years dating from the passage of the National Bank Act of 1863. It was substantially modified and improved by the passage of the Federal Reserve Act in 1913, and by the Banking Act of 1933, which created the Federal Deposit Insurance Corporation and included the basic provisions of law ultimately embodied in the Federal Deposit Insurance Act of 1950.

The evolutionary process of modification and improvement has resulted in an interchange of banking and bank supervisory concepts originating both at the state and federal levels. Although the process has been slow and not infrequently carried forward in what could be described as the method of trial and error, it has had as its objective the creation and maintenance of a strong, viable, and competitive commercial banking system capable of continuous adaptation to meet the changing conditions of a growing economy. The success of the evolutionary process must be measured by the present strength and prospects of our commercial banking system

and our economy. Any proposal to consolidate all banking supervision and regulation in one body would need to be appraised on the
basis of whether the advantages would sufficiently outweigh the
disadvantages to warrant disrupting established relationships.

Part Two

THE TREASURY ANSWERS

QUESTION I

How much should fiscal policy be relied upon to achieve
our national economic objectives among varying circumstances?

ANSWER I

An appropriate fiscal policy -- using the term as the over-all
relationship between federal expenditures and revenues -- is fundamental in this nation's efforts to achieve the maximum sustainable
rate of economic growth, maintain abundant employment opportunities, and assure reasonable stability in the value of the dollar. Although informed observers generally agree as to the strategic importance of fiscal policy in our efforts to achieve our economic
objectives, considerable disagreement exists with respect to the
manner in which such policies should be formulated and applied.

A sizable group of economists argues that fiscal (or "budget")
policy, in coordination with monetary and debt management policies,
should be used strongly and overtly to counter cyclical trends. According to this view, a period of actual or threatening inflation,
arising from pressures of demand, would call for a substantial surplus in the federal budget. This surplus would be achieved by an
increase in tax rates (or imposition of new taxes), by a decline in
expenditures, or by some combination of the two. Such a surplus,
it is argued, would help dampen total demand for current output,
inasmuch as federal government spending would fall short of revenues.

Consistent with this countercyclical approach, the program would
be consciously reversed during a recession. Reductions in tax rates

and increases in expenditures would contribute to a large budget deficit. Such a deficit, it is argued, would help to enlarge total demand for current output and promote recovery, inasmuch as federal government spending would exceed revenues.

Although this approach to the problem of countering cyclical swings in order to promote sustainable growth has considerable merit in principle, it has some serious shortcomings in practice. Such shortcomings do not involve the desirability of achieving budget surpluses in prosperous periods and of shifting toward deficits in recessions but relate instead to the difficulties encountered in the use of budget policy in the described manner.

Important practical difficulties arise from the fact that decisions as to taxes and spending programs often, and quite properly, reflect many factors other than broad economic considerations. Moreover, the timely use of budget policy as a conscious countercyclical weapon is also complicated by the fact that authority over taxation and spending is not centered in any one branch of the government but is the joint responsibility of the Executive and the Congress.

Furthermore, experience in the postwar period indicates that it is much easier to achieve a deficit in a recession than a surplus in a boom. Large deficits in recessions, only partially offset by modest surpluses in periods of high and rising activity, complicate the task of achieving sustainable growth in two ways. First, the net deficit of the federal government over a period of years is likely to add to inflationary pressures and to increase the burden borne by monetary policy in promoting our economic goals. The lack of adequate surpluses in the prosperous years following World War II -- resulting in an increase of almost $30 billion in the public debt since 1946 -- has meant that monetary policy has been called upon to bear more than its proper share of the burden in avoiding inflation and promoting sustainable economic growth. This unavoidably heavy reliance on monetary policy may have contributed to wider swings in interest rates and capital values than would have been necessary if budgetary surpluses had been adequate.

In the second place, the complications that may arise in managing a growing public debt, reflecting net deficits over a period of years, are likely to impair further the flexible and timely administration of monetary policy. It is probable that excessive expansion in the highly liquid short-term portion of the federal debt could be prevented more readily if the debt were steady or declining rather than growing. If the public debt tended to grow in size and to become constantly shorter in maturity, Treasury financings would occur more frequently and in larger amounts, thereby tending to disrupt the Government securities market and also to restrict the freedom of action of the monetary authorities.

A large public debt can place a burden on future generations. Although the real cost of government spending (in terms of the resources absorbed in government use), must be borne largely by the current generation, the economic effects of managing a large public debt and the impact of the taxes that must be levied to service it can be shifted to future generations. The transfer operation involved in interest payments on the debt (now about $9 billion per year) is hardly frictionless; it involves additional budget expenditures and, of primary importance, has a significant effect on incentives in the private sector of the economy. We cannot, therefore, accept the false comfort of the view that, simply because "we owe most of the debt to ourselves," a large public debt is of no real economic concern.

Attempts to vary tax rates and spending to help smooth the business cycle may well have perverse effects. Changes in fiscal policy may sometimes take so long to plan, legislate, and put into effect that many months may elapse from the time the need for action becomes clear until the change in budget position affects total spending. By the time the actions become effective, the economy may have changed radically, with the result that large deficits may have their major impact during periods of rising business activity and surpluses may be achieved when business activity is declining. This criticism applies especially to large federal spending programs which require lengthy periods for planning and for completion. The suggestion has been made that the federal government build up a backlog of such projects which could be initiated on short notice. While this proposal has some merit in principle, the practical difficulties involved are formidable. Once the basic plans for construction had been completed, local pressures would be exceedingly strong to embark upon such projects, regardless of the state of the economy. Moreover, it is highly doubtful that such programs could be used in a truly countercyclical manner, inasmuch as they would probably be very difficult, if not impossible, to discontinue once the need for additional stimulation to the economy had passed.

In view of these considerations, any overt fiscal policy action to dampen cyclical fluctuations should be confined primarily to variations in tax rates rather than changes in public spending programs; but even this approach involves some important practical difficulties, stemming largely from the nature in which tax legislation is conceived and passed under our form of government. Some observers have suggested that this difficulty could be overcome through administrative variation in tax rates to counter cyclical trends, such as vesting additional authority in the President. Such proposals do not seem to be feasible, or desirable, under our form of government. The delegation of such great authority to one man, by transferring a traditional legislative function to the Executive, would not only represent a radical change in our governmental system but would also greatly increase the opportunity for use of the taxing power for political purposes.

These considerations do not imply that our only alternative is to attempt to achieve a rigorous balance in the budget, year in and year out. The goal of a surplus in the budget during prosperous periods and, on the average, over a longer period of time also is highly desirable. Moreover, in view of large automatic swings in tax receipts and spending over the business cycle, budget deficits of moderate size are probably unavoidable -- and, indeed, desirable -- during periods of declining business activity.

Consequently, serious consideration should be given to operating under some variation of the stabilizing budget proposal; year in and year out, budget policy would be geared to the attainment of a surplus under conditions of strong business activity and of relatively complete use of economic resources. On this basis, during a recession, the automatic decline in revenues and increase in expenditures -- reflecting in part the operation of the so-called "built-in stabilizers" -- would generate a moderate deficit. In prosperous periods, tax receipts would automatically rise, and certain types of spending would contract, producing a surplus. Then, over the period of a complete business cycle, a surplus for debt retirement could be achieved without the disrupting effects of attempts to balance the budget in recessions. Variations in tax rates or spending programs for cyclical purposes would thus be kept to a minimum, although conditions might well arise in which such variations would be desirable.

The technique of aiming for moderate surpluses in inflationary periods and then of permitting automatic declines in revenues and increases in spending to provide the major contribution of fiscal policy in fighting recessions has been criticized on two bases. In the first place, it is sometimes argued that the automatic shift in the budget position during a recession will not create a sufficiently large deficit to be meaningful in promoting economic recovery. Before this criticism can be evaluated, it is important to understand that the impact of fiscal policy on over-all demand during a given period of time should be measured not by the absolute size of a federal surplus or deficit but by the extent of the net shift in the government's fiscal position during that period of time. Thus, an automatic shift from a $6 billion surplus to a balanced position, or from a $3 billion surplus to a $3 billion deficit, provides approximately the same amount of stimulation to total demand as a shift from a balanced budget to a $6 billion deficit, or from a $2 billion deficit to an $8 billion deficit. And it should again be emphasized that, as long as the avoidance of inflation continues to be our major long-run stabilization problem, the achievement of a net surplus over a period of time greatly reduces the burden that must be borne by monetary policy in combating inflation. Moreover, the achievement of such a surplus would minimize difficulties involved in debt management, inasmuch as the public debt gradually would be decreasing rather than rising.

A second major criticism of the stabilizing budget approach (in which primary reliance is placed upon the operation of the built-in economic stabilizers) emphasizes the time required to move automatically from a surplus to a deficit in the federal budget. Again, primary emphasis should be placed on the extent of the net shift in the budget position rather than the early attainment of a deficit in the budget. Moreover, experience with the built-in stabilizers in 1957-58 indicates clearly that automatic shifts toward deficit in a recession do indeed occur rather quickly and in large amounts. It should be recalled that, during this period, the peak of business activity preceding the recession was reached in the third quarter of 1957. The trough of the recession was reached early in the second quarter of 1958. Throughout this period, the built-in budget stabilizers were operating strongly, as is shown in the attached table.

Between the third and fourth quarters of 1957, the federal government's position on national income and product account (the most useful measure of the contribution of fiscal policy to over-all demand) moved from a net surplus of $2.6 billion to a net deficit of $0.9 billion, representing a total expansive shift of $3.5 billion.[1] This shift occurred even though federal purchases of goods and services declined by $600 million. The main factors contributing to the movement from net surplus to net deficit were a $2.1 billion decline in corporate income tax accruals and a $1.2 billion rise in transfer payments to persons, particularly unemployment compensation.

It was not until the first quarter of 1958 that overt fiscal actions to stimulate recovery, including a tax reduction and a large build-up in federal spending programs, came under serious discussion. (In its Report dated February 27, 1958, the Joint Economic Committee recommended an acceleration of certain federal spending programs, but counseled against a tax reduction at that time.) By this time, however, the federal government's net deficit on income and product account (on an annual rate basis) had risen to $8.1 billion, representing a net expansive shift of $10.7 billion from the third quarter of 1957. Although government purchases of goods and services had risen by $600 million over the period as a whole, the major factors in the $10.7 billion shift toward deficit were declines of $4.9 billion in corporate tax accruals and $1.4 billion in personal income tax receipts and a $2.4 billion rise in transfer payments to persons.

---

[1]All figures cited are seasonally adjusted annual rates.

It is also significant that the major built-in stabilizers (individual and corporate income taxes) reversed their movement in the second quarter of 1958; which marked the low point of the recession, and rose strongly thereafter. Transfer payments to persons continued to rise through the third quarter, but declined in succeeding quarters. This experience indicates that the built-in stabilizers react quickly at both the downward and upward turning points of the business cycle. On the other hand, it should be noted that federal spending for goods and services and grants-in-aid to state and local governments, reflecting the major overt spending programs to counter recessionary trends, did not rise significantly above the levels of the third quarter of 1957 until after the trough of the recession had been reached in April 1958.

Thus, the experience in the recession of 1957-58 lends strong support to the judgment that automatic shifts in the federal government's fiscal position can provide a powerful and timely stabilizing force in our free enterprise economy. Moreover, this experience demonstrates the slowness with which overt fiscal actions operate and the possibility that they will have perverse consequences because their effectiveness is delayed and their reversal is difficult. If the tax cuts or speed-up in federal spending programs advocated by some observers in early 1958 had been put into effect, this perversity, other things equal, would have been even more pronounced and the budget deficit for fiscal year 1959, which totaled $12.4 billion, would have been considerably larger. Although situations may well arise in which discretionary changes in tax and spending policies will be desirable in order to help dampen pronounced cyclical swings, it seems clear that we should continue to place major reliance on the built-in flexibility in the federal fiscal position.

QUESTION II

Should changes in the tax structure be made for the purpose of increasing the effectiveness of the financial system?

ANSWER II

The basic function of the tax system is to provide revenues to meet budgetary requirements and to distribute as equitably as possible the burden of the cost of government. In the early days of our

TABLE I-1

Federal Government Receipts and Expenditures on National Income and Product Accounts*

(Billions of dollars at seasonally adjusted annual rates)

	1957		1958			
	3rd quarter	4th quarter	1st quarter	2nd quarter	3rd quarter	4th quarter
Federal government receipts	$82.5	$79.7	$75.4	$76.5	$79.4	$83.1
Personal tax and nontax receipts	37.6	37.4	36.2	36.3	37.1	37.4
Corporate profits tax accruals	20.2	18.1	15.3	16.1	18.1	21.0
Indirect business tax and nontax accruals	12.3	12.0	11.7	12.0	11.7	12.1
Contributions for social insurance	12.4	12.2	12.2	12.1	12.5	12.6
Federal government expenditures	79.9	80.6	83.5	87.4	90.0	91.4
Purchases of goods and services	50.0	49.4	50.6	51.8	53.7	54.3
Transfer payments	17.2	18.7	19.6	21.7	22.2	22.2
To persons	16.0	17.2	18.3	20.4	21.0	20.6
Foreign (net)	1.2	1.4	1.2	1.3	1.2	1.6
Grants-in-aid to state and local governments	4.2	4.2	4.8	5.4	5.6	6.0
Net interest paid	5.8	5.7	5.6	5.5	5.5	5.7
Subsidies less current surplus of government enterprises	2.8	2.6	2.9	3.0	3.0	3.0
Surplus or deficit (-) on income and product account	2.6	-.9	-8.1	-10.9	-10.6	-8.2
Cumulative change from 3rd quarter of 1957	--	-3.5	-10.7	-13.5	-13.2	-10.8

*Data as of November 1960.

federal income tax, revenue legislation was primarily directed to obtaining the necessary funds for the operation of the government through tax laws which were designed to be certain and simple, to impose the burden equitably, and to permit the collection of revenues with a minimum of cost. Tax rates were low and the total federal revenues constituted such a small proportion of the Gross National Product that only limited attention was required to be given to the question of the comparative economic effects of a particular tax. Today there is necessarily a different emphasis in appraising tax legislation. The tax structure must also be evaluated in terms of its impact on the economy, including the financial and credit system.

The present magnitude of the tax burden emphasizes the importance of the tax structure to the effectiveness of the financial system and the general performance of the economy. In the current fiscal year (1960-61), it is estimated that the federal government will collect from individuals and businesses about $97.1 billion, or an amount equal to about one-fifth of the Gross National Product and one-fourth of the national income. The bulk of this sum represents amounts collected to pay for the 1961 Budget expenditures. The balance consists of taxes collected to maintain the trust funds, through which the social security and highway construction programs are financed. In addition state and local taxes together add almost $40 billion to the nation's tax bill.

In discussing possible future changes in the tax structure, it is important to recognize that the Internal Revenue Code of 1954 made many structural changes which reduced the deterrent effects of the federal tax system on the economy. These structural changes included more realistic depreciation allowances, more liberal carryover of business losses, better integration of corporation and individual taxes through partial relief from double taxation, more realistic and favorable treatment of earnings accumulations by closely held business, sounder rules for the treatment of corporate distributions, as well as many others. These structural changes reduced taxes annually by $1.4 billion. Other changes in 1954 brought the total reduction to $7.4 billion annually. These changes included the elimination of the excess profits tax which reduced the nation's tax burden by $2 billion; reductions in excise taxes which accounted for $1 billion; and reductions in individual income tax rates which amounted to $3 billion.

In addition to the $3 billion reduction resulting from lower individual rates, individuals shared to a substantial extent in the savings from the excise tax reductions as well as in the benefits provided by the structural changes in the tax laws. These changes allowed individuals to retain more of their earnings. Some of the changes in par-

Substantial relief for small business was provided by the Small Business Tax Revision Act of 1958, including more liberal loss deductions for investors in certain small business corporations, a further extension of the net operating loss carryback to three years, an additional first year depreciation allowance, an option to pay estate tax attributable to a small business interest over a period of ten years, and an increase in the specific exemption of earnings of a small business which may be accumulated without being subject to tax on improper accumulation of surplus. In addition, legislation in 1958 permitted certain small corporations at their option to be taxed much like partnerships, thus removing the double tax on dividends. This option also helped to eliminate tax considerations as a factor in the choice of legal form in conducting business.

All these tax changes are believed to have made a substantial contribution to our economic development in recent years. To meet the needs of a fast changing economy during the next decade, we will have to review the tax system methodically to determine possible changes which might help to reduce the adverse or distorting effects of taxes on capital markets and on the allocation of resources and also to determine those changes which will encourage individuals to invest their savings in new and expanding enterprises.

In its statement on the mission and policy issues assigned to Task Force B, the Commission on Money and Credit cites a number of specific structural areas which are of special interest in considering the effect of the tax structure on the flow of savings, on the mobility of capital, and on business financing. Some of these areas as well as related topics are discussed briefly below.

Capital Gains

Capital gains have traditionally borne a lower tax because they have special characteristics and because taxation has a deterrent effect on the sale of appreciated investments. Even the present reduced rate of tax on capital gains has various undesirable results, including a freezing effect on the sale of capital assets and on the flow of investment funds. The proper tax treatment of capital gains remains an important and complex problem involving matters of definition, holding periods, loss offsets, realization rules, and many others, as well as the applicable rates of tax.

Discussions of the capital gains problem frequently assume that capital gains arise mainly through the appreciation of securities or real estate. Such investments are important sources of capital gains. Over the years, however, capital gains treatment has been accorded to a considerable number of special forms of income. There are proposals to extend similar treatment to still other forms of income. In the area of corporate distributions, there are problems of distinguishing between dividends which are taxable as ordi-

nary income and the return of investment on liquidation of an enterprise which is treated as capital gain. Any basic change in the structure of the capital gains tax, such as a substantial reduction in the
tax to minimize the so-called "locked-in" effect on realized gains,
would add to the pressures and to tax avoidance problems in this
area.

To minimize the "locked-in" effect of the tax on realized gains,
various proposals have been made to defer the tax on realized gains
which are reinvested in capital assets. This type of proposal, generally termed the "roll-over" approach, has some precedent in the
existing tax deferment provisions for reinvestment of funds derived
from involuntary conversions and for the replacement of a personal
residence. Moreover, a similar approach has been used recently in
connection with the advance refunding operations undertaken by the
Treasury in June and September 1960, as discussed in the reply to
Question 5. However, extension of the "roll-over" approach to other
assets would involve many difficulties of practical application.

Depreciation

Depreciation allowances are an important source of funds for
business capital expenditures. Corporate depreciation is nearly
twice the amount of retained corporate earnings at present levels.
Both the adequacy of depreciation funds and their continuous flow
into investment are important factors in our efforts to achieve
balanced economic growth. The Treasury is in favor of liberalizing
business approaches to depreciation for tax purposes; the question
is how to achieve such liberalization. Since significant short-run
revenue effects are involved in the timing of depreciation, one of
the major problems in speeding up depreciation allowances is how
to minimize short-run revenue losses.

The Treasury is convinced that liberalized depreciation procedures can make a major contribution in neutralizing the deterrent
effects of high tax rates on investment. Properly designed liberalized
depreciation would have the special characteristic of providing its
benefits to those who invest in productive plant and equipment, which
in turn plays a key role in the growth of productivity. It would be
of special significance to many small, new, and growing businesses.

Liberalized depreciation allowances would raise the level of
investment in plant and equipment both immediately and over the
long run. This result, with its accompanying increase in employment
and productivity, is a basic objective of depreciation reform. Since
this form of tax revision would be expected to stimulate business
capital expenditures for modernization and cost cutting, it would also
tend to offset somewhat the fluctuations in capital expenditures for
expansion. This increased emphasis on modernization spending in

all of the varying phases of the economic cycle would not only contribute to the production of better products at lower costs but would
also help stabilize employment inasmuch as total business capital
expenditures would be less subject to wide cyclical swings.

Important improvements in depreciation allowances were made
in the 1954 Code and in the Small Business Tax Revision Act of
1958. In addition to these legislative changes, the Treasury has made
significant changes in administrative policy in the past several years
that provide greater recognition to technological improvements and
rapid economic changes in the determination of obsolescence and
depreciation rates. Under the new policy, the Internal Revenue Service will not disturb depreciation deductions unless there is a clear
and convincing basis for change.

Earlier this year (1960) the President recommended to the Congress legislation which would treat the income from the sale of depreciable business property as ordinary income, rather than as a
capital gain, to the extent of the depreciation deduction previously
taken on the property. An important objective of such legislation was
to make it possible for revenue agents to accept more readily business judgments of the taxpayers as to the useful life of depreciable
property. With the possibility removed of converting ordinary income into capital gain through excessive depreciation deductions,
depreciation would then be primarily a matter of timing. In the
absence of such corrective change in the capital gain rules, administrative decisions to permit faster depreciation would not only impair revenues but also encourage artificial and wasteful transactions
in depreciable property. Problems of equity would also arise.

The proposed legislation on capital gains would facilitate better
administration of the existing law and would also contribute to a
better climate in which to consider further legislation.

The Treasury is now conducting a survey of the depreciation
practices and opinions of American business. This study, in which
the congressional tax committees have expressed interest, is designed to obtain a better factual basis on which to evaluate further
proposed changes for the liberalization of depreciation allowances.

Double Taxation of Dividends

The 1954 Internal Revenue Code provided partial relief from
double taxation of dividends through an individual dividends-received
exclusion and credit. In so doing, it recognized the fact that under
the existing tax structure earnings of a corporation are taxed twice
-- once as corporate income and again as individual income when
paid out as dividends to stockholders. This double taxation results
from the fact that dividends, unlike wages or interest, do not

constitute a deduction to the corporation. In spite of some uncertainty about the incidence of the corporation income tax, there is a consensus that some part of its aggregate burden rests on the corporation, thus making dividend income subject in fact to some degree of double taxation.

In addition to the question of fairness involved, this double taxation is believed to have had undesirable effects on equity investment and on the choice of corporate management as between debt and equity financing.

The present provisions for partial relief from double taxation are a modest step toward correcting these problems. In recent years proposals have been considered by the Congress to repeal the existing partial relief from double taxation. The Treasury has opposed such legislation.

Withholding on Dividends and Interest

During the 86th Congress the Senate Finance Committee instructed the staff of the Joint Committee on Internal Revenue Taxation, in cooperation with the Treasury, to study the possibility of withholding tax on dividend and interest income as a means of dealing with the underreporting of these types of income on tax returns. Studies to date indicate that it would be extremely difficult, if not impractical, to institute an adequate withholding system for interest payments at this time. While the mechanics of withholding are less difficult for dividends, here, too, there are a number of difficult problems.

A significant portion of dividend and interest payments is received by individuals not required to file income tax returns, nontaxable individuals filing returns, and tax-exempt organizations. Withholding would work a hardship on these groups, particularly for elderly and retired persons, many of whom are in the low-income brackets and would not owe any tax. They would have to apply for refunds and would undoubtedly experience some delay in receiving their full income.

From the standpoint of proper administration, a withholding system would appear to require dividend and interest payers to furnish a form similar to the W-2 form used with wages. However, this would impose heavy burdens upon payers of dividends and interest and would add appreciably to the cost of dividend and interest disbursements. The increased costs would be particularly significant where the amount of these payments to individual depositors or stockholders is small. In many instances there are interposed between the payer and the recipient a number of levels or tiers, such as transfer agents, nominees and fiduciaries. In addition, there is a large turnover in shareholder accounts.

Without a W-2 type form, the Internal Revenue Service would be faced with a serious problem. The Service would no doubt be pressured to make refunds promptly, as in the case of wages, but without the benefit of a simple check against the taxpayer's copy of the withholding form and without time to make an audit of the claimant's tax return.

The development and utilization of electronic data processing machines, which will facilitate the Service's matching of information returns filed by payers of dividends and interest against the returns of taxpayers, may provide the solution to the problem of underreporting. Or, if withholding is considered advisable, these facilities will make it more practical than at the present time.

Much of the gap in reporting of dividends and interest appears due to negligence, although some of the failure to report may be willful. The Treasury last year (1959) called upon many groups active in the dividend and interest field to cooperate in an educational program designed to improve voluntary compliance in the reporting of dividend and interest income. Excellent cooperation was given by corporations, banks, and individuals. In addition, the Department of Justice is cooperating with the Service in a vigorous enforcement program. There is evidence of the program's success from District Directors' offices, from examination of selected tax returns before and after the program was initiated, and from the increase in tax receipts from individuals on nonwithheld income.

Deductibility of Interest

Proposals to disallow the deduction of interest under the federal corporate income tax have been made from time to time over the years. Among other related objectives, this type of proposal is intended to broaden the corporate income tax base, increase revenues, and discourage debt financing so as to promote a more recession-proof financial structure for corporate business. More recently, suggestions have been made to disallow the interest deduction as a means of increasing the cost of borrowing and thus reinforcing monetary policies.

Since the income tax should generally be neutral in its treatment of various forms of legitimate business expense, there would be serious doubt as to the desirability of instituting this kind of tax change for purposes of monetary or credit control. There would also appear to be questions as to the effectiveness of the plan as a credit control device. The proposal would apparently enlarge the area of double taxation of corporate earnings to include nondeductible interest. Thus the disallowance of the interest deduction would render debt financing unattractive to both borrower and lender, since common stockholders would in effect be required to absorb the tax burden on income paid to bondholders while the security of a loan would be reduced because of the prior tax load. There would appear to be doubt whether the resulting reduced level of borrowing would be more responsive to increases or decreases in interest rates. Even if such a plan served to discourage borrowing, the further question is posed: would it necessarily accomplish the underlying objective of restraining business expenditures during periods of inflationary pressures, whether financed by equity issues or borrowed funds?

QUESTION III

Does the present size of the federal debt threaten the attainment of our national objectives so that the government should strive to reduce it?

ANSWER III

Any judgment concerning the appropriate size of the federal debt relates primarily to fiscal policy, inasmuch as surpluses in the federal budget result in a declining debt and deficits result in a rising debt. As was emphasized in the reply to Question 1, an appropriate fiscal policy would result in net surpluses in the budget over the full period of the business cycle, which would be reflected in a gradually declining public debt. This, in turn, would enable monetary policy and debt management to make a maximum contribution toward our national economic objectives.

Although the absolute size of the federal debt ($286.5 billion on June 30, 1960) does not in itself seriously threaten the attainment of our national economic objectives, it is important to recognize (as discussed in the reply to Question 1) that a large debt involves an economic burden resulting from the taxes that must be levied to cover the interest payments on the debt. The fact that interest payments are transfer payments, rather than those which exhaust resources, does not alter the fact that such expenditures must be financed by the federal government, either through taxation or borrowing.

From the standpoint of debt management, the absolute size of the federal debt, although important, is at the present time less significant than its unbalanced maturity structure. As is emphasized in the reply to Question 5, the concentration of the marketable debt in securities of relatively short maturity can interfere with the use of monetary and debt management policies as instruments of economic stabilization. Frequent and large-sized Treasury financings--the corollary of a large debt unduly concentrated in short maturities -- make debt management more difficult and interfere with effective monetary policy actions.

QUESTION IV

How much should debt management policy be relied upon to achieve our national economic objectives under varying circumstances?

ANSWER IV

The ability of the American economy to achieve our national economic objectives, namely, to sustain orderly growth without inflation, to generate increased employment, to provide sufficient real capital to finance expansion, and to function as a source of strength for the entire free world -- all of this depends on the maintenance of responsible financial policies. Debt management is one of the three main links in the chain of federal financial responsibility. The two strongest links in this chain are a sound fiscal policy -- in terms of the relationship between revenues and expenditures -- and two, flexible monetary policy administered independently within government. Without strength in these areas there is little that debt management alone can do. Combined with effective fiscal and monetary policies, however, appropriate debt management can contribute substantially to our over-all financial strength. Inappropriate debt management inordinately increases the burdens on fiscal and monetary policy.

Debt management policy has three major objectives. First, management of the debt should be conducted in such a way as to contribute to an orderly growth of the economy without inflation. In a period of rapid expansion accompanied by inflationary pressures, as much of the debt as is practicable should be placed outside of the commercial banks (apart from temporary bank underwriting) and should include a reasonable volume of intermediate- and longer-term securities. In a recessionary period particular care must be taken

THE TREASURY ANSWERS

to exercise restraint in the amount of long-term securities issued in order not to pre-empt an undue amount of the long-term investment funds needed to support an expansion of the economy. A related aim should be to minimize, as far as possible, the frequency of Treasury borrowings so as to interfere as little as possible with necessary Federal Reserve actions or with corporate, municipal, and mortgage financing.

A second important objective of Treasury debt management is the achievement of a balanced maturity structure of the debt, one that is tailored to the needs of our economy for a sizable volume of short-term instruments and also includes a reasonable amount of inter-mediate- and long-term securities. There must be continuous efforts to issue long-term securities to offset the shortening of maturity caused by the lapse of time, which otherwise results in an excessively large volume of highly liquid short-term debt.

A third objective of debt management relates to borrowing costs. While primary weight must be given to the two objectives just noted, the Treasury, like any other borrower, should try to borrow as cheaply as possible. Unlike other borrowers, however, the Treasury must consider the impact of its actions on financial markets and the economy as a whole. Consequently, the aim of keeping borrowing costs at a minimum must be balanced against broader considerations of the public interest. (For further discussion see the reply to Question VI.)

These several objectives are not easily reconcilable at all times; nor can a priority be assigned to one or another of them under all circumstances.

There is some merit, for example, in the view that Treasury debt management policy should be geared solely to cyclical considerations -- pressing long-term securities on the market to absorb investment funds when the economy is expanding and, conversely, issuing highly liquid short-term securities in a period of recession. Yet in practice it has proved both impracticable and undesirable to adhere strictly to this view in disregard of other considerations. The Treasury's first obligation is to secure the funds needed to meet the government's fiscal requirements; these requirements cannot be postponed. A pressing need for cash may force it to market short-term issues even when the economy is expanding rapidly. The constant shortening in the maturity of the public debt, however, forces the Treasury to take advantage of every reasonable opportunity to issue long-term securities despite the cyclical aspect. From a purely housekeeping standpoint the Treasury needs to do some funding of short-term debt into longer-term securities whenever market conditions permit.

Similar difficulties arise with respect to following only the objective of keeping borrowing costs as low as possible. Any gain in terms of interest cost must be weighed against the loss in terms of economic effects. For example, aggressive issuance of long-term securities in recessions, when interest costs are low, would absorb too large a part of the investment funds needed elsewhere for recovery and could even prevent desirable reductions in interest rates; it would unduly increase the burden on monetary policy and necessitate much greater monetary ease, complicating the subsequent problem of curbing the excesses that may develop in a boom. On the other hand, exclusive reliance on short-term financing during recessionary periods could create parallel problems that would result in a large build-up of near-term maturities which might have to be refinanced in a period of rapid business recovery. Moreover, the liquidity represented by the increase in short-term debt, which would provide considerable scope for a rise in the velocity of the money supply, might unduly complicate public policy actions to promote sustainable growth with price stability during the succeeding business expansion.

One way of minimizing these difficulties during a recession would be to rely heavily on new Government security issues of intermediate-term maturity. Such issues tend to be bought by commercial banks in their attempts to bolster earnings in the face of slackening loan demand and falling interest rates. As banks purchase these obligations with reserves made available by an expansive monetary policy, bank credit and the money supply tend to grow, thereby helping to counter recessionary pressures. If in a later period of business expansion interest rates rise and market values of these intermediate-term issues decline, the continued holding of the obligations would become more attractive to banks that wish to avoid taking losses. The holding of intermediate-term issues by banks would help reinforce a monetary policy designed to prevent total spending in the economy from rising at an unsustainable pace.

Clearly, the Treasury must follow a middle course in attempting to reconcile its various objectives. Its concern with the public interest requires that minimum reliance be placed on short-term financing during periods of expansion. Similarly, financing in a recession should be handled so as to minimize interference with national efforts to promote economic recovery without unduly intensifying the subsequent problem of preventing an unsustainable upsurge in economic activity. At all times, attention should be given to the objective of borrowing as cheaply as possible consistent with the other objectives. Finally, constant effort must be directed toward achieving a balanced maturity structure of the debt.

QUESTION V

What debt structure should the Treasury have as a target?

ANSWER V

Treasury debt management should have as one of its principal goals the achievement of a balance in the maturity structure of the public debt. A balanced maturity structure is one that is tailored to the needs of our economy for a sizable volume of short-term instruments and also includes a reasonable amount of longer-term securities. Continued issuance of long-term securities is essential to offset the shortening of maturity caused by the lapse of time, which otherwise results in an excessively large volume of highly liquid short-term debt. Minimizing undue concentration of maturities, particularly in the short-term area, can provide the Treasury with much needed flexibility so that in its operations it can avoid interfering with effective monetary policy.

A balanced maturity structure of the public debt is not easily achieved. Long-term securities, with the passage of time, grow constantly shorter and bring about a relentless tendency toward a rising short-term debt. Despite persistent efforts in recent years to offer longer-term securities (about $50 billion maturing in over five years were sold from the beginning of 1953 through mid-1960), as of June 30, 1960, almost 80 percent of the marketable public debt of $184 billion matured within five years, as contrasted with less than 50 percent at the end of 1946 and 67 percent in December 1952. Moreover, if the total amount of marketable debt does not change, and no securities of more than five years' maturity are issued, the under-five-year debt will swell to nearly 85 percent of the total by the end of 1964. Obviously this maturity structure -- both present and prospective -- is far too heavily concentrated in the under-five-year maturity area. However, the $70 to $80 billion of debt maturing within one year does not appear to be a major problem since the liquidity needs of the economy require a very short-term debt of this general magnitude; the real problem is the excessive amount of securities maturing in one to five years.

The undue and growing concentration of the public debt in the under-five-year area has important implications both for the money and capital markets and for the economy as a whole. If the composition of the debt is permitted to grow continuously shorter, Treasury refunding operations will occur more frequently and in larger amounts. The Treasury might often be forced to refund excessively large maturities under unfavorable conditions with unduly large

repercussions on the structure of interest rates. This type of refunding would increase the cost to the Treasury and would tend to
interfere with orderly marketing of corporate and municipal bonds;
it might also disrupt the market for real estate mortgages. Moreover, the emergence of a larger amount of highly liquid, short-term
government debt could create inflationary pressures. Excessive
liquidity in the economy and frequent and large Treasury operations
in the market can unduly complicate the flexible administration of
Federal Reserve credit policies essential to sustainable growth.
A balanced maturity structure of the debt, therefore, can make a
major contribution toward sound financial policy by reducing the
frequency, size, and adverse consequences of Treasury financings,
by helping to forestall potential inflationary pressures, and by enabling monetary policy to function more effectively.

The clear need for a more balanced maturity structure of the
marketable public debt in turn raises the question as to the possible
means of accomplishing the necessary debt extension. Advance refunding is a promising method of bringing about significant debt
lengthening, so essential in the light of the unbalanced debt structure.
In advance refunding all individual and other holders of selected
issues of existing U.S. Government securities are offered the opportunity to exchange their securities, some years in advance of
maturity, for new securities on terms mutually advantageous to the
holder and to the Treasury. By this management technique the debt
could be substantially lengthened with a minimum of adverse market
and economic effects. Alternatively, the Treasury could offer long-
term bonds for cash or in exchange for maturing issues of Government securities. Although both of these techniques may be useful
under certain circumstances, under present conditions (1960)
advance refunding appears to be the most effective device for
achieving a better maturity structure of the marketable public debt.

The relative advantages of the advance refunding technique are
discussed in considerable detail in, Debt Management and Advance
Refunding, U.S. Treasury Department (Washington, D.C., September
1960.)[1] In brief, advance refunding avoids absorbing funds that otherwise would be available for investment in other types of long-term
securities, has much less market impact than a cash offering (or
an exchange at maturity), and on balance, the cost is significantly
less than if an equal amount of long-term securities were sold for
cash or in direct exchange for maturing issues.

In recent weeks (September 1960) the Treasury successfully
used the advance refunding technique to achieve a better maturity
structure and ownership distribution of the marketable public debt.

[1]Reprinted as an Appendix to Part II.

Total subscriptions of $3,972.1 million (including $3,388.4 million from public holders and $583.7 million from Government Investment Accounts) were received to three issues of 20- to 38-year $3\frac{1}{2}$ percent Treasury bonds included in an offering by the Treasury to the holders of four issues of outstanding 7- to 9-year $2\frac{1}{2}$ percent Treasury bonds, aggregating $12.5 billion. All subscriptions to the $3\frac{1}{2}$ percent bonds were allotted in full and the bonds were issued on October 3, 1960.

These results of this first major effort to lengthen the maturity of the marketable public debt through advance refunding were very satisfactory. As indicated, some $4.0 billion of securities scheduled to mature in 7 to 9 years were shifted to long-term issues maturing in 20 to 38 years. This increase in the amount of long-term bonds outstanding is especially significant when viewed in comparison with total sales of only $9.2 billion of over 15-year securities in the entire postwar period. As a result of the advance refunding, the amount of outstanding bonds with maturities beyond 15 years increased by nearly one-half, from $8.5 billion to $12.5 billion. Correspondingly, the average maturity of the marketable public debt was extended from approximately 50 months to 57 months.

This substantial amount of debt extension was achieved with a minimum of market impact as evidenced by the relatively small changes in the prices of the affected issues at the time of the announcement of the offering, by the small amount of market churning that occurred, and by the absence of any appreciable effect on the market for long-term Government, corporate, or municipal bonds. This evidence serves to confirm the judgment that the advance refunding technique permits substantial debt extension with a minimum of adverse market and economic effects. The modest amount of market trading in the affected issues also suggests that speculative purchases were minimal. The absence of speculation, in turn, indicates that the participants in the exchange were primarily long-term investors who were interested in extending the maturity of their holdings.

Another question frequently raised and directly related to the appropriate debt structure is that of the proper distribution of the debt between marketable and nonmarketable forms. The nonmarketable debt is essentially in two forms -- savings bonds and special issues to the trust funds. Almost half of the nonmarketable debt is in the form of savings bonds, consisting of over $42.5 billion of Series E and H Bonds (which are the only types now being sold) and less than $5 billion of the older Series F, G, J and K Bonds (which are now in the process of being redeemed). Most of the remaining nonmarketable debt is in the form of special issues to the various Government trust funds and agencies. These funds are invested in accordance with the legal requirements for each account. Most of these trust fund investments represent the re-investment of individuals' savings placed in Social Security, Veterans Life Insurance, Railroad Retirement, and Government Employee Retirement Funds. The nonmarketable debt also includes about $7 billion of investment bonds, the bulk of which grew out of the 1951 issuance of Series B Investment Bonds in exchange for 1967-72 marketable bonds at the time of the Federal Reserve-Treasury Accord.

The existence of both savings bonds and special issues facilitates debt management. It is obvious that there would be serious objections to placing the investments of Government Investment Accounts entirely in marketable securities. There are very large monthly fluctuations in investment requirements of the trust funds which would necessitate equally sizable purchases or sales. In the present Government securities market, sales or purchases in such sizable amounts would cause violent price fluctuations and disrupt the market.

Nor is there any question about the need for a strong and vigorous program to attract savings from millions of Americans through the E and H Savings Bond program. The average dollar invested in E Bonds stays with the Treasury for approximately seven years, considerably longer than the average dollar invested by the general public in marketable securities. Since the end of World War II financing the volume of E and H Bonds outstanding has grown from $30 billion to $42.5 billion, representing one area in which there has been significant Treasury success in selling Government securities to long-term savers.

In addition to its value as a debt management instrument, the savings bond program has undoubtedly added to the net amount of savings generated in the United States during the past 20 years. This has been accomplished largely as a result of the payroll savings plan, through which more than 8 million American workers are now buying bonds on a regular basis.

Nonmarketable securities are entirely appropriate in the structure of the public debt as far as trust funds and E and H Bonds are concerned. The demand feature of savings bonds does not constitute an important threat to the stability of the public debt. Redemption patterns in savings bonds follow a reasonably predictable course and are not substantially affected by recessionary trends in the economy. Sales and redemptions respond only gradually over a period of months to changed terms or economic conditions.

The Treasury's experience with nonmarketable securities in other than these two areas has led to the conclusion, however, that the nonmarketable instrument is subject to serious reservations in broader application. During World War II and for a number of years therafter, the Treasury sold nonmarketable savings notes running two or three years to maturity but redeemable on demand at a predetermined schedule of redemption values. These securities were helpful, during a period when the Government securities market was supported by the Federal Reserve, in assisting corporations to invest their tax reserves. With the advent of a freer market in 1952 and 1953 it became increasingly apparent that, since it was not administratively feasible to revise the terms of savings notes from month to month, the Treasury would always be in the awkward position of either experiencing a flood of sales and small redemptions at a time when savings note rates were well above market rates for comparable maturities, or -- more serious -- would find itself faced with large redemptions and negligible sales at a time when market rates became relatively attractive. As a result, note sales were discontinued in the latter part of 1953.

Although short-term rates fluctuate much more widely than do rates on longer-term securities, the Treasury also reached the conclusion two years ago that it was inadvisable to continue to sell the types of savings bonds designed for larger investors (Series F, G, J and K). Like savings notes, these securities were popular during World War II but became increasingly less adaptable as market movements were amplified in more recent years. Again, heavy redemptions of F and G Bonds (and the successor J and K Series) typically occurred when long-term interest rates were high, and under such conditions their refinancing constituted a problem to the Treasury. As a result, their sale was discontinued in 1957 and the amount outstanding has shrunk from $23 billion at the peak in 1951 to less than $5 billion at the present time.

On balance the amount and types of nonmarketable debt appear to be an appropriate part of the present debt structure. There seems to be no clear case for altering the present relationship between the marketable and nonmarketable debt although, as indicated, the savings bond program plays a particularly vital role in contributing not only to a better structure of the public debt but also in contributing to better thrift habits among millions of Americans.

QUESTION VI

Should the Treasury attempt to minimize the interest cost of the debt?

ANSWER VI

The objective of keeping borrowing costs at a minimum is, as pointed out in the answer to Question 4, a major goal of debt management. It should be reiterated, however, that the Treasury must consider the impact of its actions on financial markets and the economy as a whole. Consequently, the aim of keeping borrowing costs at a minimum must be balanced against broader considerations of the public interest. Against any gain in terms of lower interest cost there must be weighed the possible loss in terms of economic effects. For example, excessive issuance of long-term securities in recessions when interest costs are low would absorb too large a part of the investment funds needed elsewhere for recovery and could even prevent desirable reductions in interest rates. It would unduly increase the burden on monetary policy and necessitate much greater monetary ease, which would complicate the problem of curbing the excesses that might develop later in a boom.

In this context of the broader public interest, however, economical borrowing remains an important goal of Treasury debt management. The Treasury does not agree with the view that interest payments on the debt are of no real significance for the economy as a whole -- a too narrow view premised on the point that interest payments are not exhaustive in terms of economic resources but merely represent transfers from taxpayers to bondholders. As noted in the reply to Question 1, such transfer payments do exert important economic effects, particularly as related to incentives in the private sector of the economy.

On the other hand, the significance of the interest payment on the public debt -- now estimated at about $9 billion per year -- should not be overstressed. The average rate paid is still only about 3 1/4 percent, and the total amount of interest is only about 2 1/4 percent of current national income -- not much higher than 20 years ago and somewhat lower than in the years 1946-50. Moreover, about 30 percent of the interest on the public debt is paid on securities held by the Federal Reserve banks -- which return to the Treasury net earnings after dividends and surplus adjustments -- and on securities held in Government investment accounts. In addition, a substantial portion of the interest paid on securities held by commercial banks and business corporations is recouped by the Treasury through the 52 percent income tax which applies to these investors.

Although Treasury interest rates are higher now than for a number of years, the rates are among the lowest for any central government in the free world. Both here and abroad interest rates have risen substantially during the entire postwar period in those nations which rely upon free market processes and effective monetary and credit policies for promoting economic stability. The greatest degree of price stability has prevailed in the countries where interest rates (and debt costs) have been permitted to respond to the impact of market forces and an appropriate monetary policy.

Too much emphasis on minimizing interest costs as a goal of debt management can easily lead to long-run difficulties. One of the major dangers is that excessive use will be made of short-term securities, on which the interest rate is usually lower than on longer-term issues. This use of short-term issues can lead to a piling up of short-term debt which later might severely complicate debt management and monetary policy. Also, experience has clearly demonstrated that reliance on money creation to prevent interest rates from rising during a period of strongly rising business activity and credit demands can only result in inflation. The goal of holding down interest charges on the debt cannot be allowed to take precedence over the important objectives of promoting sustainable economic growth with stable prices.

In addition, it may be noted that interest minimization in itself may be variously defined. There is general agreement that the Treasury should always strive to market a particular issue at the lowest possible rate of interest. But choosing between types of issues on a cost basis alone involves difficult market judgments as to future rate movements. If long-term rates are currently lower than short rates but falling, minimization of cost over the long run would suggest temporary resort to short-term financing. Yet continued concentration of financing in the short area ratchets the costs in that area and may on balance result in a higher interest cost over a period of time. There is a constant danger that too much emphasis on interest minimization per se will lead to overuse of short-term financing involving both upward pressures on costs and, even more important, the complications noted previously with regard to effective debt management and monetary policy.

Apart from interest minimization from a cost standpoint, it may be noted that while the Treasury does not have specific aims with respect to influencing the level or structure of interest rates in its debt operations, it should and does take into account the differing impact of alternative borrowing programs on interest rates in the context of the current economic conditions.

QUESTION VII

Should Congress reduce or expand the Treasury's authority to manage the public debt and market new issues?

ANSWER VII

The authority granted by the Congress to the Treasury for management of the public debt is quite broad and, except for the 4 1/4 percent interest rate limitation on new marketable bond issues, the present authority is sufficiently broad to permit any debt management operations presently envisaged. The Treasury regularly reviews its statutory authority, however, and suggests changes when they are necessary. In 1959, for example, such a review resulted in congressional action broadening the possible scope of Treasury operations in the debt management field even though the most important request -- removal of the interest rate ceiling -- was not granted.

Congress provided in 1790 that the President had the power to borrow money on the credit of the United States for specific purposes including the payment of the foreign debt, funding of the existing domestic debt, and assumption of the debts of the several states. This authority was delegated by the President to the Secretary of the Treasury, Alexander Hamilton, and this power continued, in general, until the early Civil War period. In 1861 the Congress directly authorized the Secretary of the Treasury to conduct the financing of the War through the issuance of bonds, 1-year notes, and demand notes.

Prior to World War I, however, the Secretary of the Treasury had little discretion in the actual carrying out of public debt operations and Congress typically specified the terms and conditions of each new issue of Government obligations. In World War I, however, with the tremendous expansion of the debt, Congress recognized the increasing impracticability of specifying terms and conditions of each issue and gave the Secretary of the Treasury much broader authority to determine all terms and conditions except the total amount of the debt and the maximum interest rate on Treasury bonds.

The Treasury's positions with regard to both the interest rate ceiling and the dollar amount of the debt limit are well known. In our judgment, the interest rate ceiling on Treasury bonds has no place in the financial environment in which the Treasury operates, since this ceiling can result in an arbitrary and disadvantageous distribution of new Treasury issues. During most of 1959 and part of 1960 it forced the Treasury to finance within the 5-year area and thereby contributed to a more distorted, and probably higher, structure of interest rates throughout the economy than would otherwise have existed. It remains an important impediment to debt management in the public interest.

To many observers the congressional insistence on an over-all limitation of the amount of debt outstanding may also seem arbitrary and unnecessary. The debt limit, however, represents the only focal point which the Congress can use to interpret the over-all results of its decisions to spend money and to levy taxes, and until some better method is devised for handling the government's budgetary affairs in Congress, a statutory debt limit appears to be necessary and desirable. The Treasury has consistently urged, however, that the debt limit should provide sufficient leeway to permit reasonable flexibility in the timing of its debt management operations in order always to have sufficient margin to cover contingencies, and the Congress has generally seen fit to make such provisions from year to year.

There are other current restrictions on the Treasury's authority in debt management which are entirely appropriate and desirable, for example, the position that the Congress has taken with regard to special issue investments of the various Government trust funds. The authority under which most of the larger funds operate properly contains specific language providing for a formula for the interest rate on special issues. The limitations placed in the law on the amount of funds which the Treasury can borrow directly from the Federal Reserve System are desirable.

The Treasury also strongly favors the provisions of present law which permit the issuance of only taxable obligations. Fiscal soundness lies more in broadening the tax base and tightening loopholes than in looking toward greater tax exemption. Although tax exemption would initially add to the attractiveness of the securities, it would result in a sizable loss of revenue. Furthermore, the market for tax-exempt issues is limited to those in high tax brackets; to the extent that the present supply of tax-exempt securities has already expanded to meet their needs, any additional supply would have to find a market among investors to whom the tax-exempt feature would be of less advantage. Therefore, if the market for tax-exempt securities were substantially enlarged by the addition of Federal Government securities, any existing rate advantage of tax-exempts over taxable issues would tend to diminish. The net result might be to raise the cost of borrowing to all states and municipalities rather than to lower materially the cost to the federal government.

The Treasury is also opposed to plans which would require that a certain proportion of the public debt be retired each year. The purpose behind such plans is laudable and the Treasury Department clearly would prefer to see the long-term trend of the debt to be in a downward rather than an upward direction, thus permitting greater growth of the private economy and a lessening of chronic pressures toward inflation. Nevertheless, debt reduction could not and should not take precedence in evaluating necessary expenditure programs. It is not practical to require a certain amount of debt reduction each year and at the same time enact expenditure and tax programs which are inconsistent with such a requirement.

Suggestions have also been made from time to time that either the Treasury's authority to manage its trust accounts should be broadened or that the Treasury should have additional authority to operate a fund which could help stabilize the market for Government securities, particularly around the time of new offerings. There may be considerable merit in such a proposal and the Treasury is continuing to study the problem and its implications for a freely functioning Government securities market.

In summary, except for the removal of the 4 1/4 percent interest rate limitation the Treasury does not need other major changes in legislative authority at this time. As suggested earlier, from time to time changes in authority are needed, and in 1959 Congress, in response to Treasury request, enacted some important debt management legislation. This legislation included the authority granted the Secretary of the Treasury to postpone recognition of gain or loss for tax purposes on advance refunding of Treasury obligations, and permission to improve savings bonds terms. These legislative changes have already proved exceedingly helpful in the execution of sound debt management.

QUESTION VIII

Within its present legislative authority what changes should be made to permit the Treasury to market its new issues on a more satisfactory basis?

ANSWER VIII

The Treasury has taken full advantage of its present legislative authority, including changes in such authority enacted in 1959, to market its issues on the most satisfactory basis. A number of new techniques have been adopted which have materially added to the Treasury's efficiency in managing the public debt. These include: (1) increased use of the auction technique as it relates to Treasury bills; (2) inauguration of regular 6-month and 1-year bill cycles in addition to the traditional 91-day issues; (3) pricing of new Treasury issues at slight discounts or premiums to permit closer adjustment to existing market prices; (4) advance refunding of outstanding issues to provide a better debt structure; (5) reintroduction of callable bonds; and (6) significant improvements in the savings bond program.

The Treasury is continuing to review these and other debt management techniques. The increased use of the auction technique, even within the Treasury bill area, has not proved conclusively to be economical in comparison with the offering of fixed-coupon issues. Experience with callable bonds in the offering of the 4 1/4 percent bonds of 1975-85 in April 1960 indicates that the Treasury can acquire the privilege of callability only at considerable cost in terms of investor disinterest. Similarly, despite the successful experience in advance refunding in September 1960 in shifting some $4 billion of securities maturing in 7 to 9 years into issues maturing in 20 to 38 years, more remains to be done in utilizing this technique to relieve the congestion in the 1- to 5-year maturity range.

Within the past year (1960) the Treasury has departed from earlier practice by resorting to a cash refunding of maturing securities -- under the traditional procedure the holders of the maturing issues have a pre-emptive right to subscribe to the new securities. The cash method of refunding is a useful tool of debt management under particular circumstances, especially when the exchange does not involve a full roll-over of the maturing securities (that is, some maturing debt is retired) or when it seems desirable to maintain closer control over possible speculation by specifying the amount of new securities of different maturity to be issued. As is pointed out in answer to Question 9, this method also enables the Treasury to limit speculation by requiring sizable downpayments and making percentage allotments among investor classes.

A great many other suggestions of new marketing techniques have been reviewed by the Treasury. For example, experience with the new one-year bill indicates that the auction technique cannot satisfactorily be adapted to the offering of longer-term securities without unnecessarily increasing the costs of debt management. Issuance of bonds guaranteed as to purchasing power is an unacceptable approach, since it would unduly augment inflationary pressures. With respect to underwriting of new issues, the device of selling Government securities to commercial banks by credit to tax and loan accounts appears to be clearly superior either to procedures which would involve paying substantial commissions to underwriters of Government securities or attempting to utilize privately formed syndicates. The Treasury does not agree with the view that Treasury marketing could be conducted much more efficiently by substituting a periodic succession of small issues for larger, more irregular offerings. Such a device would tend continuously to disturb the market; investor assurance of additions to supply could adversely affect demand and tend to ratchet the cost of Treasury financing since each successive issue would have to be attractively priced, that is, lower in price (higher in rate) than the then current market.

The Treasury also does not consider feasible the idea of funding any significant part of the public debt into perpetual issues. Treasury studies thus far indicate little investor interest in a perpetual bond. Similarly, a lottery bond, such as that used in the United Kingdom, would probably add little to the flow of savings, but would largely divert funds now used to purchase savings bonds.

It should be noted, however, that the marketing of Federal securities is an ever-changing problem, and the present status of the Treasury's review does not necessarily mean that a change in the market environment will not produce changes in the Treasury views. The Treasury would be negligent in meeting its debt management responsibilities if it failed to keep alert to the requirements of changing conditions.

QUESTION IX

What changes should be made in the Treasury securities market to make outstanding securities more readily transferable?

ANSWER IX

Before entering into any discussion of possible improvements in the Government securities market it is appropriate to comment, first, on the functions and characteristics of the market for Treasury securities as the market exists at the present time (November 1960), and second, on the performance of the market in terms of these special qualities.

Quite obviously, the Government securities market performs a unique function with respect to both monetary policy and debt management policy. These policy responsibilities make it particularly important that the market operate with a high degree of efficiency and that those who participate in it conform to the highest standards of integrity and concern for the public interest. In implementing monetary policy, the Federal Reserve should be able to buy and sell Government securities to effect the needed changes in bank reserves without fear of disrupting the market. In conducting its financing operations, the Treasury should be able to rely on the Government securities market for efficient distribution and absorption of new issues. And finally, the needs of private investors in Government securities must be met promptly and adequately.

To fulfill these varied purposes the Government securities market must be broad and active. The volume of trading should be large enough to absorb offerings of securities of the size that investors wish to buy or to sell. Such a market should also exhibit a fairly wide range of offers and bids so that new purchasers or sellers will appear at successively lower or higher quoted prices. In short, the market must be highly competitive, and those handling transactions in it must have sufficient capitalization to execute orders efficiently and without delay. Of equal importance, Government securities dealers must have access to sufficiently detailed and sufficiently recent information to provide a firm basis for reliable judgment and prompt action in performing their primary function of making markets.

Finally, the Government securities market should grow and change over the years in response to the changes in our financial mechanisms and in our economy generally. A rigid market structure, unresponsive to changes in the economy of which it is a part, would soon be unable to perform its necessary functions.

The present market mechanism for Government securities exhibits many of the elements of strength required for its successful functioning. Except under certain exceptional circumstances -- which have been carefully analyzed with a view to correction by both the market itself and by appropriate government agencies -- the Government securities market has provided an effective medium through which monetary policy actions as determined by the Federal Reserve and debt management operations as determined by the Treasury can be effectuated. From the point of view of investor needs, Government securities dealers generally maintain adequate inventories for the service of their customers. They have been able to complete substantial transactions on very short notice -- transactions that are believed to be normally far in excess of those handled on the stock exchange or through the over-the-counter market in corporate and municipal securities. The market for

Government securities is in fact the largest market in the country by a substantial margin; its daily transactions average well over $1 billion of which, of course, the preponderant part is in Treasury bills and other short-term securities.

Government dealers have demonstrated that they have the integrity and honesty that is needed in handling very large transactions, many of which are concluded without the necessity for elaborate written arrangements that would seriously impede operations. There is no question, in other words, but that the physical structure of the market as it currently operates is such that investor needs -- however large -- are met promptly and efficiently and at very little cost.

There is, of course, always room for improvement in the functioning of any market. An intensive study of possible improvements in the Government securities market was undertaken by the Treasury and the Federal Reserve System as a joint staff project in 1959. Among other matters, three major criticisms which had been leveled against the present over-the-counter market in U.S. Government securities were considered in the course of the study. These criticisms were: 1) That the market is concentrated in a relatively small group of primary dealers and therefore is not truly competitive; 2) That there is little information about the operations of the dealer market and no real supervision or formal rules governing its practices despite its special public interest; and 3) That the dealer market is highly inefficient in handling small "odd lot" transactions, and is not especially interested in doing so.

There is no question that the primary dealer market is highly competitive even though it comprises only about 12 nonbank firms and 5 bank dealers. There is spirited competition among these dealers for the available volume of business. Any offer to sell at a price even slightly below the market is quickly accepted, as are offers to buy at prices only slightly higher than existing market levels.

Government securities dealers are principally wholesalers whose customers consist of several hundred nonfinancial corporations; several thousand commercial banks submitting orders both for their own account and for customers; other securities brokers and dealers handling transactions for customers; hundreds of insurance companies, mutual savings banks, pension funds, savings and loan accounts, and other financial groups throughout the country; special funds of state and local governments; personal trust accounts; and some individuals of substantial means. These investors and traders who use the market generally are very well informed and experienced in the investment field. Each is seeking to get the best possible rate of return, and each continually compares the returns available on Government securities with those on alternative investments. Also, each of the large investors regularly uses the services of a number of dealers and constantly evaluates the relative performance of the dealers with whom he is in contact.

The dealer who succeeds in attracting business of this type must therefore be able to execute buy and sell orders promptly and efficiently, and the business must be handled in accordance with high ethical standards. Furthermore, if he is to attract and hold customers, his advisory service must stand the test of time.

Each primary dealer has nationwide contacts and some of the larger firms maintain branch offices throughout the country, since broad coverage is essential if sufficient volume is to be maintained. The responsibilities and risks involved in making primary markets call for the highest level of professional skill and training. A serious impediment to an increase in the number of primary dealer firms has been the small number of qualified and experienced personnel available to work in a new firm.

There appears to be little real substance to the charge -- based on the relatively small number of primary dealers -- that the dealer market is not competitive. The customers interviewed in connection with the Treasury-Federal Reserve Study testified to the high degree of competitiveness in the market. It should be noted that the dealer market is an informal market, not organized in any way, and it should be noted also that the dealer market is not closed in terms of its present number; any bank, other institution or individual that desires to become a primary dealer (with sufficient capital plus a demonstrated ability and willingness to make a primary market for Government securities on a national basis) would be free to become a part of the dealer market, and the Treasury would welcome this development.

With regard to the second criticism -- availability of information -- the Treasury and the Federal Reserve have agreed that more statistics should be available as to the volume and characteristics of aggregate positions and transactions. As a result of the recognition of this need, the Federal Reserve and the Treasury in early 1960 undertook a new program of gathering uniform information from the market in considerably more detail than has heretofore been available. This new information is still being gathered and processed on an experimental basis and no publication of pertinent aggregate data will be undertaken until uniformity of the statistics has been achieved.

The Treasury as a result of the study has also expanded its own survey of ownership of Government securities (which had included only banks and insurance companies since its inception in 1941) to include not only dealers and brokers but also nonfinancial corporations (including data on repurchase agreements, as well as outright ownership) and savings and loan associations. Further expansion of the survey is now under way to determine more precisely the characteristics of Government security ownership by state and local governmental units.

With respect to the charge that the Government securities market is inefficient in handling small (odd lot) transactions, it is important to recognize that most small transactions are presented to other brokers and dealers or commercial banks in the first instance; when they reach the Government securities market they are handled promptly by primary dealers at a relatively low cost (in part subsidized by the large wholesale transactions that characterize the dealer operation). Thus it is understandable that dealers view small transactions purely as an accommodation to established customers, and the dealers do not actively encourage them as original business.

As a practical matter, by far the largest part of individual investors' holdings of Government securities -- and perhaps an even greater part of current transactions -- is accounted for by United States Savings Bonds. The Treasury actively encourages small investors to buy these bonds -- usually on a regular basis through payroll savings -- so that their security ownership is completely protected against price fluctuations.

The desire of individual investors to obtain marketable U.S. Government securities in significant volume has been almost completely confined to comparatively short periods of time when interest rates rose to relatively high levels. This interest of individual investors was particularly strong with respect to the 5 percent Treasury notes issued in October 1959; such interest was also an important factor during the latter part of 1959 in the secondary market demand for other high coupon notes maturing in three to five years. The relatively high rates which greatly enhanced demand in this area were, of course, the direct consequence of the Treasury debt management being confined to the under-five-year area by congressional refusal to remove the 4 1/4 percent interest rate ceiling on Treasury bonds. The result was that substantial amounts of investment funds were withdrawn from private savings institutions within a short period of time, with a relatively sharp impact on the private long-term capital market, particularly the mortgage market.

The New York Stock Exchange has carefully considered ways in which small transactions in marketable Treasury bonds and longer notes could be actively encouraged. Its officials have concluded that it would be difficult under existing conditions to encourage Exchange specialists to take the financial risk which would be involved in making a market in Government securities.

There would also be the problem of developing adequate incentives for handling Government securities on the Exchange through a commission schedule that would be competitive with the narrow spreads prevailing in the over-the-counter market. Stock Exchange officials also believe that the only way an auction market for Government bonds could successfully be established would be for the Treasury to issue tax-exempt bonds to individuals and for the Federal Reserve to place all transactions in bonds on the Exchange which, in turn, might involve some official support of the Exchange market. Neither of these conditions is acceptable to either the Treasury or the Federal Reserve System.

Any analysis of the adequacy of the Government securities market should include a careful study of the credit aspects of the transactions in United States Government securities. This matter is discussed in the answer to Question X.

QUESTION X

Should speculation in the Treasury securities market be restricted or encouraged?

ANSWER X

Opinion on the subject of speculation in the Government securities market was reported as follows in the recent study of the market made jointly by the Treasury and the Federal Reserve:

> From the opinions expressed, it was clear that speculation was viewed generally as any positioning of a Government security, financed on credit or otherwise, which anticipates subsequent resale of the issue at a profit. Considered in these terms there was general agreement that speculative activity is an essential ingredient to an effectively functioning securities market since it lends continuity and facilitates the sale and distribution of new issues.[1]

---

[1]See "Role of Speculation in the Market," Part I, page 16 of the Treasury-Federal Reserve Study of the Government Securities Market, July 1959.

It was further noted in the study that most discussants reporting opinions on this matter were doubtful as to how the differentiation between useful market speculation and excessive speculation could be accomplished in practice.

Any consideration of the use of credit in the Government securities market must take account of the fact that dealers operate very largely on borrowed funds and must continue to do so if they are to stay in business. The very fact that they are continually turning over a huge volume of credit, and the fact that they report daily to the Federal Reserve Bank of New York, provide the Treasury and the Federal Reserve with the data needed in appraising the over-all credit structure of the dealer market.

There have been instances in the past, notably in the summer of 1958, when there were examples of improper extension of credit which encouraged individuals to finance speculative purchases of Government securities on an extremely thin margin. These instances pertained principally to a few banks and corporations rather than to Government security dealers.

Steps have already been taken to make certain that loose credit practices are minimized in the future. The New York Stock Exchange has taken action against one of its member firms which failed to meet the Exchange's margin requirements. The Comptroller of the Currency has issued instructions to Chief National Bank Examiners throughout the country prescribing minimum margin requirements on transactions involving the purchase of Government securities, and the New York State Banking Department has taken parallel action. Leading banks and corporations have been cautioned about the unfortunate consequences of undermargined credit, and the Treasury will not hesitate to warn them against any credit extensions which appear to contribute to excessive speculation if and when such excesses should threaten to recur. The Treasury believes that much of the undermargined credit extension in 1958 was an unwitting contribution to speculation and that the officers of banks and non-financial corporations so involved are anxious to avoid any repetition of those events.

The Treasury has also indicated that it intends to remain completely flexible in handling the refinancing of maturing issues to make either an exchange offering (with pre-emptive rights) or a cash offering, whichever seems most desirable in the light of market conditions and related circumstances. Use of a cash offering discourages the accumulation of speculative positions in "pre-emptive rights" to new issues. It also makes it feasible for the Treasury to require sizable downpayments and percentage allotments among investor classes as a further bar to excessive speculation. It is especially useful when the refinancing involves debt retirement as in August 1960, at which time the Treasury resorted to a cash refunding.

The Federal Reserve and the Treasury are continuing to study other suggestions which have been put forward for improving the Government securities market. These include the broad question of the possibility of encouraging or requiring primary dealers to organize themselves to insure more uniform practices.

The Treasury is also continuing its study of the repurchase agreement mechanism, since the joint Federal Reserve-Treasury Study of the Government securities market served both to point up some of the dangers in the abuse of the repurchase mechanism and to review the feasibility of limitations. Although the Treasury is confident that the actions already taken will substantially minimize the problem of undermargined credit extension, there is the possibility that it might be necessary at some future date to adopt a broader approach in order to minimize undesirable speculation and to seek legislative authority to set margin requirements along the lines of the present Federal Reserve Regulations T and U.

In summary, we emphasize again that the present Government securities market is an efficient, competitive market and has proved to be so under widely varying circumstances. As a result we continue to adhere to the principle that the market's strength stems from its basic freedom from government regulation.

QUESTION XI

Should the Treasury securities market be insulated from the rest of the capital market?

ANSWER XI

In recent years various proposals have been made for "insulating" the Government securities market from other credit markets. In the early postwar period, most of these proposals (particularly those that would provide for "secondary reserve requirements" for commercial banks) were designed primarily as a supplement to general credit controls. Such devices were offered as a new technique for controlling bank credit expansion without contributing to disruption of the Government securities market. In addition, "insulation" has been advocated, through the establishment of Government securities reserve requirements applicable both to banks and other financial institutions, for the purpose of offsetting the relative decline in the attractiveness of Government securities to various types of investors.

The Treasury is strongly opposed to such proposals. Experience since the Treasury-Federal Reserve Accord in 1951 indicates that a flexibly administered monetary policy is feasible in the postwar environment, and that such policy need not be supplemented by further specific controls such as a Government securities reserve applicable to financial institutions. Indeed, such a supplemental control is not only unnecessary but may have highly undesirable effects in terms of market allocation of credit and mobility in the flow of credit to promote economic growth.

Any actions that would attempt to improve the "competitive position" of Government obligations by forcing individuals or institutions to purchase and hold the securities would actually militate against the long-run goal of promoting a more self-reliant market for Government securities. Furthermore, the existence of a large "captive market" for Government obligations would enable the Treasury to avoid a true test of the market in its debt management operations, thereby increasing the danger of excessive reliance upon borrowing, rather than taxation, to meet federal government expenditures.

QUESTION XII

To what extent are fiscal and debt management policies influenced by such international considerations as the U.S. balance-of-payments position on current accounts, the direction of long-term international lending, and shifts by foreigners between their holdings of dollar assets and gold?

ANSWER XII

Recent developments in the international economy provide convincing evidence of the need to maintain a strong dollar while pursuing our complementary economic goals relating to growth and employment. The world economy of today is markedly different from that of the early postwar years Reconstruction of war-torn industrial economies abroad has been largely achieved. These industrial nations have made impressive progress in rebuilding, improving, and enlarging their productive facilities. The result has been a marked increase in the competitive capacities of these nations. The financial counterpart of this change in the international economy has been a remarkable strengthening of the currencies of these industrial countries, and the disappearance of most of the foreign exchange difficulties that earlier plagued them.

These important economic and financial developments, coupled with a large outflow of dollars from this country in the form of private long-term capital, government loans and grants, and military expenditures abroad, have been reflected in a series of deficits in this country's international balance of payments. These deficits, measured by gold and liquid dollar gains by foreigners in their transactions with the United States, have occurred in each year since 1950, with the exception of 1957, rising to $3.4 billion in 1958 and $3.8 billion in 1959. Trends during the first three quarters indicate that our deficit in 1960 will be in roughly the same magnitude.

These circumstances have required a reorientation of thinking with respect to our international economic and financial policies. Moreover, domestic actions relating to fiscal policies and debt management must now be assessed in the light of our position in the international financial system.

Two aspects of this new situation deserve special emphasis. In the first place, the generation of these deficits during the past ten years has resulted in the accumulation of a large volume of highly liquid foreign claims on the United States. These claims, which now total about $17.5 billion, consist primarily of deposits in American banks and investments in short-term securities of the United States Government and American businesses. More than half of these short-term liabilities are held by foreign governments and central banks and thus represent a direct claim on our gold stock. The remaining liabilities represent an indirect claim on our gold, inasmuch as they can become official holdings simply by transfer from private hands to foreign governments or central banks.

In the second place, the official short-term dollar holdings of foreign countries represent a large share of their basic currency reserves, supplementing gold for this purpose. Thus the dollar has become the major reserve currency of the free world and the interconvertibility of gold and the U.S. dollar has come to form the keystone of international exchange rate stability. As a consequence, confidence in the dollar is important to the monetary systems of the free nations of the world. If confidence in the dollar is ever impaired, the results would not be confined to this nation, but would be felt throughout the free world.

The close and continuing dependence of international confidence in the dollar's basic worth upon our domestic financial policies has been strikingly demonstrated in recent years. The $12.5 billion budget deficit that occurred in fiscal year 1959 appeared at the time to convince many foreign observers that this nation would be unable to avoid a resurgence of inflationary pressure, with consequent weakening of the dollar both here and abroad. However, the massive shift from the budget deficit of fiscal 1959 to a $1.2 billion surplus in fiscal 1960 evidently was a major factor in convincing these observers of the firm intention of this country to maintain fiscal discipline.

Unfortunately, an undertone of concern developed again in the summer and autumn of 1960, reflecting not only the continuance of a substantial deficit in our balance of payments but also concern over the financial policies that might be followed by a new national administration. This concern was reflected in pronounced speculation in some of the world's free gold markets (principally in London), which drove the price of gold higher than the official United States price of $35 per ounce.

These examples of recent experience are cited to emphasize that appropriate financial policies in this country underlie the economic strength, not just of the United States, but of the entire free world.

QUESTION XIII

Should changes be made in the management of Treasury cash balances?

ANSWER XIII

We believe that the Treasury's cash balances are currently managed in an efficient manner and that further changes in the handling of Treasury cash are not necessary at this time. Treasury practices and techniques in the management of its cash balance are, of course, under continuing review. Within the broad authority under which the Treasury operates, practices are changed from time to time to make management of the cash balance both as responsive as possible to the rapidly changing needs of the Treasury and as attentive as possible to the impact of cash operations on the monetary policy actions of the Federal Reserve.

The Treasury has two principal objectives in carrying on its cash management operations: (1) To maintain a cash balance at the lowest level consistent with ability to meet the day-to-day payment of the government's obligations, and (2) to neutralize the effects of fluctuating government income and outgo on bank reserves, so as not unduly to complicate the implementation at monetary policy.

As a practical matter, the procedure for the management of the Treasury's cash balance is highly complex, involving both long-range projections which extend from twelve to eighteen months ahead and day-to-day appraisals of the collections and disbursements of all agencies of the government. Long-range projections require careful analysis of budget receipts and expenditures, operations in Government trust funds and other special accounts, and transactions involved in the issue and redemption of public debt obligations. These projections must be reviewed in the light of the limitation on the amount of public debt obligations which may be outstanding at any one time and in the light of the timing and frequency of Treasury financing operations. Day-to-day appraisals in turn require knowledge of the factors influencing daily projections of these various types of activities together with the ability to make a complete analysis of the flow of funds through more than eleven thousand individual commercial bank depositaries and the Federal Reserve banks and branches.

The Treasury's operating cash accounts are carried with the Federal Reserve banks and branches. An annual volume of more than 425,000,000 checks drawn on the Treasurer of the United States by government disbursing officers flow back through banking channels and are charged to these accounts. A substantial part of the Treasury's income is deposited directly in Treasury accounts at Federal Reserve banks, but the greater part is credited to Treasury Tax and Loan Accounts maintained in more than eleven thousand commercial banks throughout the country. Proceeds of sale of most new public debt securities and several major classes of taxes are deposited in these accounts. A large portion of the funds flowing into the Tax and Loan Accounts are generated by the banks as they pay for newly issued securities or solicit their customers to make payments due the Treasury through the banks.

On the basis of frequent estimates of its cash position the Treasury withdraws funds as needed from the Tax and Loan Accounts for transfer to its accounts at the Federal Reserve banks. Thus the Treasury keeps its aggregate cash balance at the Federal Reserve banks relatively stable, even at times of sharply fluctuating revenues or expenditures, with a minimum of disturbance to the money market. The Tax and Loan Account System permits the Treasury to leave funds in the banks and in the communities in which the funds are generated until such time as the Treasury needs to disburse them. In this way the Treasury discharges a primary fiscal responsibility of handling government funds in such a way as not unduly to disturb financial markets.

Over the years numerous changes and improvements have been made in the Treasury's cash management methods. One of the significant changes in recent years was the establishment of a separate category of Tax and Loan Accounts involving the largest banks in the country, those with total deposits of more than $500,000,000. This grouping (about 50 banks) enables the Treasury to make immediate withdrawals or redeposits on any day without advance notice whenever Treasury balances in the Federal Reserve banks are expected to deviate from the desired level. Another significant improvement is the special procedure whereby large income tax payments at peak collection periods are deposited in Tax and Loan Accounts in banks on which the checks are drawn.

There is a wealth of information available as to the manner in which cash balances are handled, including material presented to the Joint Economic Committee during the hearings on Employment, Growth, and Price Levels in July 1959 (Part 6-A, Pages 1190-1205), as well as in the Treasury answers to questions on debt management submitted by Chairman Douglas and Vice Chairman Patman of this Committee in connection with the same study (see Parts 6-C and 10 of the Hearings).

More recently the Treasury completed a careful study of the activity in its Tax and Loan Account with reference to a particular request by the Comptroller General of the United States. He recommended that consideration be given to amending present laws to permit commercial banks to pay interest to the Treasury on balances maintained in Treasury tax and loan accounts with such banks and that the Treasury make direct payments to the banks for the services they render to the government. The Treasury is opposed to the payment of interest on balances in Tax and Loan Accounts for reasons that are detailed in this study which was released to the public June 15, 1960.[1] The difficulties and disadvantages inherent in a system of fees to banks are also reviewed in this study.[2] As

---

[1]Report on Treasury Tax and Loan Accounts Services Rendered by Banks for the Federal Government and Other Related Matters, Treasury Department Fiscal Service, June 15, 1960, p. 4.

[2]Ibid., p. 5. The study also clearly shows that the Treasury is adequately recompensed in the form of services rendered by the banks, and that for the majority of banks the expenses incurred in providing such services exceed their savings on Tax and Loan Account balances.

brought out in the study, experience has shown that the tax and loan account method of managing the Treasury's balances is well adapted to the United States banking system and can be used successfully to avoid the serious money market disturbances that might otherwise be a mechanical by-product of large-scale Treasury operations.

The Treasury believes, therefore, that the present system of managing its cash position, carefully developed over a period of many years, provides an efficient and economical way of transacting the government's business, and also reduces to a minimum any possible adverse effect of Treasury financial operations on the economic stability of the country. It is our conclusion that it would not be in the best interest of the government to make fundamental changes in the system.

QUESTION XIV

Granted that stability of employment and prices are conducive to economic growth, are there any ways in which fiscal policy (excluding changes in the tax system or increased emphasis on certain types of spending) and debt management policy can contribute to healthy, sustainable growth in addition to aiming at stabilizing employment and the price level?

ANSWER XIV

The technique of fiscal policy suggested in the reply to Question I, which would result in a net surplus in the federal budget over the full period of the business cycle, would also contribute directly to healthy, sustainable economic growth because the budget surpluses would be largest during periods of prosperity, when inflationary pressures are strong and when there is a shortage of savings to finance the investment that is essential to healthy growth. The surplus funds (which reflect government saving) would be used to retire part of the public debt. Such debt retirement would increase the availability of investment funds in financial markets and contribute to lower levels of interest rates. Consequently, business expenditures for new plant and equipment, as well as other growth-producing activities, could be more easily financed at lower costs and without inflationary expansion of bank credit.

Although the role of debt management in contributing directly to sustainable growth is more limited than that of fiscal policy, it is important to recognize that appropriate debt management policies will contribute to an efficiently functioning market for Government securities. To the extent this goal is achieved, financial markets in general can be expected to operate more efficiently, which in turn would facilitate the orderly financing of growth-producing activities.

QUESTION XV

What do you conceive to be the advantages and disadvantages of having the Federal Reserve System independent of the Executive Branch of the federal government?

QUESTION XVI

Should responsibility for debt management and monetary policy be given to a single organization such as the Federal Reserve System or the Treasury?

QUESTION XVII

What degree of coordination between Congress, the Federal Reserve System, the Treasury, and other departments and independent agencies of the Executive Branch of the federal government is desirable in relation to monetary and credit policy in its broadest sense? Are present procedures adequate to provide this, and, if not, what suggestions do you have for improvement?

ANSWERS XV - XVII

Questions XV, XVI, and XVII are closely related and will be considered together.

It is sometimes argued that the Federal Reserve should be directly responsible to the President. This view is based upon the proposition that this nation must have a strong, unified economic policy and that a unified approach to economic policy is impossible so long as authority over monetary policy is vested in an agency independent of the Executive. This view calls for several comments.

In the first place, the proponents of this approach overlook an essential fact: Even if the Federal Reserve were made directly responsible to the President, such accountability would not assure a "unified economic policy" because, under our system of checks and balances, economic powers are divided within the federal government. From the standpoint of the three major federal financial policies, responsibilities are divided as follows: (1) fiscal and budget policy are the joint responsibility of the Congress and the Executive; (2) monetary policy has been delegated by the Congress to the Federal Reserve (although the Treasury does possess some monetary powers, such as those relating to gold policy and management of Treasury cash balances); and (3) debt management policy is the province of the Treasury, under the President, subject to the general limitations provided by statute. Thus, if we were to achieve a truly unified government economic policy, some arrangement would also have to be made to shift to the Executive considerable administrative powers over tax rates and expenditures. Such action seems both unlikely and highly undesirable under our governmental system of checks and balances.

Secondly, although the Federal Reserve is often spoken of as an "independent agency," it should be recalled that the System was created by Congress and is responsible to the people through the Congress. Perhaps it is more correct to say that the Federal Reserve is independent within government, rather than independent of government. Therefore, the responsibility of the Federal Reserve to Congress is on a trusteeship basis rather than on a day-to-day basis. The degree of independence from Congress enjoyed by the Federal Reserve reflects the judgment of Congress that its own long-run purposes -- which are those of the nation as a whole -- will be best served by such a temporary self-denial of a portion of its inherent prerogative, under the Constitution, "to coin money (and) regulate the value thereof . . ."[1] This arrangement is based upon the simple and convincing proposition that monetary management, involving as it does highly technical operations, should be handled by independent experts. Moreover, experience in this country and in many foreign countries indicates strongly that the highly important task of monetary management, if it is to be impartially and effectively handled, must be divorced from the "politics of the day."

---

[1]Art. 1, sec. 8(5).

Thirdly, the argument for maintaining a central banking system that is independent of the Executive is even more convincing. In our form of government, the Executive has the responsibility of meeting the fiscal requirements of the government, including the management of our huge national debt as well as the borrowing of money to meet the government's needs whenever revenues fall short of expenditures. In meeting this responsibility, the President and the Secretary of the Treasury are properly concerned with borrowing as economically as is possible, in the light of existing market conditions and the need to promote other important economic objectives. If the Executive were to possess the power over the creation of money (which is the prerogative of Congress and has been delegated to the Federal Reserve), while at the same time bearing the responsibility to borrow to meet the government's fiscal requirements as cheaply as possible, there might be considerable danger of reliance on unsound monetary policies to minimize (in the short run) government borrowing costs, at the expense of encouraging inflationary pressures. This is no idle academic theory; it has happened in this and other countries.

Do these considerations imply that the various branches of government possessing authority over economic policy are free to follow contradictory courses of action? Not by any means. The important point is that there should be basic agreement as to our national economic objectives and as to the means of achieving these objectives; the objectives are basically the province of Congress in adopting legislation, as reflected in the Employment Act of 1946, the Federal Reserve Act, and various statutes pertaining to taxation, debt management, and government lending programs. Beyond this, however, there is a pressing need for informal arrangements to provide for a free flow of information among the various responsible agencies and officials. Perhaps a brief description of the informal arrangements between the Executive Branch and the Federal Reserve, for the purpose of promoting a coordinated economic policy, would be helpful in illustrating this point.

Neither the President nor the Treasury participate directly in the formulation of Federal Reserve policy. However, from time to time and without a fixed schedule, the President, the Chairman of the Board of Governors of the Federal Reserve System, the Secretary of the Treasury, the Chairman of the President's Council of Economic Advisers, and the economic assistant to the President meet informally to discuss economic trends and developments. Moreover, the Chairman of the Board of Governors and the Secretary of the Treasury meet for informal discussion at least once each week, and there are regular weekly meetings -- as well as frequent daily consultations -- between Federal Reserve officials, Treasury officials, and senior staff members of both agencies. At these meetings, there is a free interchange of ideas and information concerning the state of the economy, credit and debt management problems, and other matters of mutual interest.

These arrangements have worked out well in practice. The important point is that as the two agencies carry out their respective responsibilities, both have the opportunity for full knowledge of the other's views.

It has frequently been suggested that these informal arrangements for exchange of information among the responsible agencies in the field of money and credit be supplanted by some type of national economic council, chaired by the President and consisting of various government officials responsible for economic policies, including the Chairman of the Board of Governors of the Federal Reserve System. While such a council might serve a useful function as a forum for an exchange of ideas and information on matters of economic policy, there is a question as to whether it would be more effective than the existing informal arrangements described above. If it were deemed desirable to establish such a body, however, its function should, of course, be purely advisory in scope, with adequate provision made for safeguarding the independence of the Federal Reserve in formulating monetary policy.

In conclusion, it should be noted that the basic question discussed in this reply, relating to the desirability of making the Federal Reserve responsible to the Executive (or to the Treasury), was intensively studied by subcommittees of the Joint Committee on the Economic Report in 1950 and again in 1952. The first subcommittee, chaired by Senator Paul Douglas, recommended that Congress by joint resolution state that:

> . . . it is the will of Congress that the primary power and responsibility for regulating the supply, availability, and cost of credit in general shall be vested in the duly constituted authorities of the Federal Reserve System, and that Treasury action relative to money, credit, and transactions in the Federal debt shall be made consistent with the policies of the Federal Reserve. (Sen. Doc. #129, 81st Cong., 2d Sess., 1950, p. 31.)

The second subcommittee, chaired by Representative Wright Patman, concluded:

> The independence of the Federal Reserve System is desirable, not as an end in itself, but as a means of contributing to the formulation of the best over-all economic policy. In our judgment, the present degree of independence of the System is about that best suited for this purpose under present conditions. (Sen. Doc. #163, 82d Cong., 2d Sess., 1952, p. 4.)

Appendix

DEBT MANAGEMENT

AND ADVANCE REFUNDING

U.S. Treasury Department
September 1960

I. SUMMARY

Debt management is an important link in the vital chain of
federal financial responsibility. The objectives of debt management
are threefold: to contribute to an orderly growth of the economy
without inflation, to minimize borrowing costs, and to achieve a
balanced maturity structure of the public debt. The latter has been
the most pressing problem confronting the Treasury as there has
been a relentless increase in the short-term debt. Related to this,
the Treasury has found it increasingly difficult to retain as customers long-term investors in Treasury bonds (pars. 1 to 16).[1]

Advance refunding makes possible significant progress toward
the twin goals of a better maturity structure and ownership distribution of the public debt. In essence, it involves offering all individual
and other holders of an existing U.S. Government security selected
for advance refunding the opportunity to exchange it, some years in
advance of maturity, for a new security on terms mutually advantageous to the holders and to the Treasury (par. 17).

Broadly speaking, two types of advance refunding may be distinguished: (a) "senior" advance refunding, in which holders of
securities of intermediate maturity (5 to 12 years) would be offered
the opportunity to exchange into long-term issues (15 to 40 years),
and (b) "junior" advance refunding, in which holders of securities
of shorter maturity (1 to 5 years) would be offered the opportunity

---

[1]The numbers refer to the paragraphs which follow the summary.

to exchange into securities in the intermediate range (5 to 10 years). The two types of operations are related and keyed to the differing investor needs and demands in terms of investments of varying maturity (pars. 18 and 19).

Prior experience with advance refunding in this country—such as the operations in 1951-52 and in June 1960—has been limited. These operations were not directly analogous to a senior advance refunding in which investors in medium-term marketable bonds would be permitted to exchange for long-term marketable securities (pars. 20 to 27).

Advance refunding offers significant advantages to the economy, to long-term investors, and to the U.S. Treasury.

Advantages to the Economy

By facilitating significant debt extension with a minimum change in ownership, advance refunding:

a. Minimizes the adverse market impact of debt extension such as that which occurs in the case of comparable cash offerings (pars. 28 to 30);

b. Avoids the absorption of new, long-term funds in cash offerings and consequently does not interfere with the flow of new savings into the private sector of the economy (pars. 28 to 32);

c. Improves the functioning of the U.S. Government securities market by contributing to a better maturity structure of the marketable public debt (par. 31);

d. Helps to minimize inflationary pressures by reducing the amount of highly liquid short-term debt, especially in the case of junior advance refunding (par. 32).

Advantages to the Investor

By participating in an advance refunding, the investor:

a. Gains an immediate increase in interest return, in consideration of his acceptance of a longer-term security (pars. 33 and 37);

b. Avoids any immediate book loss for tax purposes and, if nontaxable, in most instances is not required to take a book loss (par. 36);

c. Acquires a security whose market yield is at least equal to, and in most instances slightly higher than, that on outstanding issues of comparable maturity (par. 34);

d. Earns a rate of return over the life of the new security only equaled, if he does not exchange, by reinvesting at maturity of the old security at higher than present market yields (pars. 35 and 37 to 39).

Advantages to the U.S. Treasury

By using advance refunding as a debt management technique, the Treasury:

a. Achieves substantial improvement in the present unbalanced maturity structure of the marketable public debt (par. 40);

b. Reduces its dependence on inflationary bank borrowing (par. 41);

c. Retains its customers for long-term securities (par. 43);

d. Helps keep down the long-run cost of managing the public debt by avoiding concentration maturities in a given area (pars. 41 and 42);

e. Reduces the size and frequency of Treasury refunding operations and minimizes interference with timing of appropriate monetary policy actions (pars. 12 and 40).

An important impediment to the earlier use of advance refunding was the tax treatment of the exchanges. This obstruction was remedied by new legislation enacted in 1959 which permits the postponement of the tax consequences of any capital gain or loss resulting from the exchange (pars. 24 and 36).

Another important obstacle to advance refunding has been the 4 1/4 percent statutory interest rate limitation. Although this limitation still exists, recent declines in interest rates now permit advance refunding of selected issues (pars. 44 to 50).

Advance refunding, therefore, offers much promise at the present time as a way of implementing sound debt management policy as an integral part of federal financial responsibility (par. 51).

II. DEBT MANAGEMENT AND ADVANCE REFUNDING

1. The ability of the American economy to sustain orderly growth without inflation, to generate increased employment, to provide

sufficient real capital to finance expansion, and to function as a source of strength for the entire free world—all of this depends on the maintenance of responsible financial policies. There are three main links in the chain of federal financial responsibility. Debt management is only one, but an important one, of these links. The two strongest links in the chain of financial responsibility are a sound fiscal policy—in terms of the relationship between revenues and expenditures—and an independent and responsible monetary policy. Without strength in these areas there is little that debt management alone can do. Combined with effective fiscal and monetary policies, however, appropriate debt management can contribute substantially to our over-all financial strength. Inappropriate debt management inordinately increases the burdens on fiscal and monetary policy.

A. The Objectives of Debt Management

2. Debt management policy has three major objectives.

3. First, management of the debt should be conducted in such a way as to contribute to an orderly growth, without inflation, of the economy. This means that, except in periods of recession, as much of the debt as is practicable should be placed outside of the commercial banks (apart from temporary bank underwriting). Restraint must be exercised in the amount of long-term securities issued, particularly in a recession period, in order not to pre-empt an undue amount of the new savings needed to support an expansion of the economy. A related aim should be to minimize, as far as possible, the frequency of Treasury trips to the market so as to interfere as little as possible with necessary Federal Reserve actions and also with corporate, municipal and mortgage financing.

4. A second important objective of Treasury debt management is the achievement of a balanced maturity structure of the debt, one that is tailored to the needs of our economy for a sizable volume of short-term instruments but also includes a reasonable amount of intermediate- and long-term securities. There must be continuous efforts to issue long-term securities to offset the erosion of maturity caused by the lapse of time, which otherwise results in an excessively large volume of highly liquid short-term debt.

5. A third objective of debt management relates to borrowing costs. While primary weight must be given to the two objectives just noted, the Treasury, like any other borrower, should try to borrow as cheaply as possible. Unlike other borrowers, however, the Treasury must consider the impact of its actions on financial markets and the economy as a whole. Consequently, the aim of keeping borrowing costs at a minimum must be balanced against broader considerations of the public interest.

6. These several objectives are not easily reconcilable at all times; nor can a priority be assigned to one or another of them under all circumstances.

7. There is some merit, for example, in the view that Treasury debt management policy should take account of cyclical considerations—pressing long-term securities on the market to absorb investment funds when the economy is expanding and, conversely, issuing short-term securities attractive to banks so as to increase liquidity in a period of recession. Yet in practice it has proved both impracticable and undesirable to adhere strictly to this view in disregard of other considerations. The Treasury's first obligation is to secure the funds needed to meet the government's fiscal requirements; these requirements cannot be postponed. A pressing need for cash may force it to market short-term issues—for which there is usually a substantial demand—even when the economy is expanding rapidly. The constant shortening in the maturity of the public debt means, however, that the Treasury also must take advantage of every reasonable opportunity to issue long-term securities despite the cyclical aspect. From a purely housekeeping standpoint the Treasury needs to do some funding of short-term debt into longer-term securities whenever market conditions permit.

8. Similar difficulties arise with respect to following only the objective of keeping borrowing costs as low as possible. Against any gain in terms of interest cost there must be weighed the loss in terms of economic effects. For example, aggressive issuance of long-term securities in recessions, when interest costs are low, would absorb too large a part of the investment funds needed elsewhere for recovery and could even prevent desirable reductions in interest rates. It would unduly increase the burden on the Federal Reserve and necessitate much greater monetary ease, complicating the subsequent problem of curbing the excesses that may develop in a boom.

9. Clearly, the Treasury must follow a middle course in attempting to reconcile its various objectives. Its concern with the public interest requires that minimum reliance be placed on short-term financing during periods of expansion. Similarly, financing in a recession should be handled so as to minimize interference with national efforts to promote economic recovery. At all times, attention should be given to the objective of borrowing as cheaply as possible consistent with the other objectives. Finally, constant effort must be directed toward achieving a balanced maturity structure of the debt.

B. The Problem of the Short-term Debt

10. For some time, the most pressing debt management problem facing the Treasury has been that of securing a better maturity

structure of the public debt. Long-term securities, with the passage of time, grow constantly shorter, bringing about a relentless increase in the short-term debt. Despite persistent efforts in recent years to offer longer-term securities (some $51 billion maturing in over five years have been sold since the beginning of 1953), as of June 30, 1960, almost 80 percent of the marketable public debt of $184 billion matured within five years, as contrasted with less than 50 percent at the end of 1946 and 71 percent in December 1953. Moreover, if the total amount of marketable debt does not change, and no securities of more than five years' maturity are issued, the under five year debt will swell to 87 percent of the total by the end of 1964. This obviously is a maturity structure—both present and prospective—which is far too heavily concentrated in the under five year maturity area. However, the $70 billion of debt maturing within one year is not a major problem since the liquidity needs of the economy require a very short-term debt of this general magnitude; the real problem is the excessive amount of securities maturing between one to five years. (See par. 19, which explains how both senior and junior advance refundings assist in reducing the concentration of maturities in this range.)

11. Chart A-1 illustrates the changes in the maturity distribution of the marketable public debt since 1946. The most significant changes, of course, are the decline in the five-year-and-over maturity category from $97.5 billion in 1946 to $40.5 billion in 1960 and the rise in the maturities between one and five years from $24.5 billion to $73 billion.

12. The undue and growing concentration of the public debt in the under-five-year area has important implications both for the money and capital markets and for the economy as a whole. If the composition of the debt is permitted to grow continuously shorter, Treasury refunding operations will occur more frequently and in larger amounts. The Treasury might often be forced to refund excessively large maturities under unfavorable conditions with unduly large repercussions on the structure of interest rates. This would tend to interfere with orderly marketing of corporate and municipal bonds. Moreover, the emergence of a larger amount of highly liquid, short-term government debt than the economy requires could create inflationary pressures. Excessive liquidity in the economy and frequent and large Treasury operations in the market can unduly complicate the flexible administration of Federal Reserve credit policies essential to sustainable growth. A balanced maturity structure of the debt, therefore, can make a major contribution toward sound financial policy by reducing the frequency, size, and adverse consequences of Treasury financings, by helping to forestall potential inflationary pressures, and by enabling monetary policy to function more effectively.

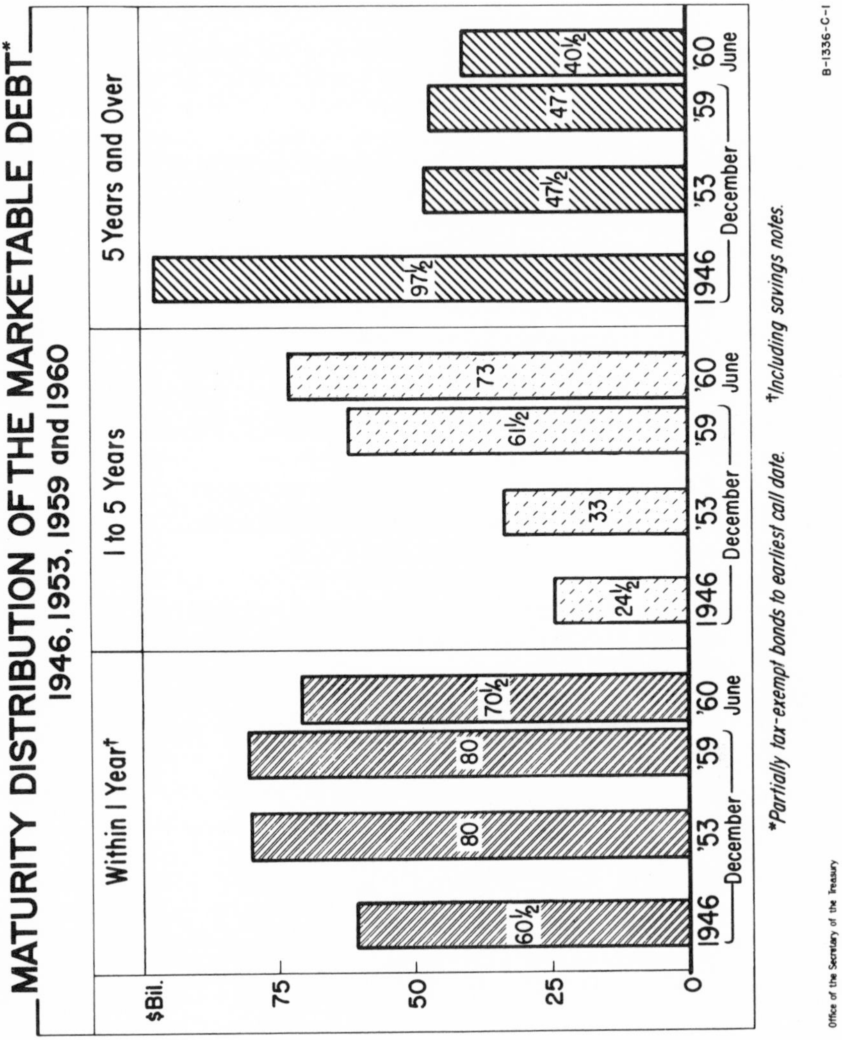
MATURITY DISTRIBUTION OF THE MARKETABLE DEBT*
1946, 1953, 1959 and 1960
$Bil.
Within 1 Year†
1 to 5 Years
5 Years and Over
75
50
25
0
60½
80
80
70½
24½
33
61½
73
97½
47½
47
40½
1946
'53
'59
'60
December
June
*Partially tax-exempt bonds to earliest call date.
†Including savings notes.
Office of the Secretary of the Treasury
B-1336-C-1

CHART A-1

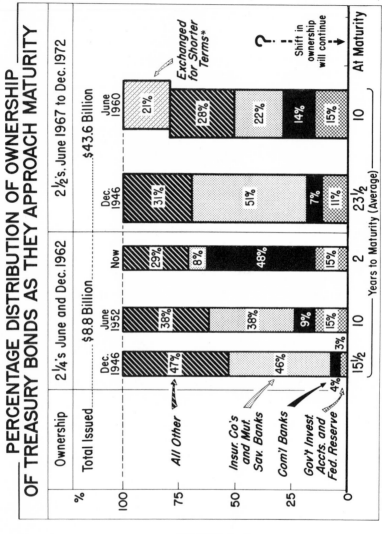

PERCENTAGE DISTRIBUTION OF OWNERSHIP
OF TREASURY BONDS AS THEY APPROACH MATURITY

*Including redemption for estate taxes.

Office of the Secretary of the Treasury

B-1376-A

CHART A-2

C. The Problem of Retaining the Treasury's Customers

13. The constant shortening of the debt also has very practical consequences for the Treasury, since it has made it difficult to retain as customers many long-term investors who once were buyers of Treasury bonds. Long-term investors who have found their holdings of Government securities moving nearer to maturity have had a tendency to dispose of them and to turn to other types of long-term investments. As a result, the Treasury has found that it has lost customers as the passage of time has eroded the long-term characteristics of Government bonds. The securities that were once long-term but which have become short-term have passed into the hands of commercial banks, nonfinancial corporations and other short-term investors, while holdings of Government securities by long-term investors—savings institutions and individuals—have been reduced. Even in those cases where the securities have been retained by long-term investors, such investors have tended to regard them as part of their liquid holdings. Consequently, by maturity there is little demand for new long-term Treasury bonds from the holders of the maturing securities.

14. The case of the 2 1/4 percent bonds maturing in June and December 1962, as shown in Chart A-2, illustrates what has happened to the ownership of Treasury bonds with the passage of time. When these bonds were originally sold during World War II, they were in the 15- to 20-year maturity area and were purchased largely by longer-term investors. At the end of 1946, almost half of them were held by insurance companies and mutual savings banks. Most of the remainder were held by individuals, some savings and loan associations, pension funds, etc. Only 4 percent were held by the commercial banks.

15. The picture is strikingly different today. Commercial banks now own 48 percent of the 2 1/4 percent bonds of 1962, and holdings of savings institutions and individuals are down very sharply. As is shown in Chart A-2, much the same sort of shift in ownership has been taking place with respect to the 2 1/2 percent bonds maturing between 1967 and 1972; but with maturity still some time off, the shift has not gone so far.

16. These changes in ownership distribution over time illustrate the problem that the Treasury has in retaining its customers, but the statistics alone do not tell the whole story. In many cases, as longer-term Government bonds shorten up, they come to serve a liquidity function within the portfolios of savings institutions and other long-term investors. On maturity, consequently, little replacement demand for long-term securities may be expected from these holders.

D. Advance Refunding—A Significant Step Toward Solution

17. Advance refunding is a debt management technique that makes possible significant progress towards the twin goals of a better maturity structure and ownership distribution of the public debt. In essence, it involves offering all individual and other holders of an existing U.S. Government security selected for advance refunding the opportunity to exchange it, some years in advance of maturity, for a new security on terms mutually advantageous to the holder and to the Treasury. Such exchanges promote debt lengthening with a minimum change in ownership, thus helping the Treasury to retain its customers for long-term securities. Advance refunding contributes to these objectives with a minimum of adverse effects on the financial markets and the economy as compared with alternative ways of debt lengthening. In turn, the investor is offered an opportunity to exchange for a new, longer-term bond with a higher coupon rate and without an immediate taxable capital gain or loss.

Types of advance refunding.

18. Within the context of the current debt structure there are two separate but related types of advance refunding that are of particular interest to the Treasury. They are (a) "senior" advance refunding, in which holders of securities of intermediate maturity (5 to 12 years) would be offered the opportunity to exchange into long-term issues (15 to 40 years), and (b) "junior" advance refunding, in which holders of securities of shorter maturity (1 to 5 years) would be offered the opportunity to exchange into securities in the intermediate range (5 to 10 years).

19. The relationship between these two types of operations is important in the successful use of advance refunding at certain times to implement needed debt lengthening. To accomplish best the major purpose of advance refunding the use at different times of senior and junior type advance refunding seems desirable. The reasons for this rest on the fact that securities in the 1- to 5-year range are not suitable obligations for advance refunding into long-term bonds; yet it is the relatively large amount of securities ($73 billion) maturing in 1 to 5 years that constitutes the hard core of the debt management problem. These securities are now held primarily by short-term investors, such as commercial banks and business corporations, which for the most part would not desire to exchange for long-term issues. Consequently, a two-phased approach, sometimes described as a "leapfrog" process, involving over time both senior and junior advance refunding, appears necessary.

a. A senior advance refunding would be undertaken first to shift a substantial amount of the 5- to 12-year maturities into the longer-term area. For this purpose the securities most often referred to as likely candidates are the 2 1/2 percent bonds issued to help finance World War II. These securities, often referred to as the "tap issues," originally totaling $43.6 billion, are now outstanding in the amount of $28 billion; and the Treasury's ownership studies indicate that a substantial portion is still in the portfolios of the original long-term investors. Consequently, no significant changes in ownership would be necessary for a successful extension. In fact, a major purpose in an early undertaking of a senior advance refunding of some significant part of these securities would be to prevent the lapse of time from changing their ownership such that holders would no longer be long-term investors who could be attracted by a new long-term offering. In addition to forestalling the inroads of time on ownership, this senior advance refunding would provide additional space in the intermediate sector and facilitate a junior advance refunding at a later date.

b. A junior advance refunding would shift an even larger amount of securities now in the one- to five-year range into the intermediate area. Just as an example, such a shift might involve an offering of 6-year bonds to holders of an issue now maturing in two or three years; an 8-year security for issues maturing in three or four years; and so on. It should be noted that a junior advance refunding can be successfully carried out in much larger amounts due to the characteristics of the intermediate market. There is a much larger market in the 5- to 10-year area, so that some greater amount of the debt extension ultimately achieved by use of advance refunding presumably would represent a shift from the 1- to 5-year into the 5- to 10-year area, with a significantly smaller amount moved out from the 5- to 12-year area to the very long area in order to retain long-term investors as Treasury customers.

Experience with advance refunding.

20. The Treasury-Federal Reserve Accord of March 4, 1951, included an advance refunding of existing marketable bonds as one of its agreed upon provisions. In order to eliminate what appeared to be an overhanging supply of long-term marketable bonds, holders of the two longest issues of bank-restricted bonds (the 2 1/2s of June and December 1967-72) were offered—21 years before maturity of their bonds—an optional exchange into 29-year, non-marketable 2 3/4 percent Investment Series B bonds convertible before maturity into 5-year, 1 1/2 percent marketable Treasury notes. A total of $19.7 billion bonds eligible for exchange into Investment Series B bonds were outstanding, of which $13.6 billion were exchanged. (About $8 billion were exchanged by private investors and the balance by the Federal Reserve banks and Government investment accounts.) In effect, then, the Treasury did advance refund this amount of its 1972 maturities when it issued the 2 3/4 percent Investment B bonds back in 1951.

21. Although the major purpose of the 1951 advance refunding was not to extend debt, it is significant that almost $14 billion of the 1972 maturities were shifted to 1980—an extension of 8 years. However, the privilege of converting the new 2 3/4 percent bonds into 5-year marketable notes in effect reduced the accomplishment in terms of debt lengthening. In fact, since 1951 more than half of the 2 3/4 percent bonds have been so converted into the 5-year notes.

22. In May 1952 the Treasury made another offering of the 2 3/4 percent nonmarketable investment bonds to the holders of the remainder of the June and December 1967-72s and to the holders of the 2 1/2s of 1965-70 and 1966-71. About $1.3 billion was exchanged. (However, one-fourth of the amount subscribed for had to be paid for in cash.)

23. Other than as a precedent, this experience in 1951-52 is not analogous since at that time the securities involved in the first exchange were still at or slightly above par and were not much below par in the second exchange. The reluctance of investors to take capital losses was not a material consideration. Moreover, the new issue was nonmarketable and could be liquidated only under penalty.

24. In the interim period since 1951 an advance refunding of the tap 2 1/2s, for example, would not have been particularly attractive to investors because—except for short periods in 1954 and 1958—they would have had to take book losses. (See footnote to par. 36 as to investor reluctance to incur such losses.) Legislation in the fall of 1959 permits the Treasury to provide exchanges with postponement of tax consequences. This again made practicable (subject to the 4 1/4 percent statutory interest rate limitation) the undertaking of advance refunding of marketable issues.

25. On June 6, 1960, the Treasury Department offered the holders of $11.2 billion of the outstanding 2 1/2 percent Treasury bonds maturing November 15, 1961, the option to exchange—with the privilege of deferring the tax consequences—for either 3 3/4 percent Treasury notes maturing May 15, 1964 (limited to $3.5 billion), or 3 7/8 percent Treasury bonds maturing May 15, 1968 (limited to $1 billion). Holders of approximately $4.9 billion of the 2 1/2 percent Treasury bonds submitted exchange subscriptions, but the bulk of the subscriptions ($4.6 billion) was for the new 4-year note, of which $3.9 billion were allotted, and only a relatively small part (a little over $300 million) for the new 3 7/8 percent bond.

26. This advance refunding, undertaken in June 1960, provided a testing ground for use of the technique in this country under pre-

vailing market conditions and ownership characteristics[2]. This particular advance refunding was designed primarily to obviate the difficult problem that would have arisen in refunding the 2 1/2 percent bonds of November 1961 at maturity, as this issue totaled $11 billion publicly held—the largest single outstanding issue. It was not undertaken to preserve ownership nor with the expectation of achieving substantial debt lengthening of the type desired.

27. This refunding clearly demonstrated the feasibility of debt extension by advance refunding but also demonstrated the difficulty of extending beyond five years under the 4 1/4 percent interest rate ceiling in the market environment then prevailing. The significant investor response to the note offering enabled the Treasury to reduce the size of the November 1961 maturity from $11 billion to $7 billion, thus making it much more manageable at maturity. However, the interest rate ceiling did not permit a significant amount of extension beyond the seriously congested one- to five-year area because the eight year bonds could not be made sufficiently attractive to induce larger acceptance of the issue. This advance refunding also served a very useful purpose in familiarizing the market generally with the technique of advance refunding; it gave investors, dealers, and investment advisers the opportunity to study the different problems which an advance refunding offering presents.

Advantages of advance refunding to the economy.

28. Advance refunding can be accomplished in worthwhile amounts with a minimum of disturbance to financial markets and to the economy as a whole. This is because most of the new long-term bonds taken in the refunding will simply be substituted for shorter-term issues held by investors who are essentially long-term holders. Because only a small change in ownership is involved, little if any new savings will be absorbed and the impact on the markets for mortgages and corporate and municipal securities should be relatively small. (See par. 32 for further discussion of this point.)

29. In contrast, if the Treasury were to offer a significant amount of long-term bonds for cash it would capture funds that otherwise would be available for investment in other types of long-term securities, and the increased supply of long bonds

---

[2] The advance refunding technique was used in the Canadian conversion loan operation in the summer of 1958. Some $6 billion of Dominion of Canada securities having from 6 months to 8 years to run to maturity were exchanged for securities with maturities ranging from 3 to 25 years—an operation involving over half of that country's direct marketable debt. Because of the fundamental differences in the financial systems of Canada and the United States this experience is of only limited applicability in this country. No operation of similar scope in relation to the total debt of this country would be either feasible or desirable.

competing for those funds would have a marked impact on the interest rates of all such securities. Similarly, when a long-term bond is offered in exchange for maturing securities the economic and market effects are as pronounced as those on a cash offering. The maturing securities by that time are almost entirely held by short-term investors (or as liquidity protection by long-term investors) who do not want long-term bonds. This involves churning in the market as the holders of the rights (maturing securities) sell to investors who want to exchange for the long bond. Since the securities are obtained by long-term investors through their purchases of rights, there is a net absorption of long-term funds with much the same results as in the case of offering a new long-term issue for cash.

30. In an advance refunding, however, this adverse market impact would be largely avoided. Under conditions such as exist today, when the securities to be refunded are selling at a discount, the holder's motive in taking the longer security in exchange is to get a better immediate return, as well as a satisfactory return to maturity, and to do so without registering a loss on his books (if depreciation from cost exists). The combination of a higher coupon and longer maturity on the new security being offered in exchange is designed so that it will tend to sell in the market at a price comparable to that of the old security. As a result it is reasonable to assume that few of the securities taken would be sold in the market in the period immediately following the exchange, and, indeed, the greater part would probably not be sold for many years. The effect on available market supply is, therefore, distinctly less than in the case of either a cash offering or a refunding at time of maturity. Assuming that the Treasury offers investors in exchange a somewhat higher coupon in consideration for their taking a longer bond, they can better their current income and still carry the new bond on their books at the price paid for the old bond. On balance, then, much more substantial debt extension may be achieved with no more immediate market impact than would occur in the case of a cash offering of a nominal amount of long-term bonds.

31. From a longer-run standpoint, the addition to the supply of long-term Government securities, and the relief of the congestion in the area between one and five years, should also contribute to a smoother functioning market for all U.S. Government securities. The principal market improvement, of course, would eventually be reflected in the one- to five-year area, which has been distorted by the unduly heavy concentration of issues in this maturity range, but the entire market structure would be brought into better balance. The breadth, depth, and resilience of the market should also reflect the improved maturity distribution, including the additional supply of long-term issues which presumably would result in a broader and more continuous long-term market.

32. Similarly, the economic consequences of an advance refunding involving substantial debt extension would be less pronounced than cash offerings (or refundings at maturity) since such an advance refunding would not immediately result in the absorption of additional amounts of long-term funds that usually are being generated currently in relatively limited amounts. It would minimize the interference with the flow of new savings into the private sector of the economy, such as would result from an equal offering for cash. At the same time, postponing the shortening process on this portion of the debt would further reduce the possible movement of these securities into the hands of short-term investors, thus diminishing the inflationary potential of the public debt. Although this would tend to reduce somewhat the flow of funds from intermediate credit markets to long-term private (non-Treasury) investment, as long-term investors might otherwise sell their holdings in order to acquire long-term private and municipal investments, the immediate absorption of new savings still would be much less than in the case of a cash offering of equal magnitude. Stated differently, there is no denying that senior advance refunding would reduce somewhat the shift of funds from the intermediate area into long-term corporate, municipal and mortgage financing which otherwise might occur; but the impact would be spread over a period of years, in much the same manner as if the Treasury were able from month to month to market relatively small amounts of long-term bonds for cash. This latter program does not, however, seem feasible from a market standpoint.

Advantages of advance refunding to investors.

33. An advance refunding offers tangible advantages to the investor who is willing to exchange for a longer-term security. Most importantly, the investor would obtain a better immediate return on his security since the Treasury would offer a higher coupon to make the exchange attractive. One immediate advantage to the investor, therefore, is an improvement in current income—to a rate level that for many institutional investors would more adequately cover interest income requirements. The investor is guaranteed the higher coupon for the entire life of the new security.

34. It should be noted that the investor also obtains a new bond that at least is equal to, and in most instances a better value than, the current market for comparable maturity issues. In most cases the Treasury would be offering a bond with a yield slightly higher than the current market rate for existing bonds of comparable maturity when computed at the same price (prior to announcement) as the bond being exchanged in advance of maturity. Or, viewed another way—in terms of price—the price of a new bond offered by the Treasury in an advance refunding, if computed at the same yield as existing bonds comparable in maturity to the new bond, generally would be slightly higher than the current price of the old bond.

35. The increased coupon for the full term of the new issue carries an additional implication. The investor who did not elect to exchange would have to replace his existing security at maturity at higher than present market rates to net the same return as that being offered over the entire life of the new security. Reinvestment at the maturity of the old bond would be required at a coupon rate for the extension period which, if averaged with the lower coupon rate on the old security to maturity, would be equal to the coupon rate the Treasury is offering on the new security for the entire period to maturity. (See pars. 37-39 for an example.)

36. Finally, one further benefit accrues to the investor who extends in an advance refunding. Under Title II of Public Law 86-346 passed in September 1959 in preparation for advance refunding, the Secretary of the Treasury may designate an exchange of one Treasury security for another as a nontaxable exchange.[3] Generally, this means that in the exchange the value of the existing security on the books of the investor becomes the book value of the new security. Therefore, the exchange causes no immediate tax consequences and investors are not required to take a loss for tax purposes merely because they exchanged. The gain or loss is deferred until the new security is redeemed (or disposed of prior to maturity). However, if a payment to the investor—other than an adjustment of accrued interest—is involved (which might be the case in some advance refundings), the book value of the new issue would not be the same as that of the existing issue and part or all of the payment becomes immediately taxable.

37. A simple example of an advance refunding offer by the Treasury will make these added advantages to the investor clear.

---

[3]Paradoxically, this legislation was designed primarily to induce exchanges by nontaxable or partially taxable investors, regulated by federal or state authorities, rather than taxable institutions. These nontaxable or partially taxable investment institutions are usually quite reluctant to incur book losses because of the resulting decrease in the stated value of their assets. However, the regulatory authorities are typically willing to permit such exchanges with postponement of recognition of capital gain or loss on the investors' books, provided that a change in the Internal Revenue Code establishes an appropriate precedent. Thus, while the legislation directly affected only holders subject to federal income taxes, it gave sanction to an accounting practice for public authorities to apply in the regulation of certain types of financial institutions even though they may not pay federal income taxes. The advantage to such nontaxable investors is that they may be permitted to carry the new, higher rate securities at the same price as the old.

This example is purely hypothetical and intentionally has no relationship to any possible or prospective offering. Assume that nontaxable holders of a 2 1/2 percent bond due in five years were offered an opportunity, at a time when the market interest rates on ten year issues were 4 percent, to exchange in advance of maturity into a 3 1/4 percent bond maturing in ten years. The nontaxable holder of the 2 1/2s who takes advantage of the advance refunding offer has an immediate increase of 3/4 percent per annum over the period (five years) to the maturity of the original security. This would amount to $37.50 on a $1,000 bond, which could be reinvested as received at compound interest. As a result, if the nontaxable holder of the 2 1/2s did not elect to accept the advance refunding offer, he would have to reinvest the proceeds of his 2 1/2s on maturity at a rate of at least 4.16 percent on this hypothetical issue in a five year maturity to earn as much as he would by accepting the exchange offer. This 4.16 percent minimum rate of investment is the rate of return for the extension period.

38. An analysis of the advantages in return to a taxable holder of the 2 1/2 percent bonds is somewhat more complicated. The effect of tax provisions varies among different investors, depending upon the price at which the security being refunded was originally acquired and the investor's tax status and plans. On the one hand, assuming a par for par exchange of the ten year, 3 1/4 percent bond for the 2 1/2s, if the holder had originally acquired his 2 1/2 percent bonds at a price of, say, $96, he would have realized a capital gain of $40 per $1,000 at time of maturity in five years. This would involve a $10 tax liability per bond at a 25 percent capital gains tax at the end of five years. By electing to exchange for the new issue of 3 1/4s he could postpone this tax for an additional five years and continue earning interest on the amount of the postponed tax for that period. If this investor did not exchange, the capital gains tax would lower the amount he had available for reinvestment at the maturity date of the 2 1/2s; on an equivalent taxable basis he would have to reinvest at a rate higher than 4.13 percent to earn as much as he would by participating in the advance refunding. For the taxable investor who elected to exchange, the tax on ordinary income would work in the opposite direction, since the investor after taxes would net something less than the 3/4 percent additional coupon over the period (five years) to the maturity of the original security.

39. Based on the assumptions in the hypothetical example, the following table illustrates the rates at which investors who held the 2 1/2s at varying book values would have to reinvest at the end of five years to be as well off as they would be by accepting an advance refunding offer of 3 1/4s, assuming a par for par exchange.

	Cost (basis) of 2 1/2 percent bond due in 5 years	Rate of return for the extension of maturity (5 years)
To nontaxable investors (or before tax).	Any cost-	4.16 percent.[1]
To taxable investors[2]--	101------	(taxable equivalent).[3] 4. 08
	100------	4. 09
	99-------	4. 10
	98-------	4. 11
	97-------	4. 12
	96-------	4. 13
	95-------	4. 14
	94-------	4. 14
	93-------	4. 15
	92-------	4. 16

[1]Based on semiannual compounding at 4 percent (from assumed pattern of market rates).

[2]Assuming coupon income is subject to 52 percent tax and capital gain is subject to 25 percent tax.

[3]Coupon rate during extension which, combined with 2 1/2 percent until maturity of old bond (five years), would provide the same return after tax as 3 1/4 percent for ten years.

Advantages of advance refunding to the U.S. Treasury.

40. From the standpoint of the Treasury, advance refunding is the best means of achieving an urgently needed improvement in the maturity structure of the marketable public debt. An improved debt structure, which is the principal advantage accruing to the Treasury from use of advance refunding, would afford much needed flexibility in financing operations. It should also result in lower over-all costs to the Treasury over the years ahead. The size and frequency of Treasury borrowings will be reduced to the extent the debt can be funded at long term. In turn, this would minimize the interference of Treasury financings with the timing of appropriate monetary policy actions.

41. As noted, advance refunding permits substantial debt extension with a minimum disturbance to financial markets and the economy generally. It makes Government bonds more attractive to long-term investors, thus reducing the Treasury's dependence

on inflationary short-term bank borrowing. It avoids many of the disadvantages involved in selling long-term bonds for cash or in exchange for maturing issues. Specifically, it reduces market interference of heavy refundings (or of resorting to alternative sizable cash offerings) in relation to corporate, municipal and mortgage financing. As a result, the direct interest cost to the Treasury of placing a given amount of securities in the long-term area by means of advance refunding should be significantly less than if an equal amount were sold for cash or in exchange for maturing issues. This is because the market process of mobilizing the cash to redistribution that must accompany a refunding at maturity requires a relatively high interest rate commensurate with the amount issued. In an advanced refunding, however, there should be little market churning and no need for mobilization of new cash, thereby resulting in a lower interest cost than on a cash offering or routine refunding of equal amount.

42. It may be noted that only when debt operations are supported by all types of investors purchasing and holding a wide range of maturities can the Treasury finance on the most economical basis. An undue concentration of the debt in one area is almost immediately reflected in higher interest costs in the area affected and experience has shown that this tends to fan out across the maturity spectrum. This was clearly demonstrated in the past year when as a result of the interest rate ceiling the Treasury was forced to concentrate its financing in the under-five-year area. Any increased interest cost is on only a small portion of the debt and very likely will be more than offset by lower costs on subsequent routine debt operations (totaling many billions of dollars each year) as the maturity structure of the debt is brought into better balance. In addition, in viewing the cost aspect of advance refunding from the standpoint of the Treasury it should be noted that the increased coupon over the remaining life of the maturing security (e.g., five years in the case of a hypothetical issue maturing in 1965) would be offset by a lower coupon for the remaining years of the new security (e.g., the five years following 1965 in this particular case) than would have to be paid now to sell a new security at a comparable maturity.

43. Finally, keeping present holders of Treasury securities as investors in the years ahead is an important task for the Treasury in managing the debt. Advance refunding makes a major contribution toward this goal; specifically, it greatly improves the Treasury's chances of retaining its long-term customers, who in recent years have been liquidating Treasury securities, as they move toward maturity, and reinvesting in non-Treasury securities. The use of advance refunding recognizes the preference of each class of investors for securities of suitable maturity. Thus a principal merit of advance refunding is that it enables a long-term holder whose bond is shortening in maturity an opportunity to extend before the maturity

shortens to the point where he decides to sell. In effect, it enables the Treasury to keep typical long bondholders in long bonds and typical intermediate holders in intermediates.

Advance refunding and the statutory 4 1/4 percent interest limitation.

44. Advance refunding is the least costly method for the Treasury to retain its customers and to achieve a significant extension of the debt. Achieving these twin objectives involves some cost, however, and in setting the terms of an advance refunding the Treasury must consider whether the cost involved would in any way conflict with the 4 1/4 percent interest rate ceiling established by Congress on Government bonds (the only obligations the Treasury can issue maturing in more than five years).[4] Until recently, in fact, the existence of the ceiling precluded any attempt to undertake an advance refunding involving a new issue of Government bonds since the maximum return of 4 1/4 percent the Treasury could have offered was below market rates.

45. In relating the interest rate ceiling to advance refunding it is obvious that the coupon rate on the new security does not represent the true interest cost to the Treasury of obtaining the debt extension. To consider only the coupon cost ignores the fact that the Treasury could allow the existing lower coupon security to remain outstanding for whatever number of years remain to maturity under the terms of the original contract with the investor. On the other hand, the coupon that could be placed on an advance refunding, say for ten years, would normally be substantially below the ten year market rate either on outstanding bonds or new issues.

46. The following is a simple illustration—again purely hypothetical—of the dollar cost to the Treasury of a ten-year, 3 1/4 percent bond offered to holders of a 2 1/2 percent bond maturing in five years. Over ten years the Treasury would pay out in interest $325 per $1,000 bond at 3 1/4 percent per annum. On the other hand, if the 2 1/2s were allowed to run to maturity and then refunded after five years, the Treasury would pay out only $125 on the 2 1/2s for

[4]This interest rate limitation was established by Congress in 1918, in connection with a particular financing operation of World War I. Except for the years 1919-22, it did not restrict Treasury debt management until 1959, when the cost of long-term borrowing rose above 4 1/4 percent in response to strong pressures of demand in credit markets. The net effect of the interest rate ceiling, during most of 1959 and the first half of 1960, was to force the Treasury to rely almost exclusively on new issues of Treasury bills, certificates, and notes, which mature in five years or less and on which no interest rate ceiling exists.

the first five years. The Treasury could, therefore, offer a five-year bond at the maturity of the 2 1/2s and pay out $200 in interest without exceeding the total interest paid out on a 10-year 3 1/4 percent bond offered in exchange for the five-year 2 1/2 percent issue. This would be equivalent to selling a 4 percent, five-year obligation to refund the 2 1/2s at maturity. This 4 percent rate, ignoring compound interest, would be the cost of the five-year extension to the Treasury.

47. This example is oversimplified, however, since the additional coupon cost to the Treasury takes place in the first five years while the saving in coupon does not take place until the next five year period. If interest is compounded semiannually (at 4 percent per annum) the cost to the Treasury of the five year extension in advance is 4.16 percent rather than the 4 percent cost in the simplified illustration. It is this derived interest cost of 4.16 percent that the Treasury would have to take into account in determining whether or not an advance refunding issue would be within the 4 1/4 percent interest rate ceiling.

48. It should be further emphasized that this interest cost to the Treasury results only from the fact that the Treasury could have allowed the old issue to continue to maturity. In that sense it is a derived cost computed only to determine whether the advance refunding complies with the intent of the legal interest limitation. The cost of refunding five years from now cannot, of course, be determined in advance. If the cost of refunding in five years should turn out to be greater than the derived cost of advance refunding the Treasury would have made a real saving in interest costs by undertaking an advance refunding. On the other hand, if market interest rates five years from now are lower, then the additional dollar cost to the Treasury would be greater than if no advance refunding had been undertaken.

49. To illustrate these calculations graphically, Chart A-3 shows the true cost of an extension of a 2 1/2 percent, five-year bond into a 3 1/4 percent, ten-year bond. The left-hand block shows the additional cost to the Treasury of the 3 1/4 percent coupon over the 2 1/2 percent coupon for the five years to maturity. The right-hand block shows the true cost of the extension to the Treasury, i.e., 4.16 percent, which is simply the coupon rate (including compounding) which, if averaged with the 2 1/2 percent return on the security being refunded (for the five years to maturity), equals the 3 1/4 percent return the Treasury is offering on the new security for the ten-year period. The right-hand block also shows the saving to the Treasury in the extension period in terms of the coupon cost on the new issue relative to either the derived cost of extension or a 4 percent market yield (assuming that the market yield curve in the ten-year area is 4 percent).

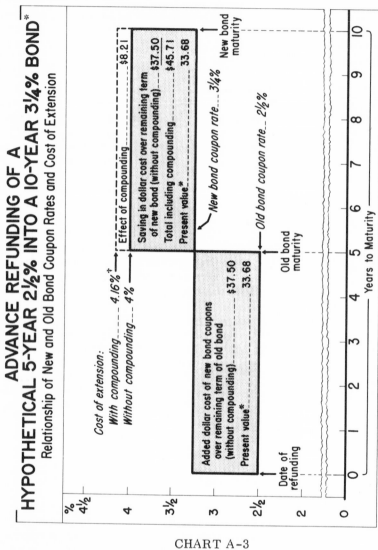

ADVANCE REFUNDING OF A
HYPOTHETICAL 5-YEAR 2½% INTO A 10-YEAR 3¼% BOND*
Relationship of New and Old Bond Coupon Rates and Cost of Extension

Cost of extension:
With compounding ---- 4.16%†
Without compounding --- 4%

Effect of compounding --------------- $8.21

Saving in dollar cost over remaining term
of new bond (without compounding) ---- $37.50
Total including compounding ----------- $45.71
Present value* ------------------------ 33.68

New bond coupon rate --- 3¼%
Old bond coupon rate --- 2½%

New bond maturity

Old bond maturity

Added dollar cost of new bond coupons
over remaining term of old bond
(without compounding) ---------------- $37.50
Present value* ------------------------ 33.68

Date of refunding

Years to Maturity

*Assuming 10-year market rate of 4%, which is also the rate for compounding or discounting to present value.
†Rounded from 4.1642%.

Office of the Secretary of the Treasury

F-623-1

CHART A-3

50. Finally, it may be noted that regardless of the actual level of market yields, alternative use of cash offerings (or refundings at maturity) to extend an equal amount of debt would exert upward pressure on yields. To obtain a substantial amount of debt extension, the coupon rate on such issues would have to be considerably higher than the market yield prior to announcement—how much above depending upon the size of the offering. On the other hand, if the amount offered were limited to avoid market impact, then a cash financing becomes relatively more "costly" in the broader context of a lesser achievement in attaining a better debt structure. Also, it is more "costly" from a broader economic standpoint, particularly during any recession when interest rates are low, to turn to cash offerings or refundings at maturity which absorb new savings that otherwise could contribute to economic recovery.

E. Concluding Comment

51. The advance refunding technique offers much promise in terms of the achievement of a better maturity structure of the marketable public debt and the retention of the present long-term holders as investors in Government securities. It is not a panacea for all the problems of debt management under all circumstances, since it is chiefly applicable when large outstanding issues are selling at substantial discounts and in a market in which there is willingness on the part of investors to extend the maturity. It is clearly the best method of bringing about significant debt lengthening, so essential in the light of the unbalanced debt structure, and at the same time retaining intermediate and long-term investors in Government securities. It would accomplish this with a minimum of adverse market and economic effects. Alternatively, the Treasury could offer long-term bonds for cash or in exchange for maturing issues of Government securities. While both of these other techniques may be useful under certain circumstances, advance refunding has great promise at the present time as a way of implementing sound debt management policy as an integral part of federal financial responsibility.

332.11U58fe
The Federal Reserve and The T...

00049801 3